RETIRING BUT NOT SHY
Feminist Psychologists Create Their Post-Careers

Editors: Ellen Cole and Mary Gergen

This book was developed by the Feminist Retirement Task Force of the Society for the Psychology of Women, Division 35 of the American Psychological Association.
Chair: Mary Gergen

Taos Institute Publications
Chagrin Falls, Ohio
USA

Retiring But Not Shy
Feminist Psychologists Create their Post-Careers

Cover Design and Layout: Debbi Stocco

Library of Congress Catalog Card Number: 2012941510

Taos Institute Publications
A Division of the Taos Institute
Chagrin Falls, Ohio
USA

ISBN-10: 0-9848656-6-7
ISBN-13: 978-0-9848656-6-6
ISBN-ebook: 978-0-9848656-7-3   Printed in the USA and in the UK

Taos Institute Publications

The Taos Institute is a nonprofit organization dedicated to the development of social constructionist theory and practice for purposes of world benefit. Constructionist theory and practice locate the source of meaning, value, and action in communicative relations among people. Our major investment is in fostering relational processes that can enhance the welfare of people and the world in which they live. Taos Institute Publications offers contributions to cutting-edge theory and practice in social construction. Our books are designed for scholars, practitioners, students, and the openly curious public. The **Focus Book Series** provides brief introductions and overviews that illuminate theories, concepts, and useful practices. The **Tempo Book Series** is especially dedicated to the general public and to practitioners. The **Books for Professionals Series** provides in-depth works that focus on recent developments in theory and practice. Our books are particularly relevant to social scientists and to practitioners concerned with individual, family, organizational, community, and societal change.

— Kenneth J. Gergen
President, Board of Directors,
The Taos Institute

Taos Institute Board of Directors

Books for Professional Series Editor
Kenneth Gergen

Tempo Series Editor
Mary Gergen

Focus Book Series Editors
Harlene Anderson, Jane Seiling and Jackie Stavros

Executive Director
Dawn Dole

For information about the Taos Institute and social constructionism visit:
www.taosinstitute.net

Taos Institute Publications

Taos Tempo Series:
Collaborative Practices for Changing Times

Retiring But Not Shy: Feminist Psychologists Create their Post-Careers, (2012) Editors: Ellen Cole and Mary Gergen

Bereavement Support Groups: Breathing Life into Stories of the Dead, (2012) by Lorraine Hedtke

Developing Relational Leadership: Resources for Developing Reflexive Organizational Practices, (2012) by Carsten Hornstrup, Jesper Loehr-Petersen, Joergen Gjengedal Madsen, Thomas Johansen, Allan Vinther Jensen

Practicing Relational Ethics in Organizations, (2012) by Gitte Haslebo and Maja Loua Haslebo

Healing Conversations Now: Enhance Relationships with Elders and Dying Loved Ones, (2011) by Joan Chadbourne and Tony Silbert

Riding the Current: How to Deal with the Daily Deluge of Data, (2010) by Madelyn Blair

Ordinary Life Therapy: Experiences from a Collaborative Systemic Practice, (2009) by Carina Håkansson

Mapping Dialogue: Essential Tools for Social Change, (2008) by Marianne "Mille" Bojer, Heiko Roehl, Mariane Knuth-Hollesen, and Colleen Magner

Positive Family Dynamics: Appreciative Inquiry Questions to Bring Out the Best in Families, (2008) by Dawn Cooperrider Dole, Jen Hetzel Silbert, Ada Jo Mann, and Diana Whitney

Focus Book Series

The Appreciative Organization, Revised Edition (2008) by Harlene Anderson, David Cooperrider, Ken Gergen, Mary Gergen, Sheila McNamee, Jane Watkins, and Diana Whitney

Appreciative Inquiry: A Positive Approach to Building Cooperative Capacity, (2005) by Frank Barrett and Ronald Fry

Dynamic Relationships: Unleashing the Power of Appreciative Inquiry in Daily Living, (2005) by Jacqueline Stavros and Cheri B. Torres

Appreciative Sharing of Knowledge: Leveraging Knowledge Management for Strategic Change, (2004) by Tojo Thatchenkery

Social Construction: Entering the Dialogue, (2004) by Kenneth J.
  Gergen and Mary Gergen
Appreciative Leaders: In the Eye of the Beholder, (2001) edited by
  Marge Schiller, Bea Mah Holland, and Deanna Riley
*Experience AI: A Practitioner's Guide to Integrating Appreciative
  Inquiry and Experiential Learning*, (2001) by Miriam Ricketts and
  Jim Willis

Books for Professionals Series

*New Horizons in Buddhist Psychology: Relational Buddhism for
  Collaborative Practitioners*, (2010) edited by Maurits G.T. Kwee
Positive Approaches to Peacebuilding: A Resource for Innovators,
  (2010) edited by Cynthia Sampson, Mohammed Abu-Nimer,
  Claudia Liebler, and Diana Whitney
Social Construction on the Edge: 'Withness'-Thinking & Embodiment,
  (2010) by John Shotter
Joined Imagination: Writing and Language in Therapy, (2009) by
  Peggy Penn
Celebrating the Other: A Dialogic Account of Human Nature, (reprint
  2008) by Edward Sampson
Conversational Realities Revisited: Life, Language, Body and World,
  (2008) by John Shotter
Horizons in Buddhist Psychology: Practice, Research and Theory,
  (2006) edited by Maurits Kwee, Kenneth J. Gergen, and Fusako
  Koshikawa
Therapeutic Realities: Collaboration, Oppression and Relational Flow,
  (2005) by Kenneth J. Gergen
SocioDynamic Counselling: A Practical Guide to Meaning Making,
  (2004) by R. Vance Peavy
*Experiential Exercises in Social Construction—A Fieldbook for
  Creating Change*, (2004) by Robert Cottor, Alan Asher, Judith
  Levin, and Cindy Weiser
Dialogues About a New Psychology, (2004) by Jan Smedslund

For book information and ordering, visit Taos Institute Publications at:
www.taosinstitutepublications.net
For further information, call:
1-888-999-TAOS, 1-440-338-6733
Email: info@taosinstitute.net

DEDICATION

We dedicate this book to the members of the Society for
the Psychology of Women (Division 35 of the American
Psychological Association), who courageously supported its
publication, and to our husbands, Doug North and Ken Gergen,
who love our title and us.

CONTENTS

THE MID-AIR PLUNGE

SPLASH DOWN AND RE-ENTRY

FOREWORD

by Ellen Cole and Mary Gergen

Ellen Cole

In 2009-2010 I had the honor of serving as president of the Society for the Psychology of Women (SPW), Division 35 of the American Psychological Association. My predecessor and awesome mentor, Dr. Martha Banks, had used her presidential year to celebrate the division's 35th birthday and its 35 year history—"35 is 35!" I decided to carry that theme forward by focusing on the present. "What's Now in Feminist Psychology!" became my guiding vision; it meant to me identifying and exploring the new and urgent topics of today. I quickly established two task forces, one on New Media, and the other—the subject of this book—on Feminist Retirement.

I saw the urgency of this topic for four reasons: (1) Retirement had not previously been addressed from a feminist perspective, at least not by SPW. (2) Many of our founding mothers were now in their 70s and beyond. Were they still working? How did they

identify themselves if they no longer had an academic appointment or a clinical practice, if they no longer received a paycheck?
What were their challenges and their joys at this stage of life? The
time was now to ask these questions. (3) These are the women
(myself among them) who just precede the baby boomer generation—sometimes called "pre-baby boomers" or "the silent
generation." But in fact we have not been silent. We are the first
generation of professional women. We created consciousness
raising groups and inaugurated the study of feminist psychology
and the psychology of women and gender. It seemed to me that
as both activists and psychologists we pre-baby boomers might
have wisdom to impart to those close on our heels who would
begin to turn 65 in 2011. (4) Finally, feminist psychologists who
were baby-boomers themselves were likely to be contemplating
their own post-career futures. What were they thinking? (I have
since learned that the U. S. Census Bureau's Population Division
estimates the number of baby boomers to be 78.2 million and that
in the year 2016, 7,918 will turn 70 each day, 330 each hour. These
are significant numbers.)

I was thrilled when Dr. Mary Gergen agreed to chair the
Feminist Retirement Task Force. One of the original founders of
Division 35, I knew that her major contributions to psychology
were in the realm of feminist and social construction theory. I had
also recently read a chapter she had written on positive aging and
I was, and am, an avid reader of the Positive Aging Newsletter, an
electronic publication she and her husband, psychologist Kenneth
Gergen, circulate bimonthly.

When Mary and I first met to discuss the task force, we thought, "Wouldn't it be great if we could ask shining lights of feminist psychology who are now heading toward, at, and past the age of retirement, to write from a very personal perspective about their lives? Wouldn't it be great if we could put together a book so that a broad audience of readers could benefit from their individual and collective experience?" *Retiring But Not Shy* had been conceived.

I want to thank Mary Gergen for her sisterhood, her artistry, and her humor. Organizing a book is a major commitment. I could not have had a better partner. I also want to thank Elizabeth McHale who joined our project at the end and helped us to consolidate what seemed like thousands of pieces of electronic paper. And of course I want to thank all of our brilliant authors, many of whom told us that this was the first time in their lives they had written so personally. I love reading and re-reading what they have written. It is from the heart, and this, for me, is why this book is special.

Mary Gergen

Ellen Cole is always a hard act to follow. But she is a wonderful compatriot when it comes to editing a book. I was delighted to be asked to chair the Task Force on Feminist Retirement for the Society for the Psychology of Women, and am very excited about the book that was born out of that collaboration. I couldn't have asked for a more creative, spontaneous, and clever partner, who never lacked courage or courtesy when engaged in the task of bringing this book to life. I would also like to laud our authors, who have been the most cooperative, generous, and talented crew I have ever worked with in creating a project of this scope. Each chapter we received was a gift of personal exploration and linguistic excellence.

Putting together this book is an intellectual endeavor as well as a personal exploration on the life transitions that constitute retirement. Ellen and I recognize that each of these stories highlights different facets of our culture's expectations about retirement, and each one also works to develop new understandings and appreciations of what it might become. Every story borrows from the repertoire of narratives available in the culture, and it also creates new potentials from that mix. Although the theme of retirement is not a new one, very little attention has been paid to how women create their lives in this transitional phase. Just as old soldiers are said to fade away, so too do women tend to fade into oblivion. Very little literature is available on how women enter and emerge from this significant life transition. Ellen and I would like to especially thank Asuncion Miteria Austria and Janis Sanchez-Hucles for summarizing important research studies on women and retirement, and especially on how these issues affect minority women, in addition to telling their own stories of retirement. As Ellen mentions, this coterie of authors is among the first professional women in psychology, and among the first in the nation. We are pioneers, and through our stories, new ways of creating post-careers are produced.

This book is part of the Taos Institute's Tempo Book Series, and is, in fact, the first book that has a feminist theme. The mission of the Institute is to promote social constructionist theory within diverse professional and personal practices. *Retiring But not Shy: Feminist Psychologists Create their Post-Careers* exemplifies a social constructionist approach in its theme of developing meaningful ways of addressing, living into, and reflecting upon the transitional phase of life we call retirement. Interestingly, one of the major motifs of these stories is how much we need some other word to describe this period of life, given that the construction of retirement as the ending of a meaningful life is so inappropriate for the experiences related by these authors. Creating new life is at the base of this period, not simply relinquishing the old.

We believe this story needs to be told and retold so that younger women thinking about their futures will not confront the end of their current careers imagining they are entering the beginnings of early death. Rather we want this book to construct for them visions of interesting, vital, and creative alternatives to the lives one currently lives. Although our message is optimistic, we have tried not to be Pollyannas, as I am sometimes called. There are definitely challenges and trials that are confronted and mostly overcome, including those related to finances, families, and finding new outlets for one's talents. Our hope is that discovering how others have dealt with these issues will be enlightening and energizing for those who will follow.

The book is organized along the metaphor of a swimmer's dive—diving into the period of life called "retirement." Our authors span a fairly large age range, approximately 30 years, and they are in different stages of their encounters with retirement. The first section includes narratives of people who are contemplating retirement, or who have just begun the process.

They are "Poised on the Diving Board." The middle section includes people who have taken "The Mid-Air Plunge" and are dealing with various aspects of their process. The third section "Splash Down and Re-Entry" relates the stories of women who are old hands at the process. Their stories are configured as both action and reflection on their experiences, what they have created and what they continue to create.

Ellen and I have tried to keep in mind the diversity of women who are transitioning into this phase of life. Our authors represent different racial and ethnic groups and sexual orientations. They are married and single, living with a partner, widowed, and divorced. They are healthy and disabled, and of diverse spiritual traditions. Together they share one trait, in that they are all professional women, with advanced degrees and successful careers in psychology. Most have held leadership roles in their professional organizations and in their communities. They all, potentially, have had a lot to lose in giving up their jobs. Because of this challenge, their stories are especially fascinating. We asked the authors to tell their personal stories so that those who will follow will have the chance to know them beyond the many books and articles they have written. We have also included their photographs so that you will encounter them more intimately. Their impressive biographies are included as a final note so that you can appreciate the paths that brought them here.

Last, Ellen and I would like to thank the "amazing" Michelle Fine, one of our favorite feminist psychologists, for her introductory remarks. We asked Michelle if she could find the time to write a sentence endorsing our book, and she came back with a "poem." She constructed our contribution in a manner that enhances our own sense that we have accomplished a meaningful goal.

We hope that you, dear reader, will find a resonance between your life and ours in this volume. Our greatest hope is that our endeavors have value for you and for future generations.

INTRODUCTION
by Michelle Fine

*W*hen I was a little girl I used to dream about discovering an attic filled with letters from elders, revealing their secrets, offering advice, unleashing the magic of their wisdom, helping me understand my existential angst. After 57 disappointed years, *Retiring But Not Shy* landed on my desk; my longed for attic could be found in these essays, penned by the most delicious gathering of feminists one could imagine. Crawling into this safe space, in the political turmoil of 2011, I found comfort in an intellectual and political spa—with old friends.

This volume is a textual pajama party of essays by the very women who pioneered feminist psychology through Division 35 of the APA; the very women whose writings disrupted and transformed the discipline of psychology insisting that gender, race/ethnicity and sexuality be central to psychological analyses; the very women whose shoulders (and minds and hearts) we all stand upon.

The writers are stunning as scholars and activists, and as a collective they are our Wonder Women. These are the women who dared to challenge disciplinary definitions of sex and gender; sexuality and identity; health and illness; beauty and femininity; science and narrative. So why am I surprised that in the tradition of radical feminism, these incredible women have also, individually and collectively, "queered" the definition of retirement?

They have, indeed, waved goodbye to the academy, vacated their offices and surrendered their paychecks. But in the name of "retirement" they are navigating wild new landscapes of personal and political adventures: fighting for welfare rights, organizing for lesbian and trans liberation, supporting Palestinian struggles, mobilizing for racial justice, traveling and staying home, meeting friends for lunch, finding new lovers and leaving (or being left by) old ones, walking on the beach, practicing yoga, learning to paint, writing fiction, designing collective housing, absorbing the cumulative pain of loss, getting a massage, hanging out with grandkids, gardening, still agitating for justice within APA.

This text is a collectively woven memoir, stretched over a generation of academics who transformed feminist thought, psychological theory and clinical practice. The volume chronicles their intellectual and professional footprints in the sand, offering a critical feminist history of psychology and advancing our understandings of aging as a stage for women's political consciousness and action.

Retiring But Not Shy captures and ignites the magic, wisdom and creativity of feminists who have redesigned retirement as a platform for: thoughtful reflection on what was (the teaching, the writing, the illegal abortion, the affairs, the marriage, the children, the mistakes and the awards); passionate engagement with politics of the moment (gender, sexuality, racial justice, welfare rights, Palestinian struggles…) and radical action toward a very different tomorrow, seeking always a world not yet…

Retiring But Not Shy makes me look forward to the next chapter… Thanks, wonder(ful) women for a delicious journey back, and forward.

Poised on the Diving Board

The Retiree as a Professor, a Woman, and an Ethnic Minority

Asuncion Miteria Austria

"Retirement can be viewed as a time for new beginnings as well as a time for continuing well-established patterns that are satisfying to the individual."
- Lorraine T. Dorfman (2005) -

*I*n the early 20th century, the average life expectancy was 47 years. Advances in medicine and resources were not available at that time; people became too sick to work and eventually died of illnesses. Only 3% of one's adult years were spent in retirement. In the 21st century, 25% of one's adulthood can be spent in retirement. As the average life expectancy in 2002 was 76 years, those retiring at age 65 could expect to spend 18 to 20 years as a retiree (The Ohio Department of Aging, 2002). The number of Americans aged 65 and over is expected to double by the year 2030. Projections indicate that by that time there will be only 2.7 people between the ages of 20 and 63 for everyone over 65 (Green, 2005).

Defining Retirement

There are varying definitions of retirement that have been used in the retirement literature, with frequent emphasis on sources of retirement income or degree of labor force participation. Webster's dictionary defines retirement as "the withdrawal from one's position or occupation or from active working life" (Merriam-Webster, Online Dictionary, 2011).

Price & Balaswamy (2009) define retirement as the termination of one's primary employment provided the participants left paid work after a minimum of 10 years of either continuous or discontinuous service. Atchley (1982) describes retirement as a process, an event, and a role. As a process, retirement constitutes the transition from the status of worker to that of non-worker and signifies the withdrawal from the work role into the somewhat vaguely defined role of retiree. To some people, retirement means the termination of a career, whereas to others, it signifies only a reduction in work hours.

McGee (2003) makes a distinction between voluntary retirement and partial retirement. Full voluntary retirement is qualitatively different from partial retirement, or leave of absence. It is not an unplanned retirement resulting from unforeseen geographic relocation, serious personal or family illness, or incapacitation. Full voluntary retirement is usually prompted by internal rather than external factors, as it derives mainly from a desire to devote time and energy to pursuits other than one's primary occupation.

The meaning of retirement has also changed. In the past, it meant a slowing down of activity and the completion of work life. Today, retirement for both men and women can mean having the opportunity to engage in hobbies, travel, start a new career, go back to school, spend time with family, take care of grandchildren or older parents, or work part-time.

It is important to note that the literature on retirement tends not to recognize the diverse employment patterns of women and neither does it consider the retirement concerns of ethnic minority women, despite demographic changes. Differences between women's and men's employment patterns include women's discontinuous work histories, lower status paying jobs, and their family responsibilities. Because of the changing demographics, the changing roles of women, the growing number of women retirees, and the fact that women constitute a majority of the older adult population, retirement can no longer be considered an issue pertaining only to men (Price & Balaswamy, 2009).

Retirement Inequities: Gender and Race

Between 1970 and 2000, the percentage of women working outside the home rose from 43% to 61%, and currently women constitute almost half (47%) of the US labor force (Population Reference Bureau, 2001). Coinciding with this expansion in women's employment is the increasingly diverse employment patterns of women. Women who work outside of the home do so in a variety of capacities with varying lengths of employment, often as a result of family and care giving responsibilities (Population Reference Bureau, 2001).

There will be an increase in retired women as growing numbers of young women and middle aged women work and retire based on their own work histories rather than on their spouse's. Despite advances in women's work histories, they continue to earn less than men and are more likely to work at jobs without pensions. In 1999, while 20% of men aged 55 to 64 and 46 % of men over 65 received a pension, only 12 % of the women 55 to 64 and 29 % of women over the age of 65 received one (Gregoire, Kilty & Richardson, 2002). Although, many researchers have investigated older women's income, few have focused on retired women, specifically, women who worked continuously or long enough to receive retirement benefits based on their own work histories. This group represents a rapidly growing population. Studies show current retirement inequities that have implications for what current working women will face when they retire (Gregoire et al. 2002).

Furthermore, research investigating retirement has historically been conducted with white middle class men. Price (2000) commented that studies on women's retirement have made direct comparison between retirement transitions of men and women, disregarding the diversity factors surrounding retirement issues for women. Despite increased workforce participation, the economic situation of single women, including white women, has worsened over time. Inequities in retirement resources are reflected in a structure of social welfare pension systems that provide public supports for the poor and private benefits for the wealthy. While women rely on Social Security, men rely more on private pensions, real estate, and other lucrative retirement investments. The percentage of women relying on Social Security increases with age and is higher among women living alone. It also increases as overall income declines. Retirement policies based on privatization will continue to adversely impact women who work at low-paying jobs, receive lower wages, and live longer than men (Gregoire, et al. 2002).

Longer life spans, lower wages than their male counterparts, and less access to pension plans make women more vulnerable in retirement (Inklebarger, 2009). Pension income provides the second largest source of income in retirement (Pension Rights Center, 2009, a,b), but less than half of all working people are covered by private pensions. A much smaller proportion of women than men, and even fewer minority women age 65 and over, received income from private pensions in 2009 (U.S. Census Bureau, 2011). Women are 9% less likely to participate in a pension plan, and women's pensions are worth less than half of a man their age, on average (Inklebarger, 2009).

Women live three to five years longer than men, and are less likely to have a pension upon retirement; thus they have more years of retirement with less money to support themselves (Inklebarger, 2009).

African Americans are less likely than others to be offered a retirement plan because they make less money and work fewer years at the same employer (John, 2010). Only 23% of African American and 12 % of Hispanic older women received pension income in 2009 (U. S. Census Bureau, 2011).

Utilizing international measures, one quarter of elderly persons in the U.S. are living in poverty (OECD, 2009). Ten percent more minority women than men are considered impoverished (U.S. Census Bureau, 2011). On average, ethnic minority women have less than half of the retirement income that men have. Asian women have less than half the retirement income of Asian men (U.S. Census Bureau, 2010).

For those working full time jobs, 38% of African American women, 26% of Hispanic women, and 38% of Asian/Pacific Islander women are covered by a pension plan (Pension Benefits, January 2003). As a whole, Social Security benefits are important to most racial /ethnic minorities. For example, about half of African Americans and Hispanics received 90% or more of their income from Social Security. These ethnic groups tend to have lower earnings on average, and thus are helped by the progressivity of Social Security benefits, with African Americans participating to a greater extent than other ethnic minority groups.

Yet, African Americans on average have shorter life spans, thus resulting in fewer years of benefit receipt.

Pension income provides the second largest source of income for retirees. But less than half of all working people are covered by private pensions. A much smaller proportion of women than men, and even fewer minority women age 65 and over received private pension in 2000 (Pension Benefits, 2003). Women were slightly less likely to participate in a pension or savings program as they are twice as likely as men to work part-time in jobs without retirement benefits. The problem is aggravated as ethnic minority women are less likely to work in jobs covered by pensions. Only 15% of African American and 8% of Hispanic older women received pension income in 2000. Minority women's lower earnings often leave them with meager resources to invest. Ethnic minority women live longer on average than ethnic minority men and need more financial resources to support themselves in retirement (U.S. Census Bureau, 2010).

An individual's gender, marital status, and ethnic background are factors affecting an older person's retirement resources (U. S. Census Bureau, 2000). For example, 13 % of women compared to 7.2 % of men over age 65 fell below the poverty line. With age, the gap widens. According to Social Security Administration (2000), 17.5% of women versus 7.6 % of men over the age 85 are poor. If one's marital status and ethnic background is considered, the income disparities widen.

When considering, non-married ethnic minority individuals, especially African Americans and Hispanics, the income disparities worsen. In a comparison between African American and White older persons, Ozawa and Huan-Yui (2000) found that while White men benefitted from more education and better jobs, African American men and African American women accrued few advantages from these achievements. Furthermore, although African American workers received disproportionately larger monthly benefits than Caucasian workers relative to lifetime earnings, when considering lifetime benefits African Americans got less of their money's worth compared to Whites, as the African Americans have lower longevity rates (Ozawa & Kim, 2001).

In sum, although more women work full-time than in the past relative to older men, these women will receive lower retirement benefits because they continue to work at jobs that pay less, they live longer, and they take more time off from work to care for children and other relatives.

Professional Women and Retirement

In 1994, age related mandatory retirement ended nationally for tenured professors in American colleges and universities. Because of this, people in academia could continue to work. The sense of loss associated with full, voluntary retirement often has the capacity to stimulate a great degree of anxiety, ambivalence, denial, and vulnerability. A full retirement represents a major life transition into a stage with many initial unknowns. Role loss occurs as a result of retirement with consequent lack of social networks. Lack of social networks can lead to feelings of loneliness and alienation and may even lead to suicide as noted among the high rate of suicide among retired White American men (Lang, 2003). It is important to note that retired African American and White women do not commit suicide as do their male counterparts, largely because they have stronger social networks (McPherson, Smith-Lovin, & Brashers, 2006).

Unfortunately, studies that have been done on retirement have been largely in the general context of work. There are very few studies specifically on the retirement of college and university faculty. In one study by Chase, et al (2003) they found that one-half of the retirees seemed to have no difficulties, and half of them had experienced negative affective responses to their new status, such as trouble adjusting to changes in image, decreased resources, and a loss of visibility. They found that "retirement shock' is a common condition which can precipitate a real identity crisis. When people are highly devoted to their work and suddenly find themselves unemployed, their self-esteem is reduced.

Retirement triggers a fear of aging. For retirees who were in positions of responsibility, retirement may mean a loss of power and authority that result in reduced self-esteem. There could also be separation from colleagues and friends at work. The sense of loss often has the capacity to give rise to an identity crisis and loss of self-esteem. For some people, retirement represents a major transition into a life change with many unknowns (McGee, 2003).

Researchers investigating the retirement experiences of professional women have found that women's work roles are an important aspect of their identities. As a result of strong work identities, professional women often view retirement as a negative life event (Erdner & Guy, 1990). Chase, et al (2003) examined women's perceptions toward retirement and found that professional women, in comparison to men, had limited interest in retirement, were not likely to consider early retirement, and were less likely to coordinate their retirement with their spouse's retirement. The women in the study also expressed interest in continuing to work past retirement and reported missing work after they retired.

Dorfman (2000) studied professors who were over 70 years old and still working. She found several factors that professors considered in continuing to work beyond 70 years of age. Among professors, work is generally a "core activity" throughout the life course and at the same time may serve as a leisure activity (Dorfman, 2005). As work is the central focus in a professor's life, the patterns of activity for professors in later life may be different from the people in other occupational roles (Dorfman, 2005). Economic factors play a crucial role in the women's decisions to continue to work or to retire. Professors have identified financial insecurity as a reason to continue to work or at least delay retirement for several years (Weiss, 2005). Health factors also play a role, as professors who were in poor health were more likely to retire than those who were in good health. Health status of one's spouse may also play a role in the decision to continue to work or to retire (Dorfman, 2000).

Research indicates that professional factors play a role in continuing to work. Highly productive research-oriented faculty, particularly those employed at research universities, are likely to remain employed longer than are less research-oriented faculty. Also, faculty who rate themselves higher in teaching and service roles rather than in research productivity are more likely to retire earlier (Holden & Hansen, 1989b). In addition, faculty who are more professionally role-oriented and who are affiliated with colleagues and professional organizations outside their institutions would be more likely to remain employed past age 70 than would faculty who are less professionally role-oriented (Boyer et al., 1994). The teaching environment and the quality of students affect faculty decisions about whether to keep working into their late 60s and beyond. Faculty who have light teaching loads and enjoy inspiring students tend to continue to work. Dissatisfaction with one's teaching assignment is associated with early faculty retire-ment. Institutional factors such as faculty who experience a poor fit with their departments are more likely to retire early. Feelings of alienation from the department and the institution have both been associated with early faculty retirement, as are having poor collegial relations and overall job dissatisfaction (Hanish & Hulin, 1990). On the other hand, high levels of work satisfaction and retention of role and status in the department are likely to result in professors continuing to work.

Reasons for Retiring

For many professionals, retirement heralds the long-awaited day when a person can leave behind the daily grind and look for-ward to a life of leisure (Pointon, 2004). People retire for these various reasons:

Intellectual Growth. Hansen and Hass (2009) studied retired people and found that people look toward pursuing intellectual growth through taking courses, private study, and participation in educationally-oriented travel. Some have undertaken considerable teaching responsibilities, and some taught part-time at the college level. Sixty four percent of psychologists who plan to retire expect to continue working part-time as psychologists (APA Monitor on Psychology, 2004, p. 82).

Spiritual Development. Retirees use the time for spiritual development. Increased prayers could be a result of declining health and increased awareness of one's mortality. But then again, retirement is a time when there is freedom to meditate and pray in an unhurried manner.

Life-long Learning. Retirement provides time to pursue creative activities such as writing, painting, and new hobbies.

Volunteer services. Retirement can be a time to give back to the community. About 52% of retired psychologists are volunteers—more than half of them in areas related to psychology (APA Monitor, 2004, p 82).

Social Networks. Continuation of social networks bodes well for more highly educated people. McPherson, et al. (2006) noted that the more highly educated people have stronger social support networks. While ethnic minorities, particularly Hispanics and African Americans, typically have lower levels of education, African American men have the smallest support network of any older group (McPherson, et al., 2006).

General Recommendations

Studies indicate that people in academia do relatively little or no planning at all for retirement. It would be helpful if universities could provide assistance with retirement planning as well as pre-retirement programs, including information on health benefits, living arrangements, and utilization of university services which would help ease the transition.

Some research universities that are losing highly productive and active faculty to retirement have developed policies to retain the faculty past the retirement age. Cornell University, for example, adopted a plan that includes stipends for retirees for a five-year period, in which they are guaranteed shared office space, opportunities for part-time teaching, continued supervision of graduate students, and the ability to apply for external grants with salary support (Dorfman, 2000).

Older professors could serve an important function as sources of resource and support for colleagues and their institutions, transmitting institutional culture and values. They have the historical and cultural background of the department and the university, and therefore can serve as important sources of departmental and institutional memory, essential to averting possibilities of "reinventing the wheel."

There are other retirement programs for retirees in academia to ward off feelings of detachment, loneliness, and uselessness. Programs could include university involvement in discussion forums or colloquia which will provide retirees continued professional identity and pursuit of scholarship (Chase, Eklund, & Pearson, 2003).

Training on computer technology should be provided to older retirees as social networking is crucial for many if they are to maintain a positive self-image. McPherson, et al. (2006) indicated that computer technology may foster social bonds. They acknowledge, however, that this may promote a wider, less localized array of weak ties, rather than the strong, tightly interconnected, confident ties like the traditional ones obtained from strong personal contacts. Nonetheless, the different digital media may provide the necessary social bonds that retirees need.

The Retiree as a Woman and an Ethnic Minority

I have wanted to retire for three years now, but have not done any serious planning about it. Work has been the central focus in my life as a professor of psychology and department chair at a Midwestern university. I have not made any distinction between work and leisure, as both activities are intertwined. I have a passion for psychology and for teaching; it is a profession in which I have invested most of my life. I grew up in a family with hard-working parents, and their work ethic has been passed on to all of their children. My family of origin consists of teachers who are considered model teachers, so the enjoyment of teaching is ingrained in me.

I now have seriously considered retiring. Health has not been a factor for me to retire as I am generally in good health. Of course I have some aches and pains, but I have not missed any day of class for health reasons, neither have I taken a sabbatical. However, I have several concerns as I approach retirement. As an ethnic minority, I am extremely proud of my professional identity. Even now, however, with my title and degree from a prestigious university, individuals who interact with me in person or on the phone sometimes have difficulties acknowledging me as a doctor or as a professor. They have difficulties calling me "Dr." despite, at times, repeated introductions of myself as a "Dr." They insist on calling me "Ms." or "Mrs." As a person of color, loss of professional identity is a serious concern during retirement. It is important to note that the ethnic minority woman once retired suffers from numerous "-isms," including ageism, which is inextricably tied to sexism and more importantly to racism. Relinquishing my professional identity that once offered me as an ethnic minority faculty a shield from perceptions of incapability, now becomes a reality, rendering me now more invisible.

I have survived the onslaught of blatant and covert racism over the many years, both from colleagues and students, especially during the early years of my professional life. However, my deep commitment to teaching and the satisfaction of having the opportunity to mentor and witness the successes of students, and the privilege of working with wonderful colleagues both at the university and in professional organizations, reinforced my commitment to stay in academia. I found continued enjoyment in my profession as I began to realize and acknowledge the contributions I have made.

I would really like to spend more time with my closely knit family, including my two children, who live out of state. I also enjoy the company of close friends who I could not spend much time with due to my school responsibilities. More often than not, my husband has assumed the role as the social representative at gatherings of family and friends. I feel fortunate that I have not been deleted from my friends' guest lists as I have not reciprocated their invitations since I developed and assumed the roles of Chair and Director of Clinical Training of the Graduate Program.

Concluding Thoughts

As I prepare for my eventual retirement, I wish I could have taken a sabbatical, which would have provided a "dress rehearsal" for being away from the rigors of daily school preparations and demands. Or, perhaps I could have worked on a part-time basis, again to serve as a "bridge" that would have been a less stressful and more gradual transition to full retirement.

I am most happy at this stage of my anticipated retirement to imagine a more relaxed schedule. I have been fortunate to be part of an institution that is dedicated to compassion, caring, and peace; and committed to serving the underserved. I have been active with the American Psychological Association for most of my professional life, a vibrant professional organization, and I envision myself continuing my involvement with the organization's activities. I look forward to continued involvement in psychology, consulting, writing, and/or advising students to maintain a sense of personal efficacy and professional identity.

References

American Psychological Association. (2004), *Monitor on Psychology*. Washington, DC.

Atchley, R. (1982). The process of retirement: Comparing women and men. In M. Szinovacz (Ed.), *Women's retirement: Policy implications of recent research* (pp.153-168). Beverly Hills, CA: Sage Publications.

Boyer, E. L., Altbach, P. G., & Whitelaw, M. J. (1994). *The academic profession: An international perspective*. Princeton, NJ: Carnegie Foundation for the Advancement of Teaching.

Bureau of Labor Statistics (2000). *Employment & Earnings, 47* (8) Washington, DC: U.S. Department of Labor.

Chase, C. J., Eklund, S. J., & Pearson, L. M. (2003). Affective responses of faculty emeriti to retirement. *Educational Gerontology, 29*, 521-534.

Dorfman, L. T. (2000). Still working after age 70: Older professors in academe. *Educational Gerontology, 26,* 695-713.

Dorfman, L, T. (2005). Leisure and the retired professor: Occupation matters. *Educational Gerontology, 31,* 341-361.

Erdner, R. A. & Guy, R. F. (1990). Career identification and women's attitudes toward retirement. *International Journal of Aging and Human Development, 30,* 129-139.

Greene, C. A. (2005). Race, ethnicity, and social security retirement age in the U.S. *Feminist Economics, 11*(2), 117-143.

Gregoire, T. K., Kilty, K., Richardson, V. (2002). Gender and racial inequities in retirement resources. *Journal of Women and Aging. 14,* (3/4), 25-39.

Hammond, P. B. & Morgan, H. P. (Eds.) (1991). Ending mandatory retirement for tenured faculty: The consequence for higher education. Washington, D. C.: National Academic Press. *Vocational Behavior, 37,* 60-78.

Hanish, K. A. & Hulin, C. L. (1990). Job attitudes and organizational withdrawal. An examination of retirement and other voluntary withdrawal behaviors. *Journal of Vocational Behavior, 37,* 60-78.

Hansen, J. & Haas, J. (Fall, 2009). Retirement: A time of significant personal growth and contribution. *The LL Review,* 87-93.

Inklebarger, T. (2009). Report spotlights retirement gap. *Pension & Investments, 37* (10).

John, D.C. (2010). *Disparities for women and minorities in retirement savings.* United States Department of Labor, Retirement Security Project: Advisory Council on Employee Welfare and Pension Benefit Plans.

Lang, H. R. (2003). Elder suicide: A selective guide to resources. *Reference Services Review, 31,* 175-184.

McGee, T. F. (2003). Observations on the retirement of professional psychologists. *Professional Psychology: Research and Practice, 34*, (4), 388-395.

McPherson, M., Smith-Lovin, L., & Brashears, M. E. (2006). Social isolation in America: Changes in core discussion networks over two decades. *American Sociological Review, 71*, 353-375.

Merriam-Webster Online Dictionary (2011) Retirement-Definition. http://www.Merriam-webster.com/dictionary/retirement.

OECD. (2009). Pensions at a Glance: Retirement-Income systems in OECD countries.www.oecd.org. publications/statistic/income-pensions.

Ozawa, M. N. & Huan, Yui, T. (2001). Differences in net worth between elderly black people and elderly white people. *Caps on Research, 24*, 96-108.

Ozawa, M. N. & Kim, H. (2001). Money's worth in social security benefits: Black-White differences. *Caps on Research, 22*, 116-128.

Pension Benefits, January, 2003. *Minority women and retirement income, 12*, 1, Aspen Publishers. Pension Rights Center(2009a). Income from pension, http://www. Pensionrights.org/publications/statistic/income-pensions

Pension Rights Center(2009b). Sources of income for older adults, http://www.pensionrights.org/publications/statistic/income-older-adults-suspension

Pointon, C. (2004). When is the right time to retire? *Counseling and Psychotherapy Journal, 15*, 4, 18-21.

Population Reference Bureau (2001). *2001 United States population data sheet* (Section 4) Washington, D.C.

Price, C. A. (2000). Women and retirement: Relinquishing professional identity. *Journal of Aging studies, 14*,(1), 21-103.

Price, C.A. & Balaswamy, S. (2009). Beyond health and wealth: Predictors of women's retirement satisfaction. *International Journal of Aging and Human Development, 68*, 3, 195-214.

The Ohio Department of Aging (2002).Senior series. http://www.state.oh.us.age

U.S. Census Bureau (2010). Annual Social and Economic Supplement. *Table PINC-09. Source of Income in 2009- Number with income and mean income of specified type in 2009 of people 15 years and over by age, race, and Hispanic origin, and sex . http://www.census.gov/hhes/www/cpstables/032010/perinc/new09 006 .htm http://www.census.gov/hhes/www/cpstables/032010/perinc/new09 018 .htm*

U.S. Census Bureau (2011) Statistical Abstract of the United States: 2011(130th Edition) Washington, DC, 2010; http://www.census.gov/statab/www/

Weiss, R. S. (2005). *The experience of retirement.* Ithaca: ILR Press.

Trading Places, Or, How One Political Moment Changed Two Paths toward Retirement and Beyond

Janis S. Bohan and Glenda Russell

he prospect of writing a chapter about what retirement looks like for feminist psychologists was initially rather daunting for us, in part because one of us is retired, but the other is not. On the other hand, we are both feminist psychologists, and as we live together, we are both looking at retirement, albeit from different perspectives. So we decided to write a story of a life shared within this somewhat distinctive context. This is a story of over a decade of change and travel, of delight and disappointment, of joint and individual work and play, of negotiation and sometimes frustration, all influenced by our differing status vis-à-vis retirement.

The title we chose describes the context of our story. As is true of many good stories, this one is based on contrasts—a contrast between the places we have each assumed (and traded), and a contrast between before and after that "political moment" that changed everything. Beneath those contrasts is another version of the story: the intersections between life paths and the continuities that persist across "before" and "after." But the kernel of the story is this changing of places that happened around a particular political moment. The story…

We were both feminist psychologists, working and living in the same geographic region, but not knowing each other. One of us, Janis, was an academic who taught at a state college in Denver.

Janis: *I had made a beeline through undergraduate and graduate work, getting my PhD early and starting my career at the age of 25. In my professional life, I was quite successful in my teaching, very involved in my department, and somewhat involved in college activities, especially those relating to women's issues. Over the years, I had managed to reinvent my career several times, includ-*

ing bringing feminist perspectives to my courses and to my writing. That process of reinvention had kept my tendency toward easy boredom at bay and had provided me with a wide range of learning opportunities and experiences. I loved my work, loved where I was working, and felt hugely privileged to have found a career that was so gratifying and such fun. In my personal life, I was a closeted lesbian and rather complacent about my comfort and safety in that status. I was out to some friends (and eventually to family), but not to colleagues or students or in any work or public setting. I participated very little in political or community activities, and I was not at all involved in LGBT political matters.

The other of us, Glenda, was a clinical psychologist in Boulder who had begun her professional career in psychology in her mid-thirties, after spending her young adulthood in jobs that were uninspiring and political pursuits that were more compelling.

Glenda: *Since high school, I had been deeply involved in community and political work, engaging in political activism around a range of issues: civil rights, the anti-Vietnam War movement, the women's movement, and LGB (and later, T) politics. I came to psychology partly by way of my activism, seeing psychology as one way to change the world, and I never entertained the notion of a separation between my professional life and my activism. When I finished graduate school, I opened a clinical practice, where I learned a lot and loved my work. In part to keep my intellectual fires burning and in part to work with a good friend, I undertook a qualitative research project in my spare time, but it was a "spare" project for my "spare" time.*

Then came the political moment when the world changed for us both. In 1992, Colorado voters passed the soon-to-become-notorious Amendment 2, a popularly initiated amendment that would legalize discrimination against lesbian, gay, and bisexual people.

Janis: *When I heard on the morning news that Amendment 2 had passed, my personal and professional life changed dramatically. I was prepared to be horrified if, as the polls predicted, almost half of voters supported it, but I had never dreamed that the amendment would pass. Stunned, angry, and resolute, I decided that my complacent life needed to change. In the next two days, I leapt from the closet: I came out to my colleagues in a long and passionate letter, came out in all my classes, and started wearing a pink triangle pin everywhere I went. I actively sought out opportunities to be involved in lesbian, gay, bisexual, and (later) transgender (LGBT) politics, and I also began looking for ways to have an impact through my role as an educator.*

Glenda: *I had been very active over the previous year working on the campaign against Amendment 2. I was well aware of the pervasiveness of homophobia and heterosexism, so I was certain it would pass. It was important to me to know that I had done everything I could to resist it. During the campaign, I debated, organized, ran a field office, raised funds, gave talks, and generally devoted all my free time to the effort. The passage of Amendment 2 also changed the course of my life, although the impact was quite different from its effect on Janis. After the passage of Amendment 2, I realized that my expertise as a social scientist could bring some clarity to the enormous impact of this event on LGB people (and their allies). So I began a research project designed to assess the psychological consequences of the amendment on lesbian, gay, and bisexual Coloradans. That project launched a new direction in my career, one that led me toward increased involvement in research, writing, and speaking and toward work within the institutions of the profession related to psychology's position on LGBT issues.*

And this is the moment when we met. As one major step in her new "out" life, Janis developed a course on the psychology of sexual orientation, thinking she could thereby use her tenured position teaching in a state college toward good ends. She heard about Glenda's research on the psychological impact of Amendment 2 and invited Glenda to give a guest lecture in the new course. Soon, we became friends. Through Glenda, Janis began to learn about LGBT politics and to meet people who were involved in the LGBT political movement in the state (and beyond). Through Janis, Glenda picked up tips about publishing and met people in the academic feminist psychology community. Before long, we were working together on research, writing papers, and presenting together at conferences; with time, we wrote a book together. And eventually, our writing partnership developed into a romantic relationship and then partnership in life. Not long after these events, which unfolded over several years, Janis reached retirement age.

Janis: *I could, of course, have worked longer at this position that I so loved. But I was a bit burned out after 30 years of teaching four classes every semester, along with all the other tasks that accompany being a faculty member. And I was ready for a change of direction, ready to do the things that my life thus far had not allowed. My new exposure to the world of politics and community involvement that followed Amendment 2, combined with all I was learning from Glenda and from our work together persuaded me that I was ready to change course. I still wanted to do a bit of writing, maybe a touch of research, perhaps a little speaking. But mostly I wanted to feel free to do the things that spoke to this new version of me and to ease back on the throttle after a fairly pressured career. In retrospect, I was, in essence, entering a life path much like the one Glenda had followed since early in her life, even as she was moving closer to the path I had followed.*

Meanwhile, Glenda, too, was ready for a change of pace, but she was not ready to retire. She is a few years younger than Janis and had begun her career later in her life. The combination meant that she had not had the opportunity to enjoy as long a career as Janis had.

Glenda: *I was not remotely ready to retire, even if I could have afforded to. I felt in many respects that I was just hitting my stride as a working psychologist. I was deeply engaged in my newfound passion for meaningful research and writing, generally trying to use my skills as a psychologist to facilitate positive social change. I was also enjoying my clinical work and learning from it, and after two decades of being a practicing therapist, I felt like I was finally able to articulate some of the nuances of the work. In addition, I was aware of an impulse toward generativity: I was intrigued by the possibility of imparting some of what I had learned in working with clients to students at the start of their clinical work. I had also been inspired to consider teaching by talking with and observing Janis, a stellar teacher who has lived the truism of touching the future through her work.*

So we were both ready for changes in our professional lives, albeit changes of very different sorts, and we were both ready for a change of scenery—Janis after an entire life in Colorado, and Glenda after 30 years there. When Glenda spotted an ideal-sounding job teaching in a doctoral program in New Hampshire, we decided to pack up and move.

Janis: *As we discussed this major move with friends and colleagues, some directed us to the "trailing spouse" literature, and some asked how I felt about being "dragged across the country" for Glenda's job. But both characterizations missed the point: I was not dutifully following Glenda down her career path any more than she was being diverted by my wanderlust. I was invigorated by the prospect of this new adventure, quite ready to build my new identity as retired-but-joyfully-busy in a new space, and her opportunity for a new professional role in quasi-rural New Hampshire looked to both of us like just the ticket.*

Clearly, we had some work to do around negotiating our apparently mismatched life courses. So much of how we have worked this out has to do with our feminist values— and with those values as honed by lesbian feminism. We were to move several times, and a big factor in each move was where Glenda could find interesting and challenging work. But at no point did I ever consider our choosing our place of residence according to Glenda's work to be a capitulation or a denial of my equal role in making decisions about our joint life.

Glenda: *As feminists, we would both chafe under such expectations, and as lesbians, we had long since assumed that our lives would be dictated by our own choices rather than by social norms about the propriety of gender roles, including a role like the "trailing spouse." Neither Janis nor I assumed that she would become the "housewife" because she was retired and I was not. Instead, I assume that her time and her interests and her skills are of equal importance to mine, and there is no doubt that we agree on that. We share life-maintenance tasks, dividing them according to skills and interests instead of gendered assumptions about role-appropriate tasks or about whose time is "free." So our moves, like the rest of our shared life, were not dictated by norms about the working (primary) spouse and the non-working (secondary) spouse, but were a product of many discussions and shared eagerness. The job in New Hampshire sounded like a great match. Janis and I had just returned from attending a conference in New Hampshire and we had found the state beautiful. We looked forward together to living there.*

And so the peripatetic period in our life began. Over the next six years, our joint willingness to adventure our way through life, finding worthwhile work, engaging pastimes, and new friends along the way would take us on a circuitous journey from Colorado to New Hampshire, Massachusetts, Michigan, San Francisco, and back to Colorado.

Glenda: *My own path during these moves was largely determined by the positions I took in each place. In all of them, I found much to like and much to learn. I worked in two full-time teaching jobs, in a think tank doing research on LGBT issues in the public policy sphere, and as the clinical director of a community mental health center serving the LGBT community. I enjoyed many aspects of my work in all the places where we lived during our travels. I relied greatly on Janis' experience and wisdom as a teacher in all of my work, but naturally especially so in my faculty positions. I was living with a master teacher who happily talked with me, encouraged me, and challenged me in my own teaching. I worked hard, and I was most definitely not retired. But Janis was, and since the theme of this book is retirement, she should share some of the activities that have comprised what I think of as a model for creative retirement.*

Janis: *Our relocations have been shaped around Glenda's jobs, but to me, they have been grand adventures (if somewhat complicated by the complexities of cross-country moves). Once the inevitable hassles of packing and unpacking our lives were put aside, I got to invent a new way of being wherever we had landed. In each new place, I spent a couple of months getting settled, learning my way around, hanging shower curtains, and doing fix-it chores (always a favorite pastime). During this period, I would just watch and listen, waiting for opportunities that captured my interest to emerge. And it has always happened, sometimes more slowly than others, and it has always involved a combination of things that I have found challenging and gratifying. Glenda has helped me enormously with the process of finding and creating the "right" opportunities, sometimes suggesting possibilities (often the things she would do if she were retired), and always offering support and input when I needed it. I have also made a point of keeping some time "in reserve" so that I can respond to new opportunities that arise—community events, joint projects with Glenda, spontaneous travel plans, or major political upheavals.*

While we were in New Hampshire, I volunteered at the community kitchen, providing meals and food boxes to poor people, and at the recycling center, which I liked to say represented working both ends of the food chain. At Glenda's suggestion (and with her credibility as my ticket), I spent two weeks volunteering on a team of political organizers working on a LGB-rights election in Oregon.

When we moved to Northampton, Massachusetts, I very soon found myself deeply involved in the community. Still interested in helping meet folks' basic needs, I delivered meals on wheels, and I worked with the American Friends Service Committee, an opportunity to be involved in broader issues of peace and justice. My professional work with Glenda, especially our joint interest in lesbian, gay, bisexual, and transgender (LGBT) issues, also shaped my community work there. In Northampton, I did a volunteer stint managing the finances of the Institute for Gay and Lesbian Strategic Studies (where Glenda was acting as Interim Director while the Director was on sabbatical leave). I also volunteered at the drop-in center for LGBT youth and worked with the Western Massachusetts LGBT Political Alliance, the last at Glenda's suggestion and with the guidance and experience of her long background in such activities. The opportunity to be so thoroughly "out" in this setting (Northampton has been called "Lesbianville, USA") was invigorating, to say the least!

And my most exciting gig in Northampton, launched by Glenda's explicit encouragement, was as a volunteer news intern with a local DJ, whose wit and intellect we both appreciated hugely. Glenda says she was after the comp tickets that were sure to flow if I had a position at this station that sponsored a lot of musical events, but whatever the motivation, her suggestion gave me a grand year of working closely with Rachel Maddow, right before she left for NYC and fame at Air America and then MSNBC.

Rachel and I had great fun together. I once played the part of Dick Cheney, hiding in a "secure, undisclosed location," and listeners were invited to win a prize by finding me; we had a putt-putt tournament on the sidewalk in front of the courthouse, and I got to lead warm-up exercises in the 10-degree weather. Rachel and I also did some fine political organizing in Northampton. Given that this all occurred in the year when same-sex marriage became legal in Massachusetts, her exposure (and popularity) gave us a great platform to organize rallies. On the day that the Massachusetts Supreme Court announced its ruling making same-sex marriage legal in the state, we managed to gather about 150 people on 12 hours' notice for a rally on the courthouse steps—complete with police escort, street barricades, and statewide news coverage. And I got to blog it all, as some months earlier, I had been invited by the local newspaper to write a blog (the very idea of which was novel at the time), which provided a non-academic and delightful forum for me to vent about whatever was on my mind. Not surprisingly, social issues, feminist issues, LGBT issues, and assorted conversations with Glenda shaped many of those posts—along with the Hubble telescope and thoughts about the shaping power of language.

The next move was to Michigan, where I had a harder time finding my pace. But when I did, themes similar to those that ran through my earlier activities emerged there as well. I signed up again to volunteer with the American Friends Service Committee and with the local peace and justice organization (cleverly called "Peace Works"). I volunteered virtually full time for the presidential campaign, for obvious reasons: this was 2004. With some entrees to the LGBT community through Glenda's campus contacts, I worked on a task force trying to build coalition among multiple and sometimes-splintered LGBT rights groups throughout the state.

And then we were off to San Francisco, many people's dream of a perfect place to live. One of my first involvements in San Francisco was with the LGBT-rights organization Equality California. I started off doing voter ID work on the phone and on street corners and soon graduated to managing the phone banks one evening a week. One very satisfying part of that work was that we took an active and vocal stand for ballot measures on behalf of a range of underpowered groups—taking on Arnold Schwarzenegger...and winning! I also volunteered with the Department of Public Health doing HIV and hepatitis testing at street fairs. And, in a reprise of the theme of working to meet basic needs, I undertook training as a literacy teacher and taught reading skills to non-reading adults.

Then, after six years and homes in four states, we decided to return to Boulder. This decision was based on many considerations, perhaps the most compelling being our (and especially Janis') desire to be back in Colorado. Neither of us regrets all that moving about. We view it as a wonderful way to have gained some perspective on reality—or rather, on the variability of "reality" as defined in different locales. We made many friends along the way, some of whom we still see regularly when we visit them, or vice versa. When we returned to Colorado, some of that earlier wanderlust had settled, and we knew that we were here by choice instead of by default. We already had friends and community connections in Colorado, and settling into a new life and a new rhythm was not as difficult as it had been elsewhere.

Janis: *Back in Boulder and with the benefit of old contacts, I quickly gravitated to the Boulder Valley Safe Schools Coalition, a community advisory group that works to make the schools safe and welcoming for LGBT folks (students, staff, and parents). In this work, especially, I am aware of the value not only of Glenda's broad and deep understanding of LGBT issues, but also her experience working with community groups and her savvy about the processes of institutional change. I also started very soon to volunteer for several shifts per week at Boulder's women's bookstore, "Word is Out." The store was owned by a long time friend and former political-activism partner of Glenda's and served as a sort of feminist haven as much as a bookstore, until it sank, like so many women's bookstores, under the weight of Amazon, the slow demise of print media, and the virtual disappearance of women-specific spaces. That volunteer work brought me in contact with a range of folks and familiarized me with many community resources I had not known about before. My other primary volunteer role these days, working first with a woman only a couple of years my senior who is living with early-onset Alzheimer's and more recently with a woman only slightly older who lives with Parkinson's disease, is a reminder both of the importance of being present with others and of my/our own finitude along every dimension.*

As Janis was leaving behind (most of) her professional involvement and becoming immersed in volunteer community and political work, Glenda was moving into deeper involvement with her academic/professional role and finding less time for political and volunteer work. For Glenda, as for Janis, the trajectory of her life comprised a series of changing life experiences.

Glenda: *Part of what drew me to clinical psychology had been the prospect of a career that encompassed many possibilities: clinical work, research, and teaching. I was also interested in community psychology and consulting, and I took courses in the Graduate School of Public Affairs. During most of the first two decades after graduate school, I engaged in all of these activities. But my work life was always anchored by my being a clinician in private practice, a very private role in many ways. As we moved among four states and I among four jobs, I assumed different roles—full-time teacher, full-time researcher, and full-time clinical administrator. Each required a new focus, and each necessitated that I limit my activities in other areas. I struggled with the latter. I am as easily bored as Janis is, and I yearned to be able to keep my multiple professional pie plates spinning. The most expansive part of my life seemed to be not with the jobs (for the most part), but with pursuing a different kind of role as a psychologist working with the American Psychological Association. I served on the Committee for LGBT Concerns and later became involved in the task force that revised APA's* Guidelines for Psychotherapy with Lesbian, Gay, and Bisexual Clients. *In many respects, these activities answered my felt need for engagement in a process of generativity more than (most of) the jobs did. Here again, Janis was a perfect sounding board for all my activities. I felt that although this service clearly demanded significant time and energy, she unfailingly encouraged me to pursue it, and she helped me to do it better.*

Back in Colorado, I continue to try to include all these roles in my life. Even as I work hard at my full-time job in a university counseling center, I also conduct a private practice and try to keep up with all the research and writing projects that call me. And with my spare time, I strive to participate in meaningful ways in the world outside of work.

Throughout this decade-long process of moving about and finding new activities, interests, roles, and passions along the way, it became clear how, in a sense, we are trading places. Janis (who had been the nose-to-the-grindstone academic) has become the community-centered volunteer and activist, and Glenda (who had been the life-long activist and was a relative latecomer to professional life) has become even more deeply involved in her professional life. Yet, the simple theme of trading places is not entirely accurate. Throughout this process, each of us has continued to be actively (as well as vicariously) involved in her former role. Glenda has continued to be involved in political and community activities, and Janis has engaged in academic/professional work.

Glenda: *Some of my political and community activities have been of a less grassroots nature and more along the lines of psychologist-in-the-community. For example, I have worked on an advisory committee for national PFLAG (Parent, Families, and Friends of Lesbians and Gays) that looks at ways to help medical and mental health professionals to take on intentional roles as straight allies. Other activities have been more explicitly connected to community involvement. Once we were back in Boulder, I jumped at the opportunity to organize a half-day colloquium dedicated to Boulder's LGBT history— a fascinating history (including legal marriage licenses granted to six same-sex couples in 1975) that simply had to be part of the year-long celebration of the city's 150th anniversary. In all of these activities, Janis is a partner in my efforts. It is not unusual for us to chat about these pursuits while taking our ritual Saturday morning walk or sharing a meal out. In no time, I am taking notes on the ideas we are co-creating, both of us delighted by the project, whatever it may be, and by the opportunity to play with ideas together.*

Janis: *My continuing involvement with things academic/ professional has often represented a continuation of my pre-retirement work. For the first several years after I retired, I taught courses online. This represented a new challenge for an old-time classroom teacher, and I found it challenging and invigorating, but I really missed the contact with students. I taught a "live" course at a uni- versity located in one of our "home towns" along the way, and I taught for one semester at my former college when we returned to Colorado. I also assumed a very differ- ent role, serving as Interim Director of the GLBT Student Services program on my former campus, a role made fun by close contact with students. Recently, I have taken on a new, quasi-professional role editing professional docu- ments for people whose first language is not English. It lets me use skills honed through years of reading students' papers, it keeps me intellectually active, and it gives me an opportunity to learn things in a wide variety of fields. But most of my continuing academic/professional work has involved joint projects with Glenda. More on that later.*

The "trading places" theme should also not be taken to mean we went our separate ways. On the contrary, at each step in this process, our paths have often merged, including time for joint professional and political work as well as for leisure time. In the professional domain, our personal relationship emerged in the context of our joint professional projects, and our respect for each other's intellect and energy did not, of course, disappear as we traded places. Many aspects of professional work together relate to long-standing (and often still-ongoing) joint research and writing projects, and the precise nature of that work has often been shaped by where we have lived and who our colleagues have been at the time. Many projects have been done with students from local colleges and universities—sometimes from institutions where Glenda taught, and sometimes not.

In New Hampshire, we took the opportunity to gather data on LGBT youth in a rural area, part of a long-standing research on the changing context for LGBT youth more broadly. Several aspects of this multi-pronged research project about LGBT youth have resulted (and still do) in joint presentations and publications. In Massachusetts, we worked together on a project that merged research and theory to examine the LGBT "generation gap," an effort that has also generated several presentations and publications, and that still draws interest in the LGBT community. In Michigan, we worked together on another project that brought together research and theory about self-defense training for women, which again led to presentations and publications. We also cooperated on a theoretical paper about the relationship between theory and practice in psychology. And, at the intersection between professional work and changing the world, we wrote brief pieces summarizing the empirical research on the false conflation between sexual orientation and pedophilia and on seeing strength and fostering resilience in LGBT youth for inclusion in a Michigan State Department of Education publication. In San Francisco, we wrote a paper that used liberation psychology as the basis of an argument for the legitimate role of activism in psychology. And back in Colorado, we have continued a project that has generated papers on the long-term impact of anti-LGBT politics.

In the political/community/volunteer domain, too, we have worked together everywhere we have lived, our shared interests trumping the fact that one of us was retired and the other was not. We both engaged in work with a local chapter of PFLAG in New Hampshire, doing some training with the group and serving on a statewide LGBT committee. Our interest in LGBT youth led us both to volunteer at a queer youth center in Northampton. While we were in Northampton, we both became involved in activities related to the same-sex marriage movement, which was very active in Massachusetts while we were there. Janis lobbied (and participated in peaceful demonstrations) at the State House on several occasions; Glenda was at the State House, too, testifying as a researcher before legislative bodies. While we were in New England, we took several trips to Washington DC to participate in anti-war rallies (combining one such trip with a Joan Baez concert).

In Michigan, we participated together in a number of organizing activities, as that state was also facing an important vote on LGBT rights while we were there. In San Francisco, in addition to assorted political and community activities that spun off from Glenda's work at the LGBT community mental health center, we participated in rallies for immigrant rights and worked together on planning committees for feminist events. Back in Boulder, we have continued to work together on community and political activities—co-chairing the program committee for a regional conference focused on LGBT issues and doing training with queer youth leaders around ideas gleaned from our earlier research. And then there is the usual litany of events and fund-raisers that keep us in touch with the progressive community and the needs of the broader community.

Finally, lest we sound like advocates for the merits of an all-work-no-play life, we also find time to play together and to share time with friends. In truth, it is sometimes difficult to decipher the dividing line between work and play, as we both enjoy our work so much. So, many of our "leisure" activities have been "work"-related: speakers, workshops, trainings, conferences, documentary films, and other events focused on the topics that some might see as closer to work than to leisure.

But other recreational activities have been flat-out fun. Each place we have lived has offered different opportunities for pleasure—indeed, this has been one joy of our wandering lives. In New England, we took frequent trips to Boston (Jane Olivor at the Berklee School of Music, Ted Sorenson and Robert McNamara talking about Vietnam regrets at the Kennedy Library, the Blue Man Group blowing our minds). We also drove to New York for all kinds of reasons (or for no reason at all). We heard Paul Winter's solstice concert at the Cathedral of St. John the Divine, caught the opera, "Dead Man Walking," and saw a play about the Bush administration written by and starring Tim Robbins.

At homes along the way, we have enjoyed whatever local culture has to offer, especially in the way of folk music (we once saw Joan Baez five times in one year, which required a bit of travel) and opportunities to see and hear folks we admire: Ira Glass, Terri Gross, the broad range of brilliant people that appear at Boulder's week-long Conference on World Affairs every year. It seems like every town has a classic old theater that has been converted into a performance venue, and we virtually haunt these places: The Colony Theatre in Keene, NH; the Calvin in Northampton, MA; the Michigan Theater in Ann Arbor; the Castro Theater (home also to the greatest LGBT film festival known to humanity) in San Francisco; the Paramount in Denver; the Chautauqua National Historic Site in Boulder.

Nor have we felt confined to local diversions. We have taken the opportunity to travel when time and finances allowed. We have visited Amsterdam, spent a long weekend in Monterey, visited family in Hawaii on several occasions, taken several trips to the canyon lands of southern Utah, kicked back on a Caribbean cruise, spent a week in the Galapagos (in preparation for which Janis re-read Darwin), and traveled to New England on what has become an annual sojourn to visit friends and eat lobster on the coast of Maine. We are aware of how privileged we are to be able to take spontaneous trips—like recently to attend Pete Seeger's 90th birthday concert in New York—and to plan grand excursions—like next year to Ireland.

Among the things that we worked out in this process has been the balance between our two "outside" lives—i.e., the lives spent more or less individually, without the immediate presence of the other. The fact that one of us is retired and the other is not raises some potentially thorny issues that we have needed to consider. We have talked sometimes about whether either of us resents or is envious of the position of the other. Does Glenda resent Janis' freedom to come and go according to her own schedule, or does

Janis resent that Glenda's work interferes with our sharing that freedom? Is Janis envious that Glenda has greater public visibility in our community or that Glenda's professional work still garners attention while Janis' own work no longer does as much? Does Janis feel lonely or abandoned (or perhaps worse, bored) because Glenda is so involved in her work? Does either of us feel like Janis' being retired while Glenda remains professionally active detracts from our shared life?

The answer to these questions seems genuinely to be, no. It is not that our relationship is without conflict. But it is true that we do not have conflict about issues related to our different positions vis-à-vis retirement. Each of us takes pleasure in the successes and freedoms of the other, and, to a degree, each of us participates in the other's successes and freedoms. Of course, this balance is not without its occasional ambivalence.

> Janis: *The truth is, it was sometimes hard at first for me to step back, to not jump in and share the professional "stage" (even though I had chosen to give it up). I once sat in the front row of the audience as Glenda gave a presentation and felt (quite inappropriately) compelled to "help" her clarify a point. Clearly, I missed the visibility and the sense of efficacy that come from engaging with others in the process of exploring ideas and challenging old notions and pushing the limits of the discipline. But I was also clear that I had other things I really wanted to do, and I could not do those things and also invest the time and energy it would take to stay as "on top" of the material, which I would need to do to feel competent (the absolute prerequisite to feeling comfortable) in that role. Although I have continued to do some writing and speak-*

ing, that has slowed over the years, and the articles, book chapters, and speaking gigs are now few and far between. Slowly, I have let go of my role as a professional psychologist/academic—albeit not always easily and not always gracefully. I have found commensurate pleasure in my new place in life, and I am delighted with the gifts that retirement has brought. And as I have settled into this life, watching Glenda thrive and shine in professional roles, seeing her grow whole new areas of expertise and produce work that seems unending is very satisfying. Sometimes I still miss being on that path, but on balance, it's good.

Glenda: *I not only do not resent Janis' being retired, I gather a great deal of pleasure from it. In some respects, I feel like I get to partake of these new and stimulating activities without leaving the house. I genuinely use Janis' retirement as a prospective model for a rich retirement experience. I suppose I might have been more inclined to be envious were it not for the fact that I love virtually all aspects of my own work. It is not an exaggeration to say that much of the time, work feels no less fun to me than does play. Perhaps my biggest disappointment—if I can even call it that—is the nagging sense of loss I feel in relation to Janis' decision to have reduced her professional activities. My disappointment is not because of the direct impact on me; I am blessed with a great deal of access to exchanging both ideas and enthusiasms with her. Instead, I feel disappointed because Janis is no longer creating the products that constituted such genuine gifts to the world. I hate it, for example, that she refuses to write a second edition of her book on the psychology of sexual orientation. It was a great book, and there needs to be another, but no one else could write it as she could.*

To return to the initial theme of this book, what does this story say about the experience of retirement for feminist psychologists— or, in our case, how does being feminist psychologists shape the experience of two women sharing a life such as ours, a lesbian couple one of whom is retired and the other of whom remains deeply involved in professional work? In some senses, this has been a story about discontinuity: multiple geographic, professional, and personal changes made more complex as we have "traded places" in the midst of it all. On the other hand, there is continuity here, too, and one of the strongest threads of that continuity is the persistence of our commitment to feminist values, as has been evident in virtually every domain of our lives.

First, and probably the *sine qua non* of all other examples, the way we have managed our relationship through this process bespeaks a feminist sensibility: collegiality; shared decision making; respect for one another's expertise, needs, values, interests; the balance over the years in how major life choices have been made and how they have played out.

Then there is the content of the choices we have made. Our volunteer, community, and political activities and our professional work all enact concerns for equality, for women's rights and well-being, for the empowerment of underpowered groups, for joining with community to change the world for the better—values at the very heart of feminism. In every domain, our lives have been shaped by the lessons of feminism, so deeply shaped that it is hard to imagine what our respective lives would look like or what our relationship would look like (or if it would exist) without those lessons. Janis' retirement introduced a particular theme into this story, and that theme has had a part in how the story evolved. But, to reiterate language we used before, the impact of retirement, too, has been trumped by our common values, including those we share with other feminist psychologists.

To close, we would like to offer our responses to three questions posed by the editors in the hope of bringing some collective closure to these varied chapters:

1. What do we wish we had known before we reached this stage in our careers in terms of retirement?

   Glenda: *Because of my relationship with Janis, I am in the very privileged position of watching a very successful retirement-in-action. It has been—and continues to be—a wonderful model of what retirement can look like. I could not ask for more.*

   Janis: *I was not prepared for the awkwardness I would feel moving about the world without a professional identity as my mantle. In fact, my shedding that mantle was a rather slow process, and I still put it on occasionally. I had not been fully aware of how odd it would feel to not be who I had been, to not present the persona I had presented for so many years. Sometimes the dismantling has been freeing; often it has been uncomfortable; slowly, it has become ordinary. Usually. Sometimes I find myself searching for ways to slip who I was into conversations. But overall, settling into the new costume, like the rest of retirement, has been part of an adventurous process. I might wish away awkward moments (especially as they were happening), but I would not wish away the process.*

   On the other hand, when I consider my life with Glenda, I wish I had known that the economy would tank, leaving her to face a more extended work life than we had imagined. It's not that I think she will quit working (as opposed to going to work) when she retires, but her being free of the daily obligations of employment would free us to be more flexible in how we spend time around that work—longer vacations, greater opportunities for spontaneous adventures, more days of sleeping in. Had we known that this would happen, we would have ... done just what we did: wandered around the country until we were ready to stop.

2. What do we wish we had done differently in terms of retirement?

   Janis: *Returning to the practical, I sometimes wish I had worked a few more years so that my retirement benefits would support more adventure. But more often, I am grateful for the freedom of those extra years, and I am very aware that I am hugely fortunate to have been able to spend these years as I have.*

   Glenda: *I spend very little time looking at what I might have done, and that includes with regard to the question of where I am in my career. I remember the time in own psychoanalytic journey when it became clear to me that if I were to change my history—paste in a better "this" and an improved "that" here and there—I would no longer be who I had been. I have not since pursued the question of what I might have done differently—at least not in terms of the big questions about my life. Having said that, there is one thing I wish were different, but it occurs on a larger scale. I wish that Janis' and my relationship were formally acknowledged as are the relationships of heterosexual friends. If it were, my access to financial resources would be quite different, and I would have better options around questions of work and retirement. This is not something*

I wish I had done differently; in fact, I have worked very hard toward that end. But it is something I wish we had been successful in achieving by now.

3. What are we happy about in terms of what we anticipated and did to prepare for retirement?

    Glenda: *I am happy to have work I love, relationships that make me better than I would otherwise be, and a passion for being alive, despite creeping aches and pains.*

    Janis: *I am happy that I have always paid heed my low threshold for boredom and shifted the focus of my work when I found myself getting bored. That habit served me well in my career, and it has served me well in retirement, where I have been able to engage in a huge variety of activities, knowing that I will always find engaging things to do with my time and my skills, that I need to keep my life both full and fluid, and that it's good for me to follow that urge. I am also happy that I am in a relationship with a woman who honors (and nurtures) my eagerness for adventure and who shares the wish to keep reaching.*

The W in Work is for Women:
Facing the Early Retirement of my Spouse

Eileen L. Cooley

Beginnings

J grew up in the 50s; perhaps that sums up best where I began. My living room was filled with *Ozzie and Harriet* and *Father Knows Best*, and my mother was always home when I was home. I wore only the required skirts to high school, loved the *Beatles*, and assumed I would grow up, get married, and have a husband who would take care of me. I waited to be swept off my feet.

My father worked and controlled the money and the decisions. He "gave" my mother a weekly allowance (I remember him counting it out) and, when she graduated from college and became a teacher, he "let her work" and she, in turn, appreciated his "openness."

Work transformed my mother. She was 20 years old when she was married, dropped out of college, and had children. In her mid-20s she returned to college, and now in her 30s and a college graduate, she started to flourish. She had her job to go to, her own money, and a developing identity. She made friends that were not part of their marriage and was gone sometimes when my sister and I were home. In her first job, my view of my mother changed from someone who was there for me and our family, to someone who also maintained a role outside our family.

Although I did not realize it at the time, I was watching my mother grow up. Through watching her transformation from an inexperienced young girl to an independent adult I really learned the power of education and work. In her college graduation and first classroom job lay the seeds for my personal obsession with work. It is in her transformation that I first learned to equate work with power and strength.

I clearly was not raised in a feminist household. How I became the feminist that I am remains somewhat a mystery to me. It may have been the unfolding of the 60s and 70s, the advent of birth control, going to college, and the sparks of the times that promised the world could and would change. Whenever it started I did not immediately jump on the bandwagon, but rather slowly changed who I was. Although Webster's dictionary defines feminist theory as encompassing political, social, and economic factors that establish equal rights for women, I became particularly focused on the economic realities of inequality. I championed work as the way to personally control my equality. If I became educated and supported myself financially, I would empower myself. In my adoption of this reductionist view of feminism, work itself came to symbolize independence, and a move away from the patriarchy.

The W in Work is for Women

Although work provides independence for all people, it has special significance for women. As more women have entered the workforce and grabbed their earning potential, their options have continued to evolve. Although we may still face the glass ceiling at work and the second shift at home, employment provides a chance at the equality that was formerly denied. Of course women who are single mothers or from lower income families have always worked, regardless of the era. But for middle and upper income women with a choice, work has been a primary vehicle for elevating their status in society. So with these beliefs in hand, I pursued school, work, and a muddled course toward becoming a feminist.

▨ Marriage and Children

Marriage, by definition, can challenge equality. People usually join their names, their checkbooks, and their households and then women tend and nurture this union, often with less-than-equal status in the eyes of the world. I have even heard people say that it is impossible to be a real feminist and be married; after all it is a "property" based notion to be somebody's wife. Having children takes this 'merger' one step further and, in the end, women can lose their independence and perhaps their independent identity. Giving birth pushes many women formerly on career paths to be caretakers, to quit jobs (if they can afford to), and to cook dinner.

Long before I entered the stage of motherhood, I tried valiantly to avoid this fate. I intentionally did not learn to cook much, I was messy to a fault, and I always worked many hours, perhaps partly to avoid having time for typically feminine tasks. Therefore with the birth of our children, our house became messier, we ate more peanut butter and jelly, and I gave up friends, rather than work, to care for my children. I tried to have it all, in spite of exhaustion and resistance to feminism from my family and friends.

As my children grew, I continued to value career and employment in spite of the pressures from the outside world to do less and be at home more. As a mother I often heard it was ok to work "if you have to" or to work "part-time" while the children were young. I would have none of these. I worked full-time to satisfy my need for equality—my need for my own sense of self, purpose, and agency. As both a faculty member and licensed psychologist, I worked in two roles, often giving up sleep rather than the purpose that was sometimes fleetingly mine. At the same time, my husband worked as a director of a university business/industry program.

So we both worked full-time, and somehow we managed to love and nurture our children along the way. In some ways those childhood years were a blur of activities, appointments, and schedules, but we also made time to laugh, love, and support each other. Our Sunday evening activity became 'calendars,' a time to sit down and coordinate who did what and when for the coming week. We both seemed to value work and the role our careers played in our lives.

The Crisis: My Spouse Retires

Amidst this blur of racing to work and activities, I did not take time to carefully think about my reactions to my husband's plan for early retirement. Then, when the time actually arrived, I was caught psychologically unprepared. I remember when I first heard the specific date. I couldn't believe it. My husband was actually going to retire. I had an instantly negative, visceral reaction—my stomach churned and my heartbeat quickened. I panicked and thought to myself, but I'm just 50 years old; I don't want to and can't enter this phase of life yet! If he retires, we are together entering the third phase. As the reality sank in, I discovered that I hated the word "retirement", despised the thought of reduced activity, panicked at the thought of getting older, and then panicked at the thought that I'd be next—the next to consider leaving my work behind.

Retirement of my partner represented a threat to my life course. I did not have a say in this decision, so perhaps I was feeling out of control. His retirement profoundly affected my sense of self and my home. Our children were still in middle and high school. If work was so important to me, what did I think about having a husband who was not working?

Although I initially tried to keep his retirement a secret, the word leaked out. After all, he was proud and excited to retire. He envisioned more time with our children and wanted to experience the next phase of his life. Clearly the problem was mine. I soon found that my friends and relatives did not see his retirement in the same negative light that I did. People said he was lucky he could retire so young or commented that now we could, or would, do more things together. Still others pointed out that now he would have more time with our children, perhaps when they needed it most, as teens. But all of these positive words of wisdom fell on my deaf ears. I remained upset.

At first I could find no logical reason for my strong negative reaction to my partner's retirement. As I delved into my own thoughts and emotions, I started to understand myself and my reasoning. Over time, I identified numerous sources for my dread. Some reasons turned out to be rational and, in fact, were supported by research data examining adjustment concerns couples experience when one partner retires. Other reasons reflected my personal point-of-view. How many of these were rooted in my pro-work feminist ideology remained to be seen.

No Longer a Working Couple

Since embarrassment was one of the first emotions I felt, let me start there. It makes sense that one of my first thoughts was how my husband and I would be perceived differently. Obviously, we would no longer be a working couple. I could no longer answer the question, "What does your husband do?" without squirming. I felt this uneasiness, in spite of the fact that he remained busy and active.

In the early years he worked as a part-time consultant in economic research and throughout his retirement he has continued to exercise faithfully, plan exquisite family vacations, read voraciously, and passionately pursue his interests in sailing and hiking. Nonetheless, I found it difficult to describe his retirement without supplying this long list. In contrast, I find work titles provide a nice shorthand way of describing each of us in one or two words. One of the first questions we all ask each other is, "What do you do? " We tend to pigeon-hole each other by our jobs, our careers, our roles.

My personal reaction clearly showed me that not only did I think retirement defined my identity, I clearly thought it defined his. From this awareness, I started to realize that, in the back of my mind, I believed everyone was somehow defined by jobs and career. As the parents mingle at soccer and basketball games, would we be perceived in a new category? Perhaps I would continue to struggle in defining my husband in this new stage of retirement. I was no longer part of a working couple and my children now had a retired father.

A Workless Model?

My daughter turned 15 and my son 13 when this "change" in our family happened. After he retired, I started to worry that my children would experience my dilemma, my embarrassment, my uneasiness, when they were asked, "What does your father do?" Would they take the time to describe his list of passions and interests, or would they simply use the "R" word?

An additional concern was the impact of their father's retirement on their concept of work. Would his unemployed status be seen as positive or negative? In my own obsessive fashion, I began to worry that their view of the importance of work might be diminished. I feared my children would start to think of work as optional, and thus, through my own projections, I felt threatened. We all knew that my husband had loved his job and was attached both to his colleagues and the institution. What did it mean that he had left all of that behind? Would their father's early retirement impact their personal drive for achievement? These were some of the questions spinning in my mind.

The reality, of course, is that my teenage children probably didn't think about their father's retirement as much as I imagined they did. Since he had a pension and a very busy schedule, in their eyes his life may have appeared pretty much the same. Furthermore, their needs continued to be met. I was clearly projecting my own discomfort onto them.

The Initial Daily Adjustment

Besides abstract concepts and concerns, there is the reality of daily life. Let's start with the obvious, he was home more often. Of course this meant I had fewer chances to be alone in the house. I used to look forward to sneaking home in the middle of the day to savor a few moments with couch and coffee. But the schedule was no longer set and I could no longer assume the silence. If I was on the computer, he might be in the next room; if I was on the phone, the words were no longer private.

Of course there were some real advantages to this new arrangement. I did know where to find him more often, and the strain of coordinating our schedules lessened. He was able to pick up the kids more often or greet the worker for dishwasher repair. He was less tired and more emotionally available. He became a better listener and expressed more ideas and feelings as he relaxed and opened up.

Household Division of Labor

Besides the pros and cons of time alone and increased availability, I pondered our division of labor at home. In a traditional, middle-income situation women may not work outside the home, work fewer hours, have less significant jobs (perhaps not careers or jobs with lower salaries), or quickly "give up" their employment for the sake of the household. Their work may be considered additional, peripheral, or simply less important. As data from the real world continues to show us, women often earn less money than men, so the disposability of a women's career may make economic sense. Given these economic realities some may argue that it is under-standable for women to take on more of the household chores.

With so much of society continuing to assign women to homemaker roles, it remains difficult to implement alternative models. I remember relatives addressing all their childcare questions to me, even while my husband was standing in the room. Changing gender role expectations is not easy. It is not just ourselves we must change, but the viewpoints and blunt opinions of well-intentioned others.

Hollywood has failed to provide us with new models and continues to portray household disasters for father-headed households. Even in 2011 much of the world assumes that men have jobs and money while women work if and when they have to. This line of thinking relegates the cooking and cleaning to women even, unfortunately, when both partners work. Although I didn't clean much, most of the time I had default responsibility for meals, childcare, and household management.

So what did I expect when I kept working while my spouse retired? Unrealistically, I thought our division of labor would quickly become more even; that he would assume many more of the household tasks. Imagine my chagrin when it dawned on me that I was still cooking dinner after working all day. The feminist in me wanted to hide.

Luckily, over the years of his retirement, he has taken on more household tasks and the balance of "home" work has shifted. Altering ingrained patterns clearly takes energy and intent. Our division of labor has slowly changed from me doing the vast majority of these tasks to more balance. Although I appreciate this improved equality in our division of labor, I remain frustrated with the slow pace of these changes and the lifetime totals. In approaching an egalitarian partnership, we have continued to miss the step where I had a chance to do less than half.

The Woman as Sole Worker

Regardless of the balance at home, however, my status as the "worker" in our marriage continues to fill me with pleasure, pumping up my feminist identity. I enjoy being the one to get up for work or the one who goes into work on the weekend. I feel empowered by the contrast and can imagine that many men enjoy a similar position. I like being the one with a more hectic schedule.

Of course the financial realities still grate against my internal feminist. How could it be that, even in his retirement, he earns more money than I do? This fact detracts from my sense of financial power and diminishes my delight at my worker status. Financial inequalities continue to be a primary factor, if not the primary factor, in the feminist struggle to be on equal footing.

I'm Next: Facing my own Retirement

Besides my discomfort over issues of division of labor or my thrill to be the one who works outside the home, the real problem with his retirement was and is the realization that I am next.

This means many things to me. It forces me to confront my own conceptualization of aging, and challenges me to address my goals for the next chapter of my life. I think his early retirement raised these issues long before I had really considered the impact of my own aging. New social psychological research stresses how the behaviors and habits of others, even friends of friends, can influence our own behavior. Clearly his change to retirement status changed me.

While my anxiety increased over my own retirement, I initially found room for denial and delay. I was comforted by our age difference and by my plans to continue working for many (many, many?) more years. At first I comforted myself by savoring a sense of relief that I had many years of employment left, happy that I had married somebody older than I was. This denial of the future reality helped in the first few years, but it did not last.

Reality has a way of creeping in, especially as I moved along my own chronological path. I realized I would retire at some time, and that time was getting closer and closer. I started asking myself questions about what I really wanted. While considering options for changing types of work, travel, and writing, I clearly realized my feminist identity would also be challenged. My narrow definition of feminism had started to haunt me. I began to realize that I had boxed myself in.

The immutable equation I had created, i.e., feminism = work, is clearly at the root of my panic over retirement. Without work, how will I demonstrate my commitment to female/male equality? Is the blending of feminism and retirement an impossibility?

Need for New Models

Clearly we need new models of feminism in retirement, but there are too few models to find. After all, feminist views flourished during the late 20th century—it is only now, in the 21st century, that our feminist forerunners are addressing their retirement. We must all look to them to spark ideas about what lies ahead. As we wait to see how feminism may be defined post-retirement, we also acknowledge the right for us all to make our own way.

So in my search for new models, I found I thought again of my own mother. I am quite proud of her level of activity and involvement in her 80s; she who grew up in the very traditional environment of the early 20th century. I have mentioned her trans-

formation from wife to worker, but she really had a second transformation as well. She transformed from a teacher to an active
retiree. Although she stopped teaching more than 20 years ago,
she remains busy—screening preschoolers for visual impairments,
driving food from restaurants to shelters, attending lectures and
plays, volunteering at a nursing home, traveling, playing bridge,
and socializing. She rarely eats dinner alone and organizes outings
and trips. Perhaps my own mother is a closeted feminist, without her knowledge! She speaks her mind, does not let herself be
cheated, and most importantly, takes charge of her time and life.

Other women inspire me as well. I love hearing of new careers
for women in their 70s and 80s, seniors working in disaster relief,
Barbara Walter's life story, and women as authors, mentors, and
presidential candidates. We may not have as many models as we
need, but clearly there are more and more women to look up to
and emulate.

The Retired Feminist: Not an Oxymoron

With these limited, but powerful models, our job as soon-to-retire
feminists is to provide better examples for each other and the next
generation. We need to demonstrate purpose and equality in our
behaviors, our activities, and our values before, and most importantly, during retirement.

What will retirement mean for me personally? Must I redefine
my personal view of feminism, change my feminist = work equation? Yes and no. On the "yes" side, I do need to re-conceptualize
my concept of work to include "the work of life." My definition
must expand to include meaningful activities beyond the old 9-5

mold. I now see there are more ways than paid employment to make a mark. On the "no" side of this question, however, I believe that even in retirement women must contribute to make a difference, to be perceived as powerful and to have power.

What will I do? I feel a responsibility to be one of these new "retired feminist" models. I imagine I will be more like my mother, busy and involved in retirement. I will think more, write more, and find new causes to fight. I do not intend to give up my feminist identity. Instead, I am intent on enjoying my new definition of work, a work concept that is more flexible and perhaps more meaningful. I may travel and relax more, but I will not give up my mission.

At the same time, it is likely that the retirement years will reduce my need to fight for equality. In this third chapter of life, women can thrive and become leaders of family and community. With a retired spouse and more limited income, the economic playing field between partners becomes naturally more balanced.

Future feminists may find this transition to retirement much smoother. Their memory of the mid 20th century will be less acute and the need to forge equality for women, I hope, will no longer be necessary. In the United States, our children are growing up in a world with greater flexibility; women have fewer barriers, more opportunities, and a wider variety of family models. As the traditional, structured family becomes more of a novelty, acceptable options multiply for both women and men. As the working world provides child care, telecommuting, and self-employment booms, our definitions of work and earning power change. Recent reports suggest a growing group of women who are the major breadwinners in their families. With this new flexibility, I imagine the feminist women of the future will float more easily into retirement without facing the same identity struggle.

Conclusion

So, I must conclude this essay by thanking my husband; thank him for providing the wake-up call and the practice run forced on me by his early retirement. I'm glad he went first and I was forced to reflect on the meaning of work in my life. In my panic over his retirement, I learned how work and feminism had become synonymous in my mind, how my flexibility had been curtailed by my personal dictionary.

I have learned about my narrow conceptualization of my feminist identity. As a result of the jolt of his early retirement, I have reconsidered what work means to me and I have increased my confidence that I can be a feminist without exhausting myself on the job. Looking back to my 30s and 40s, I can see how I needed work and career to secure an equal footing for myself. Although I knew intellectually that women were broadening their careers and roles in society, I had not taken the time to update my personal history or rewrite my definitions. Now, thanks to the anxiety I experienced when my husband retired, I can broaden my feminist identity with a wider, more flexible definition of work. I can look forward to crafting my own feminist retirement—with or without a paycheck.

To Stay or to Leave:
What are Retirement Options for a Feminist
Woman of Color in the 21st Century?

Janis Sanchez-Hucles

"Bringing the gifts that my ancestors gave, I am the dream and the hope of the slave. I rise I rise I rise."
- Maya Angelou -

"Being a professional is doing the things you love to do, on the days you don't feel like doing them."
- Julius Erving -

"I used to want the words "She tried" on my tombstone. Now I want "She did it."
- Katherine Dunham -

Historically, many men and women worked at the same job until they reached retirement. Increasingly, individuals currently have five or six careers (Silverman, Skirboll, & Payne, 1996) before they are eligible to retire. As an individual who has worked at the same University for over 30 years, the question I am debating is whether to continue in the same job or try something new for retirement.

But there are many challenges in contemplating a different career path. What path do I pursue as I leave academia? Should I remain in an allied health field such as Clinical Psychology Private Practice given the changing landscape? Or should I try a new career path in consulting? What are other careers that I could actually pursue and be successful in? What about a new career as a massage therapist? Should I follow the Sports Psychology field as I have given several presentations to female coaches due to my daughter's status as a two time Olympic gold medalist? How viable would an almost 60 year-old female be in competing for a new position? How can I be ready to offer financial support to extended family members? What personal goals must I satisfy before retirement? Some of these retirement questions are impacted by my gender as a female, my race as a woman of color, my middle class income as a Professor, and the intersection of these identities.

I also recognize that I do not fit easily in to any one racial-gender description because although I identify as African American, I have a Cuban background and speak some Spanish. I also identify as a feminist which renders me suspect to some women of color who are more comfortable identifying as a "Womanist."

I recognize that my income is a key component of the family finances, so as I contemplate alternative careers, I am cognizant of the bills that must be paid. Although I know the costs of many expenses, I do not know the costs of others such as health care premiums. I also know that my work style has been dictated by being a woman of color with a mixture of unconventionally "feminine" and "masculine" work styles. In my family life I was expected to be available to pick up and care for sick children, host social events in the home, and send out holiday cards. It was not an option to be unavailable for car pooling, cooking, and caretaking. But in order to meet my personal career goals, I also have worked long hours daily away from home, had work responsibilities that included travel, and was unable to do many of the "traditional" home chores, so I often relied on a cleaning company. I remember talking to a good friend who started working in my department at the same time. When we compared notes, she laughed about the fact that her husband probably did more of the caring for children and household tasks than she did. We talked briefly about writing an article on how the lives of women of color were still different from the lives of White women, but we were unsure of how wide-spread these differences were.

In this paper, I will discuss the occupational choices that are currently available to me as I think about career options in retirement. I will offer an overview with respect to issues salient to women of color, and I will explore the topics of retirement that are of special import as I move to this next transition period. I conclude with next step thoughts for researching the area of women of color and retirement and I answer what I wish I had known before, what I wish I had done differently, what I am glad I anticipated, and words of wisdom for others contemplating retirement.

Retirement Issues for Women

It is important to first define the concept of retirement. In the past we often spoke about retirement and those of "old age", but life has changed. Fewer jobs cover the life span, relationships and marriages are less permanent, retirement age is flexible, lifestyles are more active, and there is greater longevity, which makes it difficult to describe when "old age" begins (Kloep & Hendry, 2007). Jackson and Gibson (1985) assert that retirement involves receiving benefits, a decrease in time spent in paid work, and a view of oneself as retired. In the United States, retirement became an option with the Social Security Act of 1935 and studies of retirement planning for men began to appear (Richardson & Kilty, 1989). Despite the widespread studies on retirement, there is a paucity of assistance available to help people plan for this major transition as most preparation centers on financial advice do not address social, emotional, and health changes of later life (Kloep & Hendry, 2007).

Margaret Matlin (2000) noted that there are relatively few articles in the literature that discuss female retirement and there are even fewer investigations of people of color. Ideas of retirement have focused on White males with only the recent addition of a literature on White females, as the former group was considered more significant. Theoretical and empirical research has indicated that post secondary education has an important effect on the social and economic status of women. Both African American and White women with higher educational levels have stronger economic well being and less reliance on welfare (Zhan & Pandrey, 2002). Education appears to be a long term benefit that fosters economic sufficiency.

The literature on individuals of color who may be economically disadvantaged is sparse, as many of these individuals withdraw from the labor force briefly, but return in order to maintain a decent standard of living. Women of color traditionally continue with responsibilities for working in the home and caring for others, but not for pay (Calasanti & Bonnano, 1992). There is research that indicates that Mexican American women tend to retire earlier than Black and White women, whereas Black and White men are inclined to retire earlier than Black and White women (Stanford, Happersett, Morton, & Peddecord, 1991).

Research on the work experiences of women and the 1950s culture reveals the presence of an underside where African Americans and other women of color resided. Starting in the 1940s and increasing in the 1950s, African American women left the south to escape the low paying domestic jobs that left them vulnerable to oppression (Coontz, 1992). These women did not live in suburbs, but in urban ghettoes where they faced overcrowding, crime, drugs, segregation, and discrimination. These women of color did not enjoy the "cozy housewife role" as illustrated in television fame by June Cleaver. By 1970, they were more likely to work outside of the home at a rate of 70% versus 49% for White wives (Dailey, 1998). Forty per cent of the Black women working had small children, and 25% headed their own households (Coontz, 1992). But migration to the Northeast and Midwest brought the cultural expectation that women needed to work to augment the suppressed wages of men. So these women entered the work force.

It is known that women are more likely candidates for poverty as they grow older, but the poverty rate for African Americans is at 25% and for Hispanics 20%, in contrast to non Hispanic Whites at 8% and Asian Americans at 14% (De-Navas-Walt, Proctor, and Lee, 2005). The increasing poverty rates for minorities have important implications for the future, as these populations are expected to increase as the White population decreases. Hispanics and African Americans also tend to have less education than Whites, work in low skilled areas, and face more job instability (Flippen & Tienda, 2000). With respect to net worth, African American households have less than 20 % of the worth of White households and the mean income is about 50 to 60 % of White households (Blau and Graham, 1990; Oliver and Shapiro, 2006; Wolff, 2001a; Wolff, 2001b). African American married couples have more assets than those who are single, especially female headed households (Lee, 2009).

Traditionally, marriage was considered a vital revenue source for women as they were dependent on their higher income earning husbands. Generally, marital disruption such as widowhood, divorce, and separation tends to reduce the assets of most women (Angel, Jiminez, Angel, 2007). As census studies show declines in marriage, increases in divorces, and increased participation of women in the labor force, this benefit does not exist for African American women who are less likely to be married and living with a spouse (Cherlin, 1992; Harrington, et al, 2005).

For African American women, good jobs with benefits are keys to financial security (Willson, 2003). It is also a fact that minority families are more likely to live with extended families. Approximately 42% of African American women live with others and this may engender their financial security when they strive to help family members with financial needs (Lee, 2009).

The proportion of women in the workforce has increased significantly over the last several decades as men's participation has decreased. This reflects a trend for men to retire early and societal changes that have led women to seek paying jobs (Talaga & Beehr, 1995). It wasn't until the late 1960s and early 1970s that retirement issues for females began to be explored. The findings to date have been interesting and complex.

Women, similar to men, feel committed to work, often delay retirement, and encounter difficulties in adjusting to retirement (Atchley, 1976). Research by Calasanti (1996) indicates that gender mediates the work and retirement experiences of men and women in different ways, even in jobs that appear to be equal with respect to salary and position. Research on gender and retirement has been equivocal. In early studies conducted in the mid-seventies, men and women had positive attitudes, but females were significantly more positive (Atchley, 1982. Later studies in the 1980s and 90s show women reporting less satisfaction and more stress (Floyd et al, 1992).

Retirement Theories

There are three major theories on retirement: role theory, continuity theory, and the life course perspective. Role theory asserts that retirement is a role exit that can lead to anxiety and depression due to the loss of identity (Burke, 1991). But role theory predicts a satisfying experience for individuals retiring from a job that they do not care for and if they can maintain their role identity (Quick & Moen, 1998). Continuity theory espouses retirement as a planned opportunity to maintain social contacts, life style patterns, and personal goals (Atchley, 1982). Those who plan for retirement will be happier than those who find retirement unexpected. The life course perspective posits that life transitions such as retirement occur in an ongoing life pattern and understanding the resources available and the meaning of leaving a career path reveal different paths of employment for men and women (Moen, 1996).

My personal plans for retirement should allow me to maintain my role identity as a clinical psychologist, and I can feel good about exiting my current career path as I have completed most of my personal goals and feel ready for a change. From the continuity theory, I am also very interested in being mindful of retirement plans to ensure that I stay in touch with people important to me, personal goals, and life style considerations. From the life course perspective, I have noted that I will need to be an active participant in finding new employment opportunities and that I cannot expect to simply be contacted by others as often happens to male colleagues.

Another significant term to describe work history is "orderliness." A career is termed "disorderly" if four-fifths of the work history includes unrelated jobs (Wilensky, 1961). Wilensky noted that men with orderly careers had strong attachments to community activities, integrated work and non-work spheres, and maintained longer friendships, all of which relate positively to health and well being (Moen, Dempster-Mc Clain, & Williams, 1992). We know however that many women have career paths that require moves in and out of the labor force (Moen, 1985).

I am fortunate that I have had an "orderly" career path as I have been able to stay in my current job for over 30 years. In this career path I have had several different jobs: Professor, Psychologist at the Counseling Center, Assistant Dean, Director of Clinical Training, Acting Graduate Dean, and Chair of the Department. All of these positions brought new challenges and prompted growth, but they allowed me to develop in the same university environment.

But the research on women of color suggests that definitions of work and retirement must be altered. The National Survey of Black Americans (NSBA) (Jackson, Tucker, & Gurin, 1987) demonstrated that due to fewer educational opportunities and discrimination, many minority workers continue to work as they are not eligible for pensions or benefits that are sufficient for retirement. I know that I wish to continue working, but I am fortunate that I have a high educational status and a wealth of job experiences that should help in securing future positions. These credentials help White women, but I am unsure if these credentials will be as effective for a woman of color. There continues to be a scarcity of research on African American women and retirement which underlines their invisibility in the world of work despite their long and active participation (Silverman, Skirboll, & Payne, 1996). We need research studies that track retirement for women of color based on their income and educational status.

Resistors and Anticipators

In their exploratory study of 21 African American women and retirement, Silverman, Skirboll, and Payne (1996) were able to classify these women based on their responses to retirement and their reactions following retirement. Women could be anticipators of retirement, resistors to retirement who retired, resistors still working, and individuals who knew that the time to retire had come. I believe that I am currently experiencing all of these reactions.

Typically, anticipators of retirement have a good idea of what they intend to do following retirement. I know at this time that I would enjoy continuing my work in consulting with companies and individuals and also expanding my current private practice. I also feel a sense of resistance to retirement. I know that many colleagues remain active in academia until their late sixties and there are days when I cannot imagine what life would be like without the responsibilities of writing articles and developing lectures. I also can identify with women who feel that the time to retire has come, as I have accomplished many of my personal goals over the span of my career.

The literature also posits a variety of reactions to retirement including adapting well, loss of status, or returning to work. Again, I expect to experience all three of these reactions. I expect that a change of job consistent with retirement will engender feelings of loss, change, and discomfort initially. I hope to have a plan that allows me to maintain a healthy self esteem and to feel good about what I am leaving behind. Currently, I feel excitement and anxiety about the prospect of returning to work in a different job!

Quick and Moen (1998) conducted an empirical study on over 200 men and 200 women aged from 50-72 to study factors related to retirement. They found that for women, higher retirement quality was associated with good health, continuous career, an early retirement, and a good post retirement income. For men, higher retirement satisfaction was derived from good health, an enjoyable preretirement job, substantial planning for retirement, retiring for internally motivated reasons, and low work role salience. I find this research very provocative because I have had a continuous career, but have also been challenged with health concerns during my mid fifties. Is it therefore wise to plan for an early retirement and to work out possible career paths to follow? Do I follow the suggestions for women or should I be in accord with the recommendations for men? As a woman of color, I believe that I must consider the factors for both men and women.

Multiple Models of Retirement

It has been noted that the traditional literature on retirement does not address issues faced by older women who are minorities (Flippen & Tienda, 2000). This suggests that there may be multiple models of retirement as shaped by the power relations created by race, class, gender, sexual orientation and age (Calasanti & Slevin, 2001). Historically, work on volunteerism focused on middle class individuals and individualistic roots, but the work of minorities is typically comprised of complex patterns of unpaid community work that is collectivistic (Eckstein, 2001). Although volunteer opportunities may be diverse across race, many White individuals pursue individualistic volunteer work in accord with their interests be it cooking, gardening, or becoming a docent at a museum. Women of color however are likely to volunteer for collectivistic projects such as reading programs, after school tutoring programs, or political action groups that are focused on encouraging more minorities to vote. Researchers need to explore how collectivistic volunteer work is different from individualistic patterns and why individuals choose different paths.

Kathleen Slevin (2005) conducted a study on African American women that presents unique perspectives on this population: Race, class, and gender shaped how these women created engaged and vibrant lives, remained in good health, and were not the stereotyped selfish takers of societal resources. These women all had personal experience with segregation which served as a motivator for them to help others. They committed to a diverse array of "race uplift" work in their efforts to give back to their communities and to encourage the growth of young people.

The 2000 census indicated that females had a higher rate of volunteerism than males (62% versus 49%) and Whites had a higher volunteerism rate than Blacks (58.6% versus 46.6%), but that Blacks who volunteer have higher rates of participation than Whites (4.7% versus 3.5%) (U.S. Bureau of Census, 2000). There has been a long history of volunteerism in the Black community and church by independent and powerful women.

Adjustment to Retirement

Some research has indicated that the individuals best adjusted to retirement are those with high involvement in community organizations and activities (Kloep & Hendry, 2007). This participation is not only a sign of good adjustment and high life quality, but it also enhances cognitive functioning and functional ability (Avlund, Lund, Holstein, & Due, 2004) and reduces morbidity (Hyppa & Maki, 2003). There are also a plethora of activities for retirees to commit to, ranging from paid employment, volunteering, helping families, friends, and neighbors, tending grandchildren, or travelling (Kloep & Hendry, 2007; Staats & Pierfelice, 2003).

Conclusions

There is a pressing need to better understand the retirement patterns for women and women of color. We need to look for patterns that predict when women will retire and what predicts positive adaptations to retirement. Particularly important areas to study will include career paths, salaries and benefits, health status, and plans for retirement. Continued disparities in men's and women's life paths indicate that retirement paths and decisions will vary by gender, race, and socioeconomic status. We need to explore the similarities and differences. Why is it that African American women tend not to complain about caring for families, but White women do? Why do White women retire in accord with a spouse when women of color do not? Why do women of color and their children choose to live with extended family members and often go back to work? Do work and retirement have different meanings for individuals especially when considering race and gender (Silverman, Skirboll, & Payne, 1996)?

American culture devalues those in retirement and may accord different amounts of social, emotional, and economic capital to individuals, but a critical factor to evaluate is how retired or soon-to-be retired individuals themselves regard retirement: Are they leaving exciting and enriching careers or are they leaving boring jobs and looking forward to new challenges and opportunities (Moen, 1996)?

We must continue to study the health and mental health of women as they enter retirement and to insure that they have the benefits to care for themselves and their families from their jobs and social security. This is especially important in the case of women of color as the current literature is sparse with respect to predicting the variety of experiences they may encounter in retirement.

I was surprised and dismayed by the lack of research that has been conducted on women of color and retirement, and now I alert others to this omission to encourage more research in this area. No matter how much you plan, I think that retirement reflects change and a new direction in life and cannot be accomplished without disruption to our usual routines. I think that one career path that is open to me is to apply for research grants to investigate the factors that are related to successful retirement for women of color. This research would investigate how retirement is different for women across race and what are the factors that lead to successful retirement plans.

As I try to understand this new stage of transition, I feel that it is unfolding like so many stages in my life. Even though I knew this stage was coming and tried to prepare, I don't feel completely ready! I hate saying all those inane things to myself like, "where has the time gone" and "how did the children grow up so quickly?" I clearly remember how long the years of childrearing were and feeling like our son and daughter would never leave a particular stage, but despite these memories I also feel that time has sped by.

We have put aside money for retirement, but like many others during this time, we know that given the current economic crises and depressed real estate values, we will need to accumulate more assets to ensure a comfortable retirement. I wish in retrospect that I had learned more about investments and the stock market earlier so that we would have created a stronger cushion for retirement. I would urge women and women of color to seek full retirement benefits in work rather than 401K plans. I feel that I am fortunate because I have a Defined Benefit Pension Plan that will assist in my retirement. It is also important to make specific plans for what you want to do in retirement and to recognize that retirement is not the same as taking an extended vacation.

On the positive side, I took to heart the advice I heard from many others that I could not go back to relive the time I had with my children. So despite a very busy professional career, I am grateful that I made it to almost all of the soccer, lacrosse, basketball, track, plays, and exhibits that our children participated in. We were fortunate to be able to travel with our children as they competed locally, nationally, and internationally. The feelings associated with having our daughter participate as a member of the U.S. National team in two world cups and winning two gold medals for soccer are complex and hard to describe, but they involved excitement, dread, pride, and unmitigated joy!

I am unsure of what I could have done differently to plan for retirement. I was born in the 1950s and grew up with the belief that as the female, I should be the responsible person for raising children, housework, and contributing to the family income. During the civil rights struggle I accepted the mandate that men should be the leaders and the recipients of most of the credit, although I felt uncomfortable as I noted all of the work that women accomplished. This discomfort grew as I entered my academic career and was invited to give lectures on women of color and feminism. The more I read, the more I was able to identify as a feminist although I understand why many women of color do not. I also notice today that many young women of color have different paths. Some of these women do not cook or clean and some have decided not to have children. Many are ambivalent about feminism and womanism.

I remember my first year of marriage when I worked as an academic advisor for a University, took classes to earn a master's degree, worked part time as a sales associate for a major department store, and commuted 90 miles a week to complete a practicum in clinical psychology. In retrospect, I wonder what drove me to work so hard. I remember that I grew up with the belief that to be successful, women of color simply had to do more, so I did so.

I wonder what my life would have been like if I had not pushed myself to work so hard? Would I have felt as successful? Did I feel that I had to set an example for my brothers and sisters? At this point I find myself musing on, what is success?

I think that I have tried to plan responsibly given the life challenges and resources at my disposal. I am pleased that I have several options for retiring from my University position. At this point, I plan to pursue expanding my private practice as my first foray into retirement. I will also continue to do supervision for individuals interested in becoming licensed by the State Board of Psychology. I am also interested in looking into hospice counseling as a possible career option and am trying to learn requirements for this path.

I would also like to develop perhaps a three day work schedule with flexibility for traveling. Plans for extended weekends involve renovations to our second home in a more rural locale. I am unsure of what my next big job venture will be, but I am still interested in perhaps learning how to be a professional massage therapist. Fitness continues to be an important component of my life so I am also exploring certification as a yoga instructor. As I try to develop my plans for work, I am also committed to volunteering so I will explore options that allow me to provide assistance to others in my community perhaps by working in a health clinic and providing psychological screenings and interventions. I am also intrigued by working in a hospital emergency room to provide reassurance and information to patients and their families.

I have always found myself drawn to career paths that were perfect for me, even if not exactly planned. I still rely on prayer and divine guidance to bring me to exactly where I need to be next with all the requisite skills and abilities. Is it unsettling not to know exactly what is coming next in my life? Yes. But I have trust that I will continue to be challenged and will grow with the opportunities that are presented. It is how I have lived my life so far and by and large, it has worked for me!

References

Angel, J.L., M.A., Jimenez, & Angel, R.J. (2007). The economic consequences of widowhood for older minority women. *The Gerontologist 47*, 224-234.

Atchley, R. C. (1976). Selected social and psychological differences between men and women in later life. *Journal of Gerontology, 31*, 204-211.

Atchley, R. C. (1982). The process of retirement: Comparing women and men. In M. Szinovacz (Ed.), *Women's retirement: Policy implications of current research* (pp. 183-194). Beverly Hills, CA: Sage.

Avlund, K., Lund, R., Holstein, B. E. & Due, P. (2004). The impact of structural and functional characteristics of social relations as determinants of functional decline. *Journal of Gerontology, 59B*, 44-56.

Blau, F. D. & Graham, J. W. (1990). Black-White differences in wealth and asset composition. *The Quarterly Journal of Economics, 105*, 321-339.

Burke, P. I. (1991). Identity processes and social stress. *American Sociological Review, 56*, 836-849.

Callasanti, T. M. (1996). Gender and life satisfaction in retirement: An assessment of the male model. *Journal of Gerontology, 51B*, 18-S29.

Callasanti, T. M., & Bonanno, A. (1992). Working 'overtime': Economic restructuring and class retirement. *Sociological Quarterly, 33*, 135-152.

Calasanti, T. M. & Slevin, K. F. (2001). *Gender, social inequalities and aging: Gender lens series*. Lanham, MD: Alta Mira Press.

Cherlin, A. J. (1992). *Marriage, divorce, remarriage*. Cambridge, MA: Harvard University Press.

Coontz, S. (1992). *The way we never were: American families and the nostalgia trap*. New York, NY: Basic Books.

Dailey, N. (1998). *When baby boom women retire*. Westport, CT: Greenwood.

DeNavas-Walt, C., Proctor, B. D., & Lee, C. H. (2005). *Income, poverty, and health insurance coverage in the United States; 2004*. Washington, D.C.: U.S. Census Bureau.

Eckstein, S. (2001). Community as gift-giving: Collectivistic roots of volunteerism. *American Sociological Review, 66*, 829-851.

Flippen, C., & Tienda, M. (2000). Pathways to retirement: Patterns of labor force participation and labor market exit among the pre-retirement population by race, Hispanic origin, and sex. *Journal of Gerontology: social sciences, 55*, 14-27.

Floyd, F. J., Haynes, S. N., Doll, E. R., Winemiller, D., Lemsky, C., Burgy, T. M., Werle, M. & Heilman, N. (1992). Assessing retirement satisfaction and perceptions of retirement experiences. *Psychology and Aging, 7*, 609-621.

Harrington Meyer, M., Wolf, D. A., & Himes, C. L. (2005). Linking benefits to marital status: Race and social security in the U.S. *Feminist Economics, 11*, 145-162.

Hyppa, M., & Maki, J. (2003). Social participation and health in a community rich in stock of social capitol. *Health Education Research, 18*, 770-784.

Jackson, J. & Gibson, R.H. (1985). Work and retirement among the Black elderly. In Z.S. Blau (Ed.). *Work, retirement, and social policy* (pp. 193-222). Greenwich, CT: JAI.

Jackson, J. S., Tucker, M. B., & Gurin, G. (1987). *National survey of Black Americans, 1979-1980.* Ann Arbor, MI: Inter-University Consortium of Political and Social research.

Kloep, M., & Hendry, L. B. (2007). Retirement: A new beginning? *The Psychologist, 20*, 742-745.

Lee, S. (2000). Racial and ethnic differences in women's retirement security. *Journal of Women, Politics, and Policy, 30*, 141-172.

Matlin, M. (2000). *The psychology of women* (4th Ed.). Fort Worth, TX: Harcourt Brace.

Moen, P. (1985). Continuities and discontinuities in women's labor force activity. In G. H. Elder, Jr. (Ed.), *Life course dynamics: Trajectories and transitions, 1968-1980* (pp. 113-155). Ithaca, NY: Cornell University Press.

Moen, P. (1996). A life course perspective on retirement, gender, and well being. *Journal of Occupational Health Psychology, 1*, 131-144.

Moen, P., Dempster-Mc Clain, D., & Williams, R. W., Jr. (1989). Social integration and longevity: An event history analysis of women's roles and resilience. *American Sociological Review, 54*, 635-647.

Oliver, M. L., & Shapiro, T. M. (2006). *Black Wealth/White Wealth: A new perspective on racial inequality.* New York, NY: Routledge.

Quick, H., & Moen, P. (1998). Gender, employment, and retirement quality: A life course approach to the different experiences of men and women. *Journal of Occupational Health Psychology, 3*, 44-64.

Richardson, V., & Kilty, K. M. (1989). Retirement financial planning among Black Professionals, *The Gerotonologist, 29*, 32-37.

Silverman, M., Skirboll, E., & Payne, J. (1996). An examination of women's retirement: African American women. *Journal of Cross-Cultural Gerontology, 11*, 319-334.

Slevin, K. M. (2005). Intergenerational and community responsibility: Race uplift work in the retirement activities of professional African American women. *Journal of Aging Studies, 19*, 309-326.

Staats, S., & Pierfelice, L. (2003). Travel: A long range goal of retired women. *Journal of Psychology, 137*, 483-494.

Stanford, E. P., Happersett, C. J., Morton, D. J., Molgaard, C. A., & Peddecord, K. M. (1991). Early retirement and functional impairment from a multi-ethnic perspective. *Research on Aging, 13*, 5-38.

Talaga, J. A., & Beehr, T. A. (1989). Retirement: A psychological perspective. In C. L. Cooper & I. T. Robertson (Eds.), *International review of industrial and organizational psychology* (pp. 185-211). Chichester, England: Wiley.

U.S. Bureau of Census. (2000). No. 637: Percent of adult population doing volunteer work: 1988. *Statistical Abstract of the United States.* Washington, DC.

Wilensky, H. (1961). Orderly careers and social participation. *American Sociological Review, 55*, 521-539.

Willson, A. E. (2003). Race and women's income trajectories: Employment, marriage, and income security over the life course. *Social Problems, 50,* 87-110.

Wolff, E. N. (2001a). Recent trends in wealth ownership from 1983- 1998. In T. M. Shapiro & E. N. Wolff (Eds.), *Assets for the poor,* 34-73. New York, NY: Russell Sage Foundation.

Wolff, E. N. (2001b). *Racial wealth disparities: Is the gap closing?* Public Policy Brief, The Levy Economics Institute of Bard College.

Zhan, M., & Pandey, S. (2002). Postsecondary education and the well being of women in retirement. *National Association of Social Workers, 26,* 171-184.

"Do We Have Any Mustard?": Challenges of the Retired Spouse

Stephanie A. Shields

" . . .Will you still need me, will you
still feed me when I'm 64?"

My parents had a conventional marriage, though in many
ways it was more egalitarian than the 1960s TV shows that
seem to pass for the last word on what 1950s marriages were really like. My mother, who had been the major parent figure at home
returned to full-time employment outside the home when she was
in her mid-40s. Less than ten years later my father, who was the
same age as Mom, had to take early retirement for health reasons.
When Dad retired my mother was not at all ready to kick back
with him to chill in retired bliss. Indeed, she had established herself in as an independent earner with a social network far broader
than it had been for many years. Importantly, too, the full-time
work was earning her an independent pension.

I remember Mom complaining to me that she would come
home after work to be greeted by Dad with "What's for dinner?"
The question made her crazy. Not only because it implied that
she was the only one who could figure out what dinner might be,
but because he seemed oblivious to all of the routine work that
makes a household function. Why couldn't he step up and take
some responsibility for household maintenance? Why, when he
took the initiative to prepare dinner, was it always take-out pizza?
I was a newly single assistant professor at the time. When Mom
and I talked, we would laugh about the situation. Sort of. We
recognized that my father's combined sense of privilege, studied
ignorance about things domestic, and painful drama of coming
to terms with the end of his paid work life, created a protective

wall around him. That wall shifted responsibility for his wellbeing and the wellbeing of their relationship to her. If she pressed
him to take responsibility she might risk his health further. If she
put herself first, she would feel guilt for asserting independence,
a guilt deeply embedded in the psyche of many women of the
Greatest Generation.

My mother's solution was to retire a few years sooner than
she would have liked. My parents then traveled extensively and
happily across North America in their RV. Mom invested her
energies into planning their travel, crochet, reading, birding, and
maintaining connection with friends and family.

When I contemplated my mother's situation, I was certain
that no such fate awaited me. My life was quite different from my
mother's. I never had been economically dependent on a partner.
I viewed my employment differently than had my mother. I had
worked continuously since college, and had been on by own for
a number of years before remarrying at 41. And most important,
mine was not my mother's marriage. Lew is a feminist man who
never harbored expectations that I would be the sole keeper of
the house.

So I was stunned when, soon after Lew retired, I came home
from a full day of work and was met with his earnest and sincere
question: "What's for dinner?" I could not believe it. I felt like I
had stepped into a cartoon world of bad jokes.

There is only a seven year difference in our ages. From middle adulthood onward seven years means next to nothing. It really
didn't matter that he turned 50 before I did, or even 60. What we
had not thought through, however, is that the small age difference

would push him into retirement sooner and that we would have to reckon with that difference in life stage. Two other factors complicated matters. First, Lew's retirement, though phased, came about as a result of reorganization and downsizing of the administrative office in which he worked. He was looking forward to retirement, just not at that moment. Second, Lew's transition came at the same time as my own investment in research and professional activity was at a new and exciting peak. The age difference that had meant little until now required a profound change in how we each organize our lives and make things work.

Unlike in the pre-retirement days, so far we have avoided the clash between partners that comes when one is intensely busy in some project or work or childrearing and the other is under less self-imposed or external pressure. The mismatch between career demands, for example, derails more than one grad student couple, including my own first marriage.

Lew and I have had imbalances in work commitment in the past. The most significant was early in our marriage. Lew was underemployed and looking to move from temporary faculty positions to administration. While I never understood why such a sane person would *want* to be an administrator, I supported his efforts fully. And that meant accepting that his search was every bit as important as the position I already had. I had to continually remind myself of the emotional toll that underemployment takes. It helped me enormously that my colleague, Claudia, was going through much the same thing with her partner. It helped to have someone to talk with about the mismatch between the real work (which we had) and the pretend work that we imagined the job search to be. We were working our tails off, but our partners were *only* looking for a job. It was hard not to be frustrated that household needs from grocery shopping to gutter repair were not being picked up by the job-hunter. If they weren't *really* working, couldn't they at least take care of the everyday daily-ness of home life?

At the same time that Claudia and I shared complaints, we were experiencing first-hand the soul-killing, relationship-jeopardizing, uncertainties of unemployment. Our two-person support group enabled us to cope with the frustrations with and fears for our partners. It also enabled us to be a bit better about not bringing those fears and frustrations home which would magnify an already difficult situation.

That earlier experience has helped both Lew and me to cope with this new imbalance. We both know what it takes to keep moving forward, and without actually making this a conscious plan, I think we both have made it a priority. He does not complain (much) about my busy schedule and preoccupation with work. He has been remarkably supportive of me when I revel in the deliciousness of research and the energizing effect of working with graduate students. In some ways I think our past disagreements about priorities has reduced, rather than intensified the likelihood of conflict now. For example, my priority has always been research and graduate training, while Lew's was undergraduate teaching and administration. The rivalry that occasionally tinged our discussions about work have melted away. I am thrilled that he has the opportunity to teach in Poland and the appreciation that the students show for his commitment to them. For his part,

Lew is more positively supportive of my professional commitments than he ever showed before, and this even as he is trying to
discover how he wants to structure his days and ambitions.

The change in work status still entails much careful adjusting. Even with Lew's change in work status, I am still stuck with
being the designated Keeper of All Quotidian Knowledge. My
favorite example being Lew at refrigerator with door open, plain-
tively asking, "Do we have any mustard?" I don't know whether I
am more frustrated by the fact that Lew asks when he is perfectly
capable of figuring it out himself, or the fact that I actually know
the answer without looking.

Google browsing turned up vast numbers of jokes about
retired husbands. A few years ago there was even a report widely
circulating about "Retired Husband Syndrome," a set of symptoms purported to be common among Japanese wives whose
salaryman spouses retire and then bring their managerial attitude
home, with the stress taking a toll on the woman's health. The
challenge of he's retired/she works occasionally is dealt with in
heterocentrist news articles that focus either on her envy of his
free time or the mismatch between a man who wants to detach
from paid employment and a woman who continues to enjoy hers
as fulfilling. Maybe there are articles that consider the mismatch
within same-sex couples, but I haven't found them.

A search of the scholarly research on retirement is surprisingly thin on the topic of asymmetric retirement, especially among
professional couples. Large scale surveys show a negative effect
of retired husband/working wife on marital quality, but these
studies are almost all with our parents' generation, a generation

characterized by more "traditional" gender roles in the home and different employment patterns (Miller & Yorgasen, 2009).

There have been many unexpected benefits of this transition. The best result so far is that Lew is much more calm and content. A workaholic in his career, the drivenness and accompanying impatience are mostly gone. Or more accurately, the impatience is reserved for discussions about politics, Pennsylvania drivers, and the invasive garlic mustard weed that is taking over a corner of our property.

Another unexpected benefit has come from something that we had always before found difficult—car coordination. We got rid of our second car when it needed more in repairs than it was worth and now are a one-car couple. Our comings and goings need to be much more coordinated and at times it still causes friction. For the most part, though, time together in the car has surprisingly become quality time. Before Lew's retirement, Saturday errands were the only substantial time we spent in the car together other than on vacations. Now I've got what one of my grad students calls my "Lew-mousine service." Lew brings me to campus, picks me up, takes me to yoga while he heads to Barnes & Noble for coffee and schmoozing. These 10 or 15 minute trips—if we aren't in a hurry—are quite nice and, I realize as I write, that I look forward to those nice slices of time with him.

Lew is helping in other ways, too, and I can tell he is trying to pull more weight in the home management department than he has in the past. He's always done half of the laundry and cleaned the kitchen after meals, but despite his sometimes half-hearted and sometimes sincere attempts at cooking over the years,

I have landed the position of main meal planner and meal maker. Over the past two years Lew has stepped into this final frontier of domestic competence and since last winter has taken over dinner duty. Now, instead of asking what's for dinner, he has mainly taken over that chore. Of course, this means adjustments, too. Still relatively new to cooking, he regards recipes to be as unforgiving as architectural plans. So if the recipe calls for Wegman's basting oil, there is no possibility of a substitution. His approach requires saintly flexibility on my part. I must be encouraging always and offer expert opinion only when asked. Mostly this means that I stay out of the kitchen. The cooking is going well, especially now that he understands my suggestions are not criticisms and now that I understand that, if he is the cook, he is in charge. Cooking is going well, but menu planning needs work. A few months ago he found a recipe for potatoes au gratin. That night he made cheesy potatoes for dinner. Only potatoes. And I bit my tongue rather than ask if there might be a vegetable or a salad or some fish still hiding in the kitchen, and gratefully ate a meal that I did not have to prepare. The dish was tasty, Lew was satisfied with his success, and now potatoes au gratin is in the bi-weekly meal rotation.

It turns out that Lew is like many retired husbands—at least those who post to message boards—who are proud to have taken over the main responsibility for cooking or other household chores. Still, I'd like to hear from the wives' perspective. I am sure I am not the only one who has enjoyed a meal of potatoes au gratin. Or have had new bamboo-color towels turn pink from being bleached. Or wonder why I still have to be the mustard monitor. These are small inconveniences and I try to view them as simple distractions, which I think is made much easier by the fact that we are no longer locked in a "who is busier?" mode of sorting out tasks.

I have to acknowledge our tremendous privilege which, in many ways we recognize and some we don't, eases the transition for us. Lew was in some way pushed into retirement because of a reorganization in his office, but it was a soft landing, including a semester paid leave followed by two years of teaching with no other obligations. He then followed up on an old invitation to teach in Poland for one semester. This year he has gone back for a second, and last semester. I am working full time because I want to, not solely because of economic need. Between our savings and retirement income we can be assured of a fairly comfortable life without economic stresses barring catastrophic illness or the equivalent.

Though there have been many benefits to our relationship, we are far from having this transition worked out. Lew has had great difficulty letting go of work as a core feature of his identity. He is happy in the kitchen, but not *that* happy. His teaching in Poland has been very good for him as a way to further disengage from full-time work, but the long separation strains our relationship even with the miracle of Skype. Importantly, too, it has allowed him to postpone dealing with reality and shaping the structure of an everyday life in retirement as he has more than once said. He is still in something of an in-between stage with respect to retirement. His professional identity was always central to how he organized his life, and now I see him struggle with finding a social identity that is not defined by his work role. Lew likes to say that he just wants to spend most of his retirement days reading. But as one of his friends wrote to him, there's only so much reading that can fill a day; at some point you have to figure out what to do with all those other hours.

Always a travel hound, Lew uses travel as the platform for organizing retirement. After coming home from his first semester as visiting professor in Poland, he left two months later for a two-week Mediterranean cruise, and followed that a month later with a week-long road trip in Montana. Much of the travel is motivated by doing things now while he has the health and interest. At the same time, some of the traveling is part of his postponing strategy. As long as he is on the road, he doesn't have to really figure out what retirement and the next phases of life involve.

Another area of some tension concerns our different ideas about what to expect of retirement. I have to remind myself to be supportive of him, not try to help him shape his retirement as I would my own. I think I know what I would do if I were in his place, but I am not in his place. I would have project after project, but Lew is content spending the entire day reading and websurfing. This would drive me nuts on a day after day basis. It does not drive him nuts. And if it works for him, I should be content.

Importantly, Lew's retirement gets me to think much more about my own plans than I think would be true if he were not retired. I do not resent his retirement because I am not yet ready to retire. I do, however, envy his time. Even more, I have become less patient with time wasted. For example, my impatience with unnecessary (to my mind) meetings is even greater than it used to be. Nor would I mind if I never had to face another large undergraduate class. (Undergraduate teaching, some wise soul pointed out, is the only industry in which your customer wants less, not more.) Retirement also seems to make it easier for Lew to reach out to family and reconnect with friendships he had let lapse. I don't keep up with friends nearly as much as I wish I did. So here again I envy his time.

I am happy in the life that I am living right now and when people question me about *my* retirement, it seems insensitive and presumptuous. It is easy for me to forget how quickly time ticks forward. In a few (two? three? five?) years I aim to negotiate a stepped-down contract. Watching Lew go from 70 hour week, to 30 hour week, to visiting part-time instructor shows me the benefit of easing out of a professional role that I have used to define myself since I was 22. Typical of Baby Boomers, I believe I can have it all. So I scheme to construct a retirement combining a relaxing, travel-filled time of no obligations with a continuing commitment to a fulfilling, invigorating career. I want to write the book on women, work, and emotion that has been on my gonna-do list for years, and I have ideas for oh-so many other projects. Maybe at last I will learn Spanish, too. I know that I won't be taking cooking lessons.

Reference

Miller, R.B., & Yorgason, J.B. (2009). The interaction between marital relationships and retirement. In R. Crane & J. Hill (Eds.). *Handbook of families & work* (pp. 392-408). University Press of America.

70 Candles:
I Am a Work in Progress

Ellen Cole

"I wish I could find the right language to describe this rite of passage. Retirement, that swoon of a word, just won't do."
- Ellen Goodman (2010) -

You would think that after reading all of these inspiring retirement stories I would be able to write my own with ease. Not so. Mary Gergen has been urging me to complete my chapter (as any good co-editor would) ever since we decided over two years ago to undertake this project. Here is my problem: I am in transition. I don't exactly know who I am right now in relation to work or not-work. One might say I don't, therefore, know exactly who I am, period. This is occasionally troubling, sometimes exciting, and pretty constantly perplexing. You see, I never ever made the decision to retire. Here is what happened.

Moved By Love

I began to practice psychology in the mid-1960s, before the days of licensure. Since then I have been licensed in the three states in which I've lived: Vermont, Arizona, and Alaska. A license was a necessity for me because, in addition to having spent my career primarily as an academic psychologist, I also spent about half a day a week seeing clients, mostly couples, for sex therapy. The rest of my professional time was devoted principally to teaching and administration (I've been a dean, program director, and full professor), editing and writing (I co-edited the journal *Women & Therapy* for 13 years and have accumulated a long list of publications on my resumé), professional service (I've been, for example, president of the Alaska Psychological Association, chair of the Committee on Women and Psychology of the American

Psychological Association, and president of APA's Division 35, the Society for the Psychology of Women), and political/social activism (I was an early career psychologist during the heady days of second wave feminism and then a mid and late career psychologist during the burgeoning movements of civil rights for ethnic and sexual minorities—opportunities abounded to integrate my personal values and professional expertise). I loved my career.

I also of course had a life outside of psychology, including a great husband who transitioned from being a professor of English Literature and Humanities to being a university president, first in Arizona and then in Alaska. In 2005 he announced to his board that he planned to retire five years hence. In 2010 we would return to Arizona where we kept a home and where I was already licensed. I would open a private practice and probably find an academic appointment, perhaps part-time. He was ready to retire; I was not. I told him, jokingly, "We don't have to go to Arizona. I'll be happy to move anywhere but New York state." I said that because I had been told that New York was the only state that would not license me—for a variety of reasons, mostly related to the fact that I received my PhD decades ago.

Move ahead to today. We live, quite happily I must say, in Albany, New York. But there's the question of my work life, ergo my identity. Here is the rest of the story.

In 2009 the K-12 country day school that my husband attended as a child for all 13 years needed a new Head-of-School immediately. Knowing he was near his announced retirement date, several of his former classmates urged him to apply for the position, and he and I agreed that he would. For the first few months after the job offer materialized, we continued to live in Alaska in the university president's home, and Doug commuted between Anchorage and Albany. Since the board was already well into their presidential search, Doug was soon able to move full-time to New York. I moved into (beautiful) temporary housing in Anchorage, and I continued to work at my beloved job until the end of the academic year, when I planned to join my husband in, ironically, upstate New York.

Those six months were unsettling as any transition can be, but also quite thrilling. I made and mostly emptied my Alaska bucket list which included flying in a friend's helicopter to a remote glacier. There were many good-bye parties. In my waning time in my department my colleagues and I designed a PsyD program (the first in Alaska) which has since been fully approved by the state and the regional accrediting association and has enrolled its first students. I was given the honor of being named a Professor Emerita, which came with an impressive, framed resolution delineating my contributions, and most meaningful of all, I was asked to be my university's commencement speaker—an unusual invitation (which I accepted immediately), since commencement speakers are typically strangers of renown rather than home-grown employees. The day after graduation I got on a plane and left what had been my existence for nearly 16 years.

And Then What

At the age then of 69 (I am now 70) and not ready to retire, I needed to figure out the rest of my life. I was offered and accepted two adjunct positions almost immediately after moving to Albany. The first was at a local Catholic college, teaching a course I'd never taught before, "History and Systems of Psychology." The other was teaching a four-day intensive in sex therapy to graduating PsyD students—right up my alley.

I knew these two courses wouldn't be enough. I wanted colleagues and an intellectual community. In the long run, I knew I needed to feel as though I were contributing to society. I wanted to be, as I had been, an important part of something that I believed to be important. In the short run, I decided to do something very expensive and to many of my friends and three of my four children absolutely mystifying. I applied to the University of Pennsylvania to get a Master's degree in Applied Positive Psychology (MAPP), 47 years after receiving my first master's degree. It would not get me licensed in New York, but I knew it would (and it did) provide tremendous challenge, great instructors and co-students (although I was twice the age of most of my classmates), and a daily schedule. MAPP is a hybrid model, meaning that I spent three days a month on the UPenn campus and worked electronically from home in-between. The program was perfect for me—and despite having enjoined my own students over the years to work for the learning rather than the grades, I admit somewhat sheepishly that for months I displayed my A's on the door of our refrigerator!

My Capstone Project at the University of Pennsylvania

A Capstone Project in this program is a sort-of-thesis that can take the form of a research project, a book proposal, an extensive literature review, a broad exploration of a topic, etc. Mine took the latter form; I called it "70 Candles: Women Thriving in their

Eighth Decade" and successfully amused myself by making sure it came to 70 pages precisely. In a nutshell, I first reviewed the literature on women and aging, 70 year-old women in particular, and combed the ever-expanding positive psychology writings for relevant resources. I also started, with my pal Jane Giddan whom I've known since I was 12 and she was 13, a blog suitably called 70candles.com. We solicited comments originally from our own acquaintance-circle, and then slowly began to receive submissions from as far away as Israel. Finally, Jane and I conducted what we called a "conversation group" for thirteen 70 year-old women, and I conducted a similar group by myself for ten more and then interviewed two additional women over an afternoon in my kitchen.

I had the opportunity, in all, to hear from forty-five 70 year-old women. Although we did not collect consistent demographic information from the bloggers (except for their ages), 62% of the women who attended our conversation groups had graduate degrees and most identified themselves as professionals. All had had a career at one time, including attorney, professor, biologist, business owner, real estate agent, economist, speech-language pathologist, psychologist, and concert pianist. None identified as a homemaker. A few continued to work full-time, but the rest, in just about equal numbers, were retired or worked part-time. There was great latitude in the issues the women were invited to discuss. While topics included grand-mothering, technology, physical challenges, bonds with women, and future living arrangements, the issue most often brought up, by far, was that of work and retirement.

I will include excerpts from the blog and conversation groups, to give a flavor of the breadth and depth, the meaningfulness, and the complexity of this topic for 70 year-old women today who had or continue to have meaningful careers. I wish I had the space here to include them all.

> "*I'm slowly reducing my work hours, in a career I've greatly enjoyed. I feel reluctant to stop completely, but my husband has retired, and is encouraging me to wind down....*"

> "*Now I work only three days per week, but am loathe to give up my profession, as a clinical psychologist, completely. I find that age and experience have deepened and enriched my ability to empathize, assist, and engage with my patients. By using my own life experience I am encouraging other women to expect to be similarly productive long past their 40's. And I hope I am a role model to my young clients as they tackle life's challenges.*"

> "*As the first generation of women in professions, we are very different from our mothers. They could be teachers, nurses, or secretaries; few ventured beyond limited offerings, and when they did work, the generation before us stayed in a single job until they retired. A wider range of career options opened up for us, as law schools, medical schools, business schools all started admitting more women.... Now, as we consider winding down, or retiring from our careers, we (and I) believe there is still an array of options ahead.*"

> "*It's interesting to consider how our identity has been affected by our life's work. Is our job who we are? Or is*

it a mutable facet of our being? The retired lawyer still sees nuanced issues in the world through her analytic lens. The essence of each of us is embedded in a complex fabric. Work-life, and all it provides, is but a fragment of 'I.'

"Each day contains the possibility of something new and exciting that's never happened before."

"When I reflect on my life at 70, I begin with a holistic snapshot—that includes family, friends, and recreation. I end by thinking more and more about the role of work in my life, and the role of work in the lives of other women my age. We are mothers and grandmothers and wives and partners, but perhaps above all we—I don't think I'm the only one— identify ourselves by our work. Who will I be when I no longer have a title? Who will I be without a paycheck? On what stage will I express my creativity and desire to contribute?"

"People might not listen to me if they knew I was 70, so I keep it to myself." [This is from an attorney who works full-time.]

"I think my clients listen and take advice better now because they see me as wise." [This is from a full-time clinical psychologist.]

"I don't see retirement as an ending, but rather as an expanding. At first I was getting distressed. Now I think it's more like putting new tires on a car, re-tiring, liberating."

"I taught elementary school for 32 years, retired, and after five years got so bored that I went back to work teaching college students. I love it."

"*I was Executive Director of a non-profit and not doing well with the stress at work. It was a weight on my shoulders. How good it felt after I retired; it's a gift. I think maybe being married makes it easier, more fun. Don't know if I would have retired if I was alone.*"

"*I was Dean of Students, but that's not who I am now. Someone said to me, 'when you wake up the morning after you retire you won't know who you are.' I said, 'I don't think so!'*"

"*I haven't figured out how to give back, to give to society.*"

"*There are many places where you are needed and can make a difference.*"

"*I worried about how I could continue to use my brain, but it turns out opportunities abound.*"

"*I think an issue for women our age is the discrepancy in work trajectories between us and our husbands—it's problematic when one's ready to retire, and the other isn't.*"

"*I retired from New York State seven years ago. I had a long list of things to do when I retired, like cleaning out the closet. The list keeps growing, but I never get to any of it. I'm just as busy now as I was then.*"

"*Work is not the paycheck or the W-2. Your profession is always with you—I still read things like a lawyer. I have the worldview of a lawyer even without the job title.*"

"*Although mostly retired now, I'm still a speech therapist whenever I'm with people, kids.*"

"*'I'm a photographer.' I've never, ever said that before.*" *[Before retiring, this woman was a financial analyst; "photographer" is the new identity she is developing.]*

"*I do a lot of work I'm not being paid for—boards, writing. When someone asks me what I do, I'd love to say I'm a writer, but I've never published anything so I really can't say that.*" *[This woman, too, is re-inventing herself after years as an executive.]*

"*People told me that I would know when it was time to retire, but I was skeptical. Then one day I received a call from a favorite client, for whom I had recently written a report. He said that he loved the report and wanted to have a meeting with all his colleagues so that I could present my findings and recommendations. He said he had cleared the time of Tuesday at 8AM with everyone, and looked forward to seeing me then. I responded without hesitation that I couldn't make it at 8AM on Tuesday. He sounded very surprised, and asked whether I had another client meeting at that time. I said, calmly but firmly, 'I have another commitment at that hour.' I suddenly realized that my yoga class was more important than this wonderful client, and immediately knew that this was my sign.*"

For the purposes of this chapter, I present these quotes in random order to demonstrate the variation and the complexity of this topic for so many of us. For me, personally, I ended my Capstone project with the following three conclusions.

A Determination to Celebrate Aging and Eliminate Ageism

By the end of my Capstone Project I was very proud to identify myself as an old woman and, like Simone de Beauvoir (1972) in *The Coming of Age*, I felt the same urgency to combat ageism as I felt in my earlier feminist years about combatting sexism. If you look for it, it is everywhere. Last week, for example, I heard a respectable radio newscaster say this: *"Wanna feel really old? McCaulay Culkin [star of the film "Home Alone" in 1990, when he was ten] turned 31 today! Doesn't it make you want to put your hands on your cheeks and scream?"*

I agreed with Laura Carstensen (2009) who calls the reinvention of old age "the social and biological revolution of our time," with the bottom-line premise that more and more people are living to be centenarians—more than one million by 2050 (p. 283). I learned from an article called "Longevity Increased by Positive Self-Perceptions of Aging" (Levy, Slade, Kunkel, & Kasl, 2002) that "individuals with more positive self-perceptions of aging, measured up to 23 years earlier, lived 7.5 years longer than those with less positive self-perceptions of aging" (p. 261). And so it behooves everyone, young and old, to admire the old among us, ourselves and others.

I am also looking increasingly for 70 year-old women and beyond who are thriving. A friend recently sent me an email about

Marjorie Stoneman Douglas, who retired from a successful career as a journalist only to begin a second career as an environmental spokeswoman, playing an important role in the establishment of the Everglades National Park. My friend said (personal communication, June 24, 2011), "she continued this career into her 100s and interviewed and spoke until at least 103, and I have seen her in a video at 107. She passed in 1998 at 108." What other inspirational stories can we find if we look?

The Realization that We Thrive in Our Own Company

I had so much fun pulling together the conversation groups, and I have rarely if ever experienced so much group laughter and even raucousness as I did with both of the groups. We really enjoyed laughing (and occasionally tearing up) among ourselves as we shared common issues, challenges, and triumphs. It occurred to me that this is only logical. We are the generation that invented support groups and consciousness-raising groups. We need to bring them back for ourselves as we reach the age of retirement, as we did for ourselves at age 25 and 30. The issues then were women's rights and women's empowerment. The issues now are old women's rights and old women's empowerment, to be sure, but I can't think of a better way to address the questions and concerns that come along with ending or cutting back on what was a satisfying career. Sisterhood was powerful then and it can be powerful—and helpful—now.

I Am Not Alone in My Confusion (and That Feels Good), but I Have a Ways to Go (and That's Okay)

Retirement is a transition, and transitions are challenging. The women from whom I heard wondered if they retired too soon, never want to retire, or wonder when the time will be right. And yet, all of those with whom I spoke who were already retired felt as though they were making good use of their lives and most had figured out how to continue to contribute to society in meaningful ways. They viewed retirement as an opportunity to reinvent themselves, some fearing retirement before the deed was done, and then relishing their newfound opportunities afterwards. Still, I was unique among my age-mates in that I did not leave full-time employment on my own schedule.

So Where Am I Now?

At this point I have graduated from UPenn and have lived in Albany, NY for a year and a half. I have established what I consider a lovely life. Importantly to me, I am in two book groups and have regular tennis partners and a walking buddy. There are women here whom I consider to be newfound friends. I am on the board of Upper Hudson Planned Parenthood. My husband and I continue to grow and thrive together, and I am geographically closer to children and grandchildren and other family members than I have been in decades.

My work-life is…well…in transition. Although I have been a dean, full-professor, and so on, I did not even get an interview when I applied for an Assistant Professorship at a small local college. I do not have a license to practice psychology in New York State, so I cannot open even a small private practice in sex therapy, as I wish I could. I have taught part-time at three institutions this fall, teaching doctoral students, college undergraduates, and high school students. Introducing psychology to high school seniors has felt like a huge privilege to me, outside my comfort and experience zone, but incredibly gratifying. Yet….

Although I am a positive person, and I love above all teaching, I do not really like being an adjunct. The time in the classroom is fulfilling and enjoyable, but I miss colleagues and teamwork and the challenges that come with administration. Without a license I do not feel like a "real" psychologist. Many say to me, "Ellen, you're 70 years old. Relax. Enjoy yourself." They do not understand.

Our local paper recently ran a feature story called "Social Toll of Joblessness: Unemployed Feel an Emptiness as they're Suddenly Cut Off from Workplace Friends" (Barnes, 2011). I can relate to that. I also really hate not having a decent paycheck. Adjuncts earn a paltry amount, without benefits. I understand I speak from privilege when I say I did not worry about money when I was employed full-time. If I wanted to buy an expensive meal or a little luxury I didn't think twice about it. Now I think twice. I marched for equal pay for women and have prided myself on earning my own way in life. My husband and I have kept our finances separate. We have to rethink this now, and it makes me squirm.

And yet… I have long considered myself an adventurer. Like Helen Keller, I believe "Life is either a daring adventure or nothing." There is a part of me that leaps with joy at the prospect of the unknown. I am also reassured by the literature I've read, by the Capstone Project I undertook, and certainly by the chapters in this book, that post-career years can be vital ones. I'm not there yet, but I will be.

References

Barnes, S. (2011, Sept. 4). Social Toll of Joblessness: Unemployed Feel an Emptiness as they're Suddenly Cut Off from Workplace Friends. *Times Union*, Albany, NY.

Carstenson, L. L. (2009). *A long bright future: An action plan for a lifetime of happiness, health, and financial security.* New York: Broadway Books.

de Beauvoir, S. (1972). *The coming of age.* New York: G. P. Putman's & Sons.

Goodman, E. (2010, January 1). Ellen Goodman writes of letting go in her final column. Retrieved from http://www.washingtonpost.com/wpdyn/content/article/2009/12/31/AR2009123101743.html

Levy, B. R., Slade, M. D., Kunkel, S. R., & Kasl, S. V. (2002). Longevity increased by positive self-perceptions of aging. *Journal of Personality and Social Psychology, 83*(2), 261-270. doi: 10.1037/0022-3514.83.2.261.

Retirement: Life in the "Selective Moreso" Lanes

Jessica Henderson Daniel

etirement—the word is just not me. I see myself as a high energy woman fueled by a steady stream of ideas that lead me down interesting and intriguing new paths. Thankfully, times have changed. Retirement is more an alive menu than a static life pattern. My plan: create a retirement based on my own terms.

A member in one of my reading groups shared that as we age we are "moreso." I have given this some thought. Perhaps I could become a "selective moreso" person. So who am I?

My identities include: Black, female, psychologist, mother, sister, mentor, avid reader, Air Force dependent, traveler, walker, advocate for social justice, event organizer, one who appreciates the arts—graphic and performance, cook and consumer of good food. I have a core, but my expressed identities are context dependent. Life has been an opportunity to explore and develop my identities and interests over the years. So which ones will I take with me into the "moreso" retirement lanes?

The first identity is an Air Fore dependent i.e. a person who moved every few years. During my childhood and adolescence, my father's assignments landed me in California, Bermuda, Hawaii, the Philippines and North Carolina. In all locales, being an initial outsider was the norm, only the length of time in this "sister outsider" state varied. This was true whether or not the people looked like me (a descendent of Sub-Sahara Black Africa), were persons of color but not Black or they were primarily Caucasians. Adjusting to others and learning to manage differences was the norm. Race and ethnicity have been a major part of my navigating the waters of life.

In each location, my mother appreciated the people and their cultures. As a consequence, her life was enriched e.g. enhanced leadership skills (California), bread baking skills (Bermuda), cooking skills from a Korean friend and the art of applying make-up from a Japanese friend (Hawaii) and learning to make her own dress patterns (the Philippines). For her daughters, she modeled an appreciation for diversity before it became a politically correct stance. We were not restricted to relationships with military personnel and their families (except in the Philippines due to safety issues), but attended school and church with the local people, which facilitated the formation of meaningful relationships. Making connections was not always easy, but the benefits clearly outweighed the challenges.

From the above, travel both in the US and abroad will be important for me as a retiree. I want to meet people who look like me and yet are different from me; I want to meet people who do not look like me. In this highly mobile society, some places will have both groups. I plan to visit Australia, which was once a Black continent as well as to Sub-Sahara Africa. Visiting European countries will open me up to the range of European cultures which are quite varied as Europe is a multi-cultural continent.

As a process person, I want to have in place strategies that will make this plan happen. My identity as a psychologist may help to initiate contacts. Topics that interest me include adolescent girls, mentoring and trauma. Making contacts with colleagues in various parts of the world may be a way to enter the country and to begin to learn about the culture.

I hope to display a respectful curiosity about people, observing their cultural boundaries in the process. Having opportunities to be in their private spaces i.e. their homes and in their social worlds can open up the fabric of their lives as individuals, dyads and families. Experiencing their architecture, listening to histories from various sources, and consuming meals in restaurants and private homes would be part of my visits to different places. I want to learn about their humor, the way that they live their lives and raise their children, and the treasures that they hold dear. Remaining in a city or country for at least a week and returning several times will increase the probability that this learning would occur in the context of relating to people. It will take more time to travel among the people rather than just to tourist sites. But I want to do that. I see this as a way to continue to grow and develop during my retirement years.

While visiting Senegal over 30 years ago, I spent an afternoon with a local family. It was an honor to be invited into a private home as a dinner guest. My mother was on the trip and of course talked to the matriarch who had prepared the food. She purchased spices in Senegal and we had a version of the meal when we returned to the US. We learned about the country and culture—daily lives and special occasions.

A second major part of my identity is my appreciation of the arts—visual and performance. During my retirement year, I plan to visit art galleries and museums. Viewing art removes me from the everydayness of life. I am intrigued by many forms of art. Visiting these venues is usually a solitary experience for me because it takes time to enjoy the art. I look forward to spending time at Boston's Museum of Fine Arts on a regular basis and certainly when they have special exhibits. Local galleries throughout metro-Boston will also be frequent destinations. Visiting art sites in New York City several times a year will be on my agenda. Artists are so varied; viewing art can elicit a range of feelings. Oils, acrylics, watercolors and pencil drawings all interest me. I am amazed at the creativity and skills of the artists. Sculptures are particularly fascinating to me. My one regret is that they are often untouchable despite eliciting an urge for a multi-sensory experience. When viewing art, I look for similarities and differences across time and cultures.

Performance art in the form of theatre, dance and music would be a part of my travel as well. While in Hawaii as a high school student, I fell in love with Shakespeare and attended plays alone. My parents would drive me into town and pick me up afterwards. They supported my interest even though they did not share it. My college English teacher introduced me to Greek plays. They became alive as he read them in class and then encouraged us to discuss the twists and turns of events and characters. My monolingual limitation probably means that this activity will be limited to English speaking sites. I may purchase season tickets to insure that I attend several plays a year.

Dance is an opportunity to witness the creative movements of individuals, dyads and groups on stage, in silence or in tune with music. The latter has no limitations. It can be from any part of the world. The costumes are often varied and interesting, a part of the staging of the dance performance. I want to see Alvin Ailey in New York City with an orchestra and not taped music. Revelations is the signature piece—with its incorporation of Black church life and music. Dance troupes from around the world appear in Boston. I look forward to "traveling" through dance performances.

Music comes in many forms that fuel my soul. My cultural roots include jazz; the blues; the Motown and Philly Sounds; and spirituals and gospel music. Having friends from the Caribbean has meant a steady stream of calypso and reggae music over the years. Friends from the Mother Continent shared their music as well during graduate school. Then, the most popular artists were South African. Currently, there are African musical artists from many countries. I was introduced to classical music through programming at the historically Black college I attended. While in graduate school, I was drawn to opera. The magnificent voices and elaborate staging created a spectacular event, whether comic or dramatic.

I have enjoyed watching foreign films for years. Fortunately, an arts theatre is within walking distance of my home. Sub-titles do not diminish my interest in travelling around the world via films.

The bottom line is that the arts will be a major "moreso" lane in my life.

My third identity is that of organizer. I founded two reading groups for Black women that are respectively 30 and 22 years old. For the past 19 years, I have organized an annual joint meeting of both groups with an author. It is a potluck dinner with delicious food in a beautiful home that comfortably seats some 20 women. Through the latter, I have met some wonderful authors, primarily Black women who have enjoyed meeting with this group of dynamic and smart women. At Children's Hospital Boston, I organize the annual Dr. Martin Luther King Jr. Observance Programs and the Black History Month Grand Rounds. Both feature intellectually stimulating presentations by outstanding Black scholars in medicine and other disciplines. Also, I initiated the Diversity Training through Literature Fishbowl Grand Rounds in the Department of Psychiatry. Psychologists, psychiatrists, and social workers discuss a book on stage and then the members of the audience join in the discussion. The book selected is both by and about persons of color. The focus is on the intersection of context, psychosocial issues and mental health issues that are raised by the story line.

One thing is clear—I truly enjoy intellectual stimulation across disciplines and topics. As a graduate student, I hosted dinner parties for African students at the University of Illinois-Urbana campus. Few African American graduate students were on campus at the time. The students talked through main courses of either meatloaf or spaghetti/meatballs. They had very different views of the United States and the world at large, listened to BBC on a regular basis, and talked about politics with passion. They were primarily from West Africa and represented the best and brightest in their respective countries. Some were torn about whether to remain in the US or to return to their respective countries. The discussions were lively and informative—I learned about life across the Atlantic, including Europe and Africa.

As a retiree, I look forward to having dinner parties that will allow me to listen to some particular conversations. Specifically, I frequently think "wouldn't it be fascinating to have two or more particular intellectuals talk with each other about that?" I especially look forward to unlikely combinations of scholars/intellectuals approaching topics from their unique perspectives. Ideas, agreements, disagreements, consensus and ideas on hold would all be possible results. Just the thought of this is exciting to me.

It is highly probable that one of the dinner parties will focus on a book, fiction or non-fiction as I am very passionate about reading. Having authors talk about their works and the writing process is truly fascinating.

These evenings will become precious memories for me and the guests.

My fourth identity is someone who enjoys preparing and consuming good food—delicious and well-presented food. Thankfully, I have moved beyond meatloaf and spaghetti/meatballs over the years. This venture will give me the incentive to spend time going around the world in my kitchen. At one point in the 1980s I formed a cooking group that focused on preparing dinners with recipes from around the world. It lasted three years. It was a fun and delicious time. I have some of the recipes and of course can find others. I will cook and then hire students to serve and clean-up after the dinner so I will not miss any of the conversations. About four dinners a year should do it for me—my dip into the pool of multi-disciplinary discussions. Good food and good conversation—with perhaps a musician to play the piano during dessert. My dining room table seats 8—a good number for full engagement. Boston is an academic community rich with numerous colleges and universities. Visiting scholars also come to the metro Boston area; I will keep an eye out for them. The possibilities are numerous. Having organized activities in the past, the first year may be slow—but after that, it should be full steam ahead.

The above four identities and soon to be "moreso" lanes all require energy. I look forward to being a world traveler, consumer of arts, event planner and international cuisine creator. I will reach back and move forward at the same time.

My fifth identity is not listed above, but emerged as I have thought about this time of my life. It involves nature, especially flowers, trees and water. The focus on water is from my days of living across the street from the ocean as a child in Bermuda; the trees and the flowers are from my two-year stint on the West Coast later in life. In Bermuda, the ocean was never far away. Walking on the beach was a private pleasure. Water is soothing for my spirit and I enjoy walking along the water be it the ocean, a lake or a river. I visited a colorful rose garden once and became mesmerized by the experience. From that point on, I have found walking among flowers to feel like walking through a live palette of colors—it is another form of art for me. Trees feel like live sculptures with variations in the colors, shapes and textures of the leaves. While I probably will not become a gardener, I have an appreciation of flowers. This will be a time to visit festivals that celebrate flowers, both here and abroad.

However, I will need to practice actually taking time to enjoy nature. When I visited the Montreaux Jazz Festival in Switzerland some 20 years ago, I would walk along the water almost every evening. The locals kept gently saying to me, "Madam we stroll." I would walk slowly for a few minutes, but the fast track walk would consistently emerge. So learning to vary my walking speed will be a task.

The above five identities have a minimal focus on race, ethnicity and gender, three topics that I hold dear as a social activist. These personal identities will be with me as I journey in the "moreso" lanes as they are the identities that people see and experience almost instantly. They carry with them the potential for a range of responses including acceptance, rejection and ambivalence. It is what it is—human being responding to other human beings.

But I am clear, that I will continue to mentor and advocate for persons who are often relegated to the margins of society. I will look for potential in those who may be dismissed without cause because they do not fit. I suspect that in all of the above lanes, I will have an opportunity to do that.

Finally, my desire is to attend the college graduations of all my academic and church grandchildren is very strong. (I do not have any biological grandchildren so I figured out how to have this special relationship.) Consequently, I will pay attention to health matters—eating well and walking more. It will be such a joy to witness them in their caps and gowns on their special days. I look forward to seeing the joy and perhaps relief on the faces of their parents. I probably will purchase a new hat for each graduation, but their cap will always be the cap of the day and not my hat.

In retirement, I look forward to living life to the fullest. In fact, I have started practicing for retirement at this stage. I deliberately schedule in quality time in the "moreso" lanes now so that the transition to retirement will not be abrupt.

Parting Three Questions to be Answered

What do I wish I had known before I reached this stage in my career in terms of retirement?

At times, I wish I had been able to focus my energies in just a few areas. But there were too few people (Black, female and PhD holder) like me so I felt that I had to do what was needed rather than just focus on my career. More focus might have been better. But I am not so sure. I do not regret investing in the lives of others. The connections have been and continue to be priceless.

What do I wish I had done differently in terms of my retirement?
I wish I had taken time to pay more attention to financial planning for retirement. My "moreso" lanes will require financial resources. I have prepared—I believe that I perhaps would have more financial resources if I had been more focused on earning more money than following my passions. But to be honest, I do not believe that I would have felt as fulfilled as I do at this point in my life.

What am I happy about in terms of what I anticipated and am doing to prepare for retirement?
I am living more at this stage of my life. Through sheer determination, I have been able to protect my spirit. For that I am most grateful. I have energy and a resolve to live life to the fullest. Postponement is no longer a part of my life script. I use everything now—not just for special occasions as every day is a special day, a gift.

From Anxiety to Curiosity:
Emotional Readiness for Retirement

Marcia Hill

*a*year ago, I could hardly imagine retiring. I'd thought about it for years, of course, as I've been creeping inevitably toward the traditional retirement age. I liked the idea in the abstract well enough. No work! No more insurance company hassles! More deeply, I longed to put down the burden of carrying all those souls. This job is hard; I've been taking care of people for years. What a relief it would be to stop, to do only the everyday care giving that is part of having a family and friends. I have loved doing therapy, but I have also imagined with longing what it might feel like to set aside the weight and responsibility for people in pain, people who look to me for a way out of their misery.

Worries

But then there was the dread. When the thought of retirement came up, it didn't sit easily. In fact, it scared me. When would I retire? What would I do after I retired? The "when" part seemed uncertain, but at least it had its own implicit answer. I would retire when I could afford to do so. That simple answer, though, had layers of confusion under it. How much money would I need? I didn't want to be scraping by (been there, done it, didn't much like it), but what level of income would mean enough financial latitude to have a comfortable and even enjoyable retirement? There was no point in retiring, it seemed to me, if I wasn't in a position to enjoy it. This all seemed a matter for considerable hand-wringing, but theoretically one could figure out an answer. Somehow.

The "what" part felt far more daunting. Work takes up a lot of my time, and what would I do with that time after retirement? I'd talked with a number of people who had retired, and the answer was virtually always the same: "Oh, I'm busier than ever." *Busier than ever?* Doing what, exactly? OK, so they travel a bit more and visit family. Maybe they take a yoga class or volunteer at the Red Cross. Their gardens definitely look better than mine. But how many hours do these things take? *What are they doing with their time?*

And then there's the matter of life meaning. If you're a therapist, you know what I'm talking about. Being a therapist is meaning-dense work. Years ago, I heard a colleague refer to therapists, herself included, as "meaning junkies." Admittedly, there are plenty of times when I'm just hand-holding, and plenty of times when I stumble or can't find a way to be helpful. But there are also times when someone's world shifts under her feet. I had a client say to me recently, "I feel like I've just been born." Damn, that's impressive for making me feel like my day matters, for making me feel like *I* matter. I regularly see people leave my office feeling less burdened, more themselves. I watch transformation, even if only incrementally, and I get to midwife that daily. What could possibly replace that? America's ageism is bad enough, with its subtle (well, usually subtle) messages that retirees are irrelevant. But I have been used to feeling regularly that I make a real difference, perhaps more than people do in many jobs. I imagined that in retirement, I might indeed feel irrelevant.

Therapy is not just any job. When I thought of retirement, I would think, too, of what it has taken me to come to this point in my career. I have developed wisdom, as most therapists do. I have learned to get to the heart of the matter quickly, I have learned how to make something really happen and shift. I have developed focus, and intuition, and that interesting skill that shows up in senior people in many fields: the ability to go from one point to another without the intervening steps. I have learned what I cannot do. What of all this? Am I simply to set it all aside? What a waste. What a loss, particularly to me.

So here's the Scary Retirement Scenario: I feel like I'm on vacation for the first few weeks, and then I start to feel adrift. I enroll in the obligatory yoga class. That's a few hours a week. Maybe I find something to volunteer for, although I have to say that the thought of volunteering for anything involving human services doesn't quite make sense. Wasn't taking care of others what I was retiring *from*? I visit my family more often, perhaps travel more, but what would that add up to, a few weeks a year? And then what? I presumably would visit with friends more often. Perhaps I tackle the things I never got around to when I was working: I sort through my accumulated stuff, I paint the kitchen, that sort of thing. I imagine myself starting to feel unmotivated. Why paint the kitchen this week when there's next week and next month and next year? I imagine finding excuses to run errands just to get into town and do something. I imagine feeling like my life is pointless. There's a British sitcom set in a retirement home, entitled, with typical British humor, "Waiting for God." I imagined myself in retirement feeling like I was waiting for death.

Transition

Then three things happened. One, I turned 60. Those birthdays with a zero on the end always make one sit up and take notice, but this one struck me particularly: sixty is no longer middle-aged.

Sixty marks the beginning of a transition to something else, to the third stage of life. I haven't felt scared about it, or in denial, or depressed, but simply very, very aware. Turning 60 felt like it informed everything in my life. I planned a big trip for a birthday splurge: what was I waiting for? I resigned from the last managed care panel I was with: I hated it, so why still do it? Further, they pay poorly and my time is valuable. In fact, it is more valuable than ever. I recently gave a Grand Rounds presentation, followed by the obligatory meeting with the self-important Head Honcho. Afterwards, I thought, why do this any more? I don't find it enjoyable and I don't need to say yes to requests for activities I don't like. My time here is growing shorter: what do I want to do with it?

The second thing that happened was that I finished a chunk of psychological work about the ways in which I took on the job of protecting others in my childhood home. I imagine that many therapists have some aspect of this in their psyches. We learn early how to be caregivers, to put aside our own needs and tend to those of others. We learn to hear what is unsaid. We practice the subtle art of influence. We come to this in a variety of ways, but the end result is a hunger to help, to make things right, to feel that we can ease suffering in the lives of others. I assume that in the end, we are all healing our families or our childhood selves. We choose the profession because we need it and because we're good at it. After all, we've been "practicing," many of us, since we were quite young. Easing the pain of others gave me something that no other work could: an ongoing healing of my own pain, and a symbolic healing of the pain in my childhood family.

In finishing this work about my own version of learning to take care of my family, I finally felt done with the job in some deep way. My parents are dead now. My family's struggles were difficult, but we made it through. I did what I could as a child to protect my mother and sibs, and I presume it helped. The task is over. Maybe we as therapists can finally retire when we have finished the emotional task that brought us to the work in the first place.

This has rippled out into my work, subtly but distinctly. Therapy still feels like important work. It's still satisfying to make a difference in people's lives. But it doesn't feel necessary; it doesn't feel like the *only* important thing to do. I used to feel that there was nothing more meaningful, and I suppose there wasn't (at least for me), to the extent that I was still symbolically "on the job" with the rescue of my family. But now I don't feel like I need that particular kind of meaning in my life. Perhaps I don't need any particular kind of meaning. Perhaps there is enough meaning in living with pleasure.

Finally, I rediscovered art. Isn't this interesting that this happened at about the same time as the rest of it? I have always had a knack for drawing, not great talent, but enough to get some satisfaction. I'd done virtually nothing with it, except for the occasional homemade gift or card. Then I took an art class at the local Community College. What fun! I spent way too much money on art supplies and the occasional workshop and have been completely enjoying myself. I am a raw neophyte, I know nothing about technique, but who cares? I discovered pastels, which I love. I can begin to see one thing, at least, that I might do with my time when I retire. I have lots to learn and lots of practicing to do before I can make the kind of things that I would like to make. But it will be a pleasure to get there.

So where does this leave me? I am still not ready to retire financially, although I have started working with a financial planner and can see that I'm close. And while I do not quite feel ready to retire emotionally, I can see that readiness as a possibility from where I stand now. I am watching with interest as the change plays itself out. I went with some trepidation to a Croning Ceremony at the Association for Women in Psychology meeting a couple of years ago, telling myself that if it was too weird, I would simply leave. But it was not weird at all. Women talked about what was wonderful about growing older, and what we had to say about that was considerable. Here is what is wonderful for me: I feel that I have claimed the mantle of age. I know who I am. I do not feel apologetic about, or even that I need to explain, the ways that I am powerful or the ways in which I am not in the cultural mainstream or even the ways in which I am injured and limited. I believe in the importance of kindness, but I am not especially interested in pleasing others or in whether they approve of me. That said, I also see clearly how much of human difference is superficial and that I have a great deal in common with my fellow travelers. I am coming to terms with the limitations of my life: my accomplishments are what they are and no more. My choices along the way have both freed me and constrained me. My life and capabilities are circumscribed, but I can't say that it particularly bothers me. I have an increasingly clear sense of my own personal authority. I stand in myself. Perhaps I do not, any longer, need to stand in my work.

And Now

A psychologist would say that I am decathecting from my job, albeit exceedingly slowly. Perhaps I am just noticing the moments of lesser attachment to my work, moments that were always there but ignored until the possibility of actually not doing that work started to seem more real. I am aware of the thinner places in my work, if you will, the times when I feel less engaged.

I notice the sessions with people who are hard to help. I notice the people that I care about but don't quite love. I am aware of the clients who might be just as well served, perhaps even better served, by another therapist. I am aware of the people who can only allow, or perhaps only need, something that is far less than what I am able to give. I notice the sessions that are good work without being life-changing. It doesn't quite reach the level of impatience, and I would not describe myself as burned out on the job. But I do mark the people and sessions that are less rewarding in a way that I never did before. I think: There might be other ways I would like to be spending my life energy.

I read once about someone who calculated how long he could expect to live, based on actuarial tables, and then how many weekends were in those years. He filled a jar with that many marbles, and each weekend he took one out. I am feeling a bit like that. I am sixty now. How many more clients will I meet and work with? How many more sessions of therapy will I do? Those limits, even though unknown and not at all immediate, sharpen my expectations for my work. My work life no longer feels limitless, and I feel itchy when I spend an hour with someone who barely lets me help her.

I notice, too, the prominent place of work in my life, the time it requires, the emotional commitment and energy it demands. My job defines and shapes so much of my experience. I am more aware of the other things that I might like to be doing with that emotional energy, the other ways I might like to shape my life. I am more conscious that my time and energy are bounded, and I do not wish to use them thoughtlessly. My work is a valuable use of self, but there are other valuable uses of self. I more frequently wish for balance, to diminish the great emphasis that I have given work in my life and to increase my investment in creativity and relationships and whatever other possibilities might emerge.

Retirement is a process of the heart and psyche as much as of the schedule, and I am recognizing that I have begun that process in the past year or so without any change at all in my work hours or commitment. I still don't know when I'll retire. But retirement is beginning to feel emotionally possible to me in a way that it did not a year ago. I imagine that everyone, regardless of her job, tries to find a way to feel psychologically ready to retire. But I would guess that it is particularly difficult for therapists, who must retire from such deeply meaningful work, from making a difference in people's lives in such a clear way. Retirement is a layered experience for us. It means relinquishing a particular kind of meaning and intimacy that doing therapy provides. It means letting go of the use of a lifetime's accumulation of skill. To the extent that our investment in the work stems from our families of origin, it means declaring that work finished.

More universally, retirement means a reorganization of one's life emotionally as well as practically. If work is no longer at the center, defining all the rest by its demand for a primary place, what will the new constellation of activities and meanings look like? What, in fact, would it look like to organize a life with enjoyment more primary than obligation? For the first time, I am actually looking forward to finding out.

An Update

It is perhaps a year since I wrote the essay above. My life as an artist has moved from unformed to unfolding. One of the gifts of maturity, at least for me, is that I know that I am unlikely to get what I want unless I figure out what it is and make it happen. I knew that, at this stage, it was too difficult for me to paint alone and that I needed feedback from other artists if I were ever to improve. I used to have this naïve idea that artists could make art simply because they were talented. I have since discovered that it's like doing therapy or any other complex skill: talent may get you started, but there are techniques that are learnable, and practice makes all the difference. I kept asking around until I found a couple of women to paint with weekly. That's been just right: motivation to keep painting as well as the support, comments, and suggestions of a couple of other artists. We all benefit from that. I found an experienced artist to critique my paintings, which has helped me to begin to develop my own "artist's eye," and has reassured me that I am on the right track. I made a list of goals, which helped me further focus my efforts. I set up a studio in the guest bedroom, created forms for keeping track of paintings and expenses, had business cards printed and made a website (www. marciahillart.wordpress.com).

I believe that my art is supposed to go live with people who love it, but they need to see it to know that! So I suggested to my little painting group that we have a show in a local coffee house. That idea has taken off, and we have now exhibited in several local venues. I have made perhaps twenty paintings in the first half of 2011 alone, and have sold eight. The other point of selling paintings, of course, is to meet my expenses. Art, especially framing, is not a cheap avocation! I have been astonished to discover how much time all of this takes. My painting mentor confirmed that she spends perhaps 1/3 of her art time making art, and 2/3 of the time marketing, record-keeping, and doing other art-related activities.

In addition, for all of 2010, I kept track of my expenses. Good news! While I cannot afford to retire, I discovered that I can definitely afford to cut back, and that is exactly what I did. I reduced my caseload to three days a week, and shorter days at that. I love this balance. We are very fortunate in this profession to be able to scale back our work hours gradually, at least until the point where we're not earning enough to pay for overhead. I go home no later than 4:00, some days earlier. What has been extraordinarily interesting to me is that I find myself in a similar position to the retired people I talked with a year ago. While I've done a little culling of files, I have not accomplished as much as I thought I would with four days a week of non-office time. My garden still needs attention. The kitchen has not been painted. I have not sorted through my accumulation of stuff. I am too busy with art! I have also, however, found it easier to have time with friends, and I feel that I have slowed down a bit. I have time, too, to read and putter, to savor my life.

▨ Want some advice?

We're all, if we're fortunate enough, either in retirement or on a trajectory toward it. If you are on your way, here are some things you might learn from my experience. I did not anticipate how much I would want to be retired. I do, after all, love my work; I always have. It was easy to anticipate that I'd just keep working until I could afford to retire, and that seemed fine. I have always been a good saver, and I have always lived below my means. So now, I am enormously relieved to be in a financial position to be considering retirement seriously. But had I known how much I would want the financial freedom to cut back my hours or to stop entirely, I think I would have been less relaxed and generous about setting and collecting fees. Since I have worked most of my career in private practice, I have had some control over my income. And, looking back, there were too many years during which I probably undercharged people, accepted insurances (Medicaid being the prime example) that did not pay enough to cover my overhead, and allowed people to accumulate a debt to me which then went unpaid far too often.

To the reader in private practice, I would say: calculate your per-client-hour overhead. I did this several years ago, and it was certainly eye-opening. Overhead should include not only standard business expenses, but also what you pay for medical insurance, social security, and retirement contributions. After all, if you had a salaried job with benefits and a pension, these things would be included. Divide it by the number of clients you see in a year. It's a bigger number than you expected, isn't it? For me, that information led me to stop accepting (or significantly cut back) some insurances. And, over the years, I have become much more consistent about charging for missed appointments and not allowing clients to accumulate a debt with me. I still carry some clients at reduced fees and I still accept the occasional underinsured client, but far fewer in both categories.

To all readers, I can only offer the usual advice. Fund your retirement plan as fully as you can. Live below your means, even if it means simplifying your life. I promise you, you will not be less happy. And, if like me, you are surprised at some point in your life with your eagerness for retirement, then you will be glad you're prepared.

The Mid-Air Plunge

Retired: Who Me?

Bernice Lott

*"If I can't dance—I don't want to be
part of your revolution."*
- Emma Goldman -

"Nothing will work unless you do."
- Maya Angelou -

everal years ago one of my colleagues used the term "un-retirement" to describe what she and I were both doing in the
years following our taking on of the title of Professor Emeritus
and exiting formally from our university payrolls. I would like
to take credit for this wonderful Alice-in-Wonderland concept
(remember the un-birthday party?), but I did not originate it. It
certainly provides the best clue to what the editors of this volume
would label my "post-career." For some of us, the "career" continues—albeit in a somewhat altered form.

Thus far, my un-retirement has been experienced as a relatively seamless transition. The major change in my work life was
giving up the classroom and daily contact with students—no more
formal teaching. As a symbolic act, I also voluntarily gave up my
office and lab space in the psychology department and moved
important books and notes, memorabilia, and award plaques, to
an office in my home. It was a pleasant surprise to experience
the ease with which I was able to toss reams of files and papers
and notes into bags for disposal! Digital files and computer jump
drives made this less painful than it might have been, and I am
grateful for electronic technology. As someone who has been
fortunate enough to live geographically close to my university
home, shifting the location of my "office" was accomplished with

little trauma, and I have been able to eliminate lots of unnecessary "stuff."

With my university within walking distance (when books and
papers do not weigh me down), I keep my professional mail coming to the psychology department where I go periodically to pick
it up. I also continue to make use of my department's copy and
Fax machines and to get occasional assistance from the department's gracious and competent administrative staff. Even without
a physical trek to the department or the university library, this
computer age enables me to have access to worldwide resources
from my home office so that I can keep writing and researching
and communicating with colleagues.

My un-retirement has not been accompanied by the activities many assume I would be engaged in. I have not been binge
traveling, for example. As a fortunate academic and a lover of
far-away places, I managed to get to many parts of the world and
visit and live in some countries outside of the United States during
my active teaching years. Post retirement, with its more flexible
days and weeks, does provide more travel opportunities, but I
admit to finding myself annoyed when I am greeted by questions
about where I have just been and where I am going next. The other
assumed activity is that I am now spending lots more time with
children and grandchildren. With my family scattered across the
country in California, Colorado, and Maryland, my husband Al
and I have always devised ways to visit with them several times
each year—extra time at conferences and meetings, holidays,
birthdays, and special events. That has not changed, and the visits
(to them and by them) are no more frequent, given everyone's

schedules of work and school. We call each other and email about as often as ever. What I have also not done during these retirement years is turn to painting, potting, golf, gardening, or starting a business or a new career. I'm not sure what this says about me!

Un-retirement has lured me into making time to do some of the things that have waited for years to get done—like getting my old stamp collection in shape and sending it off to my youngest granddaughter, reorganizing my books and photo albums, reducing the contents of my paper files, and organizing family and travel slides for DVDs. Other home projects are still waiting to be tackled—perhaps for un-retirement, part II. For the most part, my busy life revolves around the activities described below.

Professional Work

My professional work habits and schedule are mostly unchanged from what they have always been. I still identify myself as an experimental social psychologist, and my interests in learning, gender, social class, discrimination, multiculturalism, and social justice remain salient and strong. With no teaching responsibilities, I have more time to devote to research and writing, and in the years since 1997, when I left the classroom, I have been happily productive. I have had the good fortune to work closely, on several projects, with wonderful colleagues, including a former graduate student who is now a major voice on issues of social class in research and policy.

Work with an interdivisional American Psychological Association group has just recently ended after several conference presentations and the publication of two papers. Our project, begun a decade ago, was focused on increasing the pipeline into psychology for students of color. The group included psychologists from Maryland, California, and Texas with specialties in counseling, community, and social psychology. One member of the group is in my home department, enhancing face-to-face collaboration, but we all communicated by a phone conference once or twice a month and by e-mail. Our objective was to contribute research and advocacy to enhance the success of minority students in psychology.

Another collaborative project, initiated by APA's Divisions 9 and 35, was preparation of a report on *Resources for the Inclusion of Social Class in Psychology Curricula.* Heather Bullock and I worked with 14 psychologists from a variety of disciplines, at various stages in their careers, to produce a report that was printed by APA in hard copy as well as on-line (Report, 2008). Included are descriptions of relevant classroom exercises and course syllabi, and lists of fiction, social policy legislation, popular media (film, TV, music), scholarly books and articles, and websites. The on-line report is maintained by APA's Committee on Socioeconomic Status and is up-dated periodically.

During my un-retirement years (beginning in 1998) I have written or co-written, in addition to the task force report, 14 published articles, 6 chapters, and 8 book reviews, commentaries, or forwards. I have also co-edited one book (Chin, et al., 2007), and two special journal issues (Lott & Bullock, 2001; Rogers & Lott, 2006). A book on psychology and economic injustice that I co-wrote with Heather Bullock (Lott & Bullock, 2007) has received two national awards. My most recent book (Lott, 2010) is on multiculturalism and diversity, the result of many years of teaching and study. I also continued to serve as a PhD advisor for graduate students, helping them successfully complete their doctorates and move into careers. My last doctoral student graduated in 2009, and I am accepting no more. My first doctoral student received her PhD in 1976 and, since then, I directed 40 theses and dissertations; during the earlier years in my professional career, I worked primarily with undergraduates.

Now I am busy with two current projects. One is a collaborative investigation of whether stigmatization of the poor in the print media has declined in periods of economic stress for the middle class. The second project is a study of the relative invisibility of labor unions as a subject of interest within psychology.

I thus continue to "work," and am a bit peevish when friends or other retirees living in a different way seem puzzled by, and not quite comfortable with, how I spend my days. Never previously having enjoyed "going to lunch," I continue to decline weekday invitations. I still live in an old-fashioned way, begun in my student days, with week days spent in professional work and evenings, weekends, and holidays set aside for special events, entertainment, socializing, game playing, music, reading, movies, theater, hiking, and political action. Colleagues and friends are surprised that I typically check my email only during the times reserved for "work" and not during the times set aside for fun and relaxation. These old habits seem to suit me. (You can guess that I don't own a smart phone—that demands constant checking.)

I am pleased when younger colleagues who have read my work share their comments and questions with me. And I was awed and immensely honored by the gold medal award for life-time achievement in psychology in the public interest that was presented to me at the 2011 APA convention by the American Psychological Foundation.

Political Work: Human Rights and Social Justice

With un-retirement came a coincidental entry into the governance of the American Psychological Association as a participant and a critic. For many years I had been actively involved in the work of Division 35, the Society for the Psychology of Women, serving as its 1990-91 president, and I had also been an elected member of the Council of SPSSI (Division 9), but it was not until SPSSI elected me to serve as their representative to APA Council (COR) that I entered fully into the political work of APA. I was the SPSSI representative for two consecutive terms (2002-2007), during which I tried to do justice to SPSSI's reputation as the "conscience of APA."

Almost immediately, my co-representative, Irma Serrano-Garcia, and I introduced a new business item to have APA establish within the Public Interest Directorate a Committee on Social Class and Socio-Economic Status. This seemed like a clear follow-up to a Resolution on Poverty and Socioeconomic Status that had been approved earlier. The Resolution had come from an APA Committee on Urban Initiatives that had worked closely with a Division 35 Task Force on Poverty which I had co-chaired. Ironically, COR decided to eliminate the Committee on Urban Initiatives two years after it passed the Resolution, providing me with my first "awakening" to the rather odd politics within APA governance. It also signaled the beginning of my efforts to argue publicly for the inclusion of social class in our professional association's understanding of diversity.

The call for a new permanent committee on social class and SES was met with a variety of negative responses, rebuffs, and little support from "the leadership." As a compromise, a Task Force to study issues related to socioeconomic status was approved. It was not, however, until a fateful COR meeting in New Orleans in August 2006, a year after the Katrina tragedy, that the recommendation of this Task Force for a permanent committee was approved. It was no accident that the events of Katrina influenced the decision and prompted some impassioned vocal support from those who saw the clear relationship between social class, poverty, and the suffering of so many in the aftermath of Katrina. At the same time, at this meeting in New Orleans, a high-ranking member of APA governance urged opposition to such a new committee, commenting that social class was a subject in (and for) sociology, not psychology! But the Committee was approved, as well as a new APA Office on Socioeconomic Status.

On another front, I became deeply involved in collaborative work to change APA's policy of justification for the role played by psychologists in U.S. facilities such as Guantanamo in which enhanced interrogation methods (torture) were being used on prisoners. Beginning with the 2005 report of the Presidential Task Force on Psychological Ethics and National Security (PENS), APA exhibited a shameful reluctance to deal openly and honestly with what psychologists were doing in national security settings in which international standards of human rights were being disregarded and ignored. I was among those who worked hard and vocally in a variety of ways for positive change, for truthful reporting of relevant proceedings, and to argue that psychologists should not work in settings in which violations of human rights systematically occurred (Lott, 2007). In a referendum brought to the APA membership in 2008, a majority of respondents agreed. This referendum followed the August 2007 APA conference that included a mini-convention on ethics and interrogation that I helped to plan.

An additional issue that brought me into conflict with APA leadership was my efforts to amend a *Resolution on Anti-Semitic and Anti-Jewish Prejudice*, adopted by COR in 2005, in which criticism of Israeli government policies was linked to anti-Semitism. Such a position, I argued was not evidence-based but was, instead, shaped by main-stream political considerations and discomfort with dissent. My efforts were met with considerable hostility from many and virtually no publicly expressed support so I accepted a compromise that amended a few words in the 2005 Resolution to indicate that not all critics of the Israeli government were anti-Semites.

I think there were some in APA leadership who breathed a sigh of relief when my second term as COR representative from SPSSI was over. I, on the other hand, was happy to have had the opportunity to work closely with many impressive and committed progressive psychologists who shared a vision of an APA dedicated to improving human welfare. I was delighted and encouraged when the National Multicultural Conference and Summit honored me with an Elders Wisdom Award in 2005, perceiving it as recognition of my work in the interest of social justice.

Community

For several decades I have worked closely with the George Wiley Center (GWC), a group in Rhode Island named in honor of a Rhode Islander who organized and led the National Welfare Rights Organization in the 1970s. George Wiley had been the first African American undergraduate chemistry major at the University of Rhode Island. Later, he left a comfortable life in academia as a researcher and professor at Syracuse University to help low-income women pursue economic justice. Over the years, my connection with the GWC added depth, specificity, and authenticity to the courses I developed on the social psychology of poverty and, all during my un-retirement years, I have been a member of their Board. Our work is grass-roots activism directed toward achieving goals set by low-income persons and families to enhance the quality and dignity of their lives. We have had many successes in affecting local and state policies.

I try to bring my knowledge and background as a social psychologist to the work of the GWC through assistance with grant writing and the mediation of group process. While I was still teaching, a group of my graduate students pursued a project involving interviews of school administrators and parents about their attitudes toward a school breakfast program for low-income students. We used the information we gathered for news releases and advocacy. Post retirement, I received a grant from SPSSI's Sages Program in 2002 to conduct a study on "Issues of Importance to Low-Income Adults and Readiness for Social Action." With the assistance of two undergraduate students, we interviewed a sample of 100 low-income adults (60 women and 40 men; 18% were minorities of color) at eight different sites in one county in Rhode Island. In exchange for their willingness to answer questions about issues of concern, respondents were given a copy of a resource booklet we had prepared containing up-to-date information on public agencies offering assistance to low-income adults with food, clothing, jobs, etc. Those willing to be interviewed were asked to share the resource booklet with friends and neighbors.

Respondents were asked to rate each of eleven issues on level of importance to them personally: food stamps; minimum wage; affordable housing; public schools; medical care; welfare benefits; utility shutoffs; neighborhood jobs; police protection; public transportation; and child care. We found, at that time, that the most important issue (for 94% of all respondents, 92% of women, and 98% of men) was affordable housing. The next three most important issues were raising the minimum wage, convenient public transportation, and affordable/accessible health care. Each of these issues was considered very important personally by more than 50% of women, men, and the total group of respondents. We used the data we gathered to advocate for affordable housing in the Town of South Kingstown.

During the months leading to the presidential election of 2008, I was energized by the Obama campaign. I am not a supporter of either of the major political parties and register as either a Green or an Independent. But Obama's background, fundamental decency, and expressed values drew me into active involvement. That he was nominated and elected still strikes me as an improbable miracle, and I am determined to continue my support for him despite some expected and predictable disappointments. I believe in the vital importance of telling him and others in government how they can do better for the public good, and in supporting and prodding elected progressives.

Personal Work

Beginning in early adolescence, walking and dancing have given me immense physical and emotional pleasure. Much later, I added to the quality of my life by a regular schedule of various aerobic exercises and the practice of yoga. Now, as my body ages and I need to contend with arthritic and rheumatic intrusions, there are changes in what I can comfortably do. My new emphasis is on the stretching, muscle strengthening, and balance work best suited for "older" bodies! With the time flexibility afforded by un-retirement, I am able to take a pleasant walk when I want to and go to a near-by gym two times a week.

A disabling "freak" accident necessitated many months of intense physical therapy, and I continue doing some of what I learned. The accident occurred on late Christmas morning in 2008. Al and I were walking on the beach, as we often do, along the surf to a point where the ocean meets a river. As we were heading back toward the parking lot, two quite large and very powerful dogs—unleashed—ran toward each other and both simultaneously bumped against my left hip, knocking me down and causing serious damage to my right arm. Many emergency room and surgery hours later I learned that I had suffered two compound wrist fractures and a smashed elbow. A final third surgery was required months later. My right arm is permanently altered; it cannot be fully extended. Actions requiring flexion have profited from physical therapy and have improved greatly with stubborn effort, but limitations remain as well as varying degrees of discomfort.

The consequences of this accident and the general challenge of aging joints remind me to respect the limitations of my body and to treat it with respectful care. I have come to terms with the fact that I will never again ride my bicycle (which still hangs in my garage!) on the wonderful new bike paths in my community. I will also no longer venture out in the snow with my cross-country skis, and will forever need to cope with the untreatable annoyance of tinnitus. More serious medical issues are bound to arise.

End Notes

As end-of-life becomes a concept with greater personal meaning, I ruminate a bit more than I used to. As is true for all of us, my life has been a unique adventure. I had an illegal abortion when I was 20, and spent 7 early years in an unhappy marriage. Later, I lost a child at birth. But regrets do not enter my thoughts at this point in my life. I continue to be incredibly fortunate on so many levels and know that other choices and other circumstances might have resulted in a far different direction for my life.

I have benefited from the automatic privileges associated with white skin and heterosexuality, although not from gender or class position. I have tried to understand and work against the destructive economic, political, and psychological consequences of stigmatized and relatively powerless social categories. Because I was married to a veteran of WWII, with GI Bill benefits, I was able to pursue a graduate education. This enabled me later on to work in the stimulating and creative and largely independent environment of academia, and to achieve a comfortable level of economic security. I am in loving interconnection with a small group of wonderful supportive friends, and with children and grandchildren who are remarkably capable, thoughtful, and fun to be with, and who lead decent and exciting lives. My family is a source of joy and pride, challenge and hope. The difference between my life and that of my immigrant working-class parents is astounding, and I am humbled by it. I think of others in this country whose lives are damaged and compromised through no fault of their own.

I want to believe that I have had some positive impact on the lives of my husband, and my children, some of my students and colleagues, and that my joint efforts with others have influenced the outcome of some important local and national events. I take pleasure from books, theater, conversation, out-door hikes and explorations, dinners "out," small adventures, travel, and work. Political struggles continue in the process of working for progressive social change. I hope to enjoy my un-retirement as long as I can, and to say goodbye (grudgingly) to life and those I love with as clear a head as possible.

The editors have asked for "final words of wisdom." What I can offer is my conviction that the pursuit of feminist objectives and social justice is not age-bound but a life-long endeavor that brings joy and renewal and promise. How "to prepare" for retirement is something I never thought about (except in terms of pension security), but know that others do so and that there will be some excellent advice somewhere else within the pages of this fine book.

References

Chin, J. L., Lott, B., Rice, J., & Sanchez-Hucles, J. (Eds.) (2007). *Women and leadership: Feminist visions and diverse voices.* Malden, MA: Blackwell

Lott, B. (2010). *Multiculturalism and diversity: A social psychological perspective.* UK: Wiley

Lott, B. (2007). APA and the participation of psychologists in situations in which human rights are violated. *Analyses of Social Issues and Public Policy, 7,* 1-8.

Lott, B., & Bullock, H. E. (2007). *Psychology and economic injustice: Personal, professional, and political intersections.* Washington, DC: APA Books

Lott, B., & Bullock, H. E. (Eds.) (2001). Listening to the voices of poor women. *Journal of Social Issues, 57* (2).

Report of the Task Force on Resources for the Inclusion of Social Class in Psychology Curricula. Available: http://www.apa.org/pi/ses/final_report.pdf

Rogers, M. R., & Lott, B. (Eds.) (2005). Helping non-mainstream families achieve equity in the public schools within the context of school-based consulting. *Journal of Educational and Psychological Consultation, 16* (1&2).

Retirement:
Yet Another Stage in Life's Grand Adventure

Nancy Felipe Russo

*W*hen I began this account, it was December 2011, and the holidays were fast approaching. Where had the time gone? As of January 1, 2012, I officially retired after 25 years at Arizona State University, but have yet to "catch up" on my writing. My "retirement" chapter is at the top of the list. My assigned task is to provide some words of wisdom with the goal of providing information that will help others benefit from my experiences. This has been an unexpectedly daunting task.

Career Highlights

Retirement is a time of reflection and passing on a legacy of "lessons learned." I begin with some career highlights to put my thoughts about retirement in context and underscore some of the learning experiences that I especially want to pass on. My career has encompassed many hats: teacher, researcher, scholar, administrator, mentor, editor, leader, policy analyst, and advocate. For the last 35 years I have been in academe. I have told part of my story—highlights of my academic career—but that was nearly two decades ago (Russo, 1994). I also spent a large portion of my career outside of academe, serving about two years as a Health Scientist Administrator in the National Institute of Child Health and Human Development, and 11 years as the first head of the Women's Programs Office of the American Psychological Association (APA).

It was at APA that I learned what it truly meant to be a psychologist—academic and otherwise—and that the academic norm of "publish or perish" is important because it ensures that research universities will produce and disseminate new research knowledge. As the world's largest and oldest scientific society for psychology, APA has been a gathering place for some of the best psychological minds in the country. My first role was with the Educational Affairs Office, which dealt with all aspects of educational training in psychology, from precollege to undergraduate, to graduate and even postgraduate levels. I was able to meet psychologists from every kind of setting, inside and outside of academe, learn about their values and activities, and attend meetings where they discussed and debated roles for psychologists. It was at APA that I first worked closely with senior women in psychology and gained a feminist identity. Florence Denmark, who eventually was the fifth women to become APA president in the 100 year history of the organization and also has a chapter in this volume, became a particularly important role model and mentor for me.

Through that experience I learned about the discipline's implicit norms, and began to recognize the role of mentoring in making hidden norms explicit. In addition, my eyes became opened to opportunities that I had missed. For example, in addition to not seeking advice from available mentors in graduate school, I hadn't raised an eyebrow when my major professor told me that a fellowship was going to another student because he had a wife to support while I had a husband to support me. I considered it reasonable when someone encouraged me to go into developmental psychology "because women are naturally good with children." I could go on.... It is fascinating to me that I never noticed the sexism in such messages. I didn't think twice about the fellowship opportunity (how was I to know that holding that fellowship was an honor that would have given me an edge in the job market). I liked developmental psychology and so I double-majored in it and did my thesis on the development of nonverbal communication in children.

It wasn't until my experience at APA that I learned that there were things to learn that weren't in the books and there is a social side to achievement in addition to the traditional factors of "ability and effort." I began to devote a substantial part of my professional career spreading the word about survival strategies in academe, so that others will be able to learn more quickly what I missed. These activities included reworking APA's most popular publication, *Careers in Psychology* and editing a newsletter for high school teachers of psychology. Mentoring has been a life long commitment that I am continuing in retirement. One of my current efforts is contributing to the mentoring literature and collaborating on presentations and publications connected to *CareerWise*, an online resilience training project funded by the National Science Foundation (NSF), which is aimed at reducing attrition of female graduate students in physical science and engineering (see http://careerwise.asu.edu/).

At APA I learned about women's issues in psychology. By 1973, APA had established a standing Committee on Women in Psychology (CWP), and I became involved in CWP activities to enhance women's status in psychology and encourage research and applications of psychology related to women's lives. Spurred on by CWP, women psychologists organized to establish the APA Division of Psychology of Women to promote research on women's issues, which was established in 1973 as the 35th division of the association, and is therefore known as "Division 35."

In 1977, after concentrated lobbying by women and men who cared about feminist issues, APA established its first Women's Programs Office. Women psychologists now had an institutionalized power base for their issues. I led the office from 1977 to 1985, and then left APA to direct the Women's Studies Program at ASU.

It was during my time at APA that I began to establish a publication record that would one day enable me to return to academe. I began to write about women's lives in earnest, for I now understood the need to create and disseminate relevant knowledge if it is to be used and have an impact. I pursued my interest in women's history in psychology that began in graduate school. Promoting and preserving women's contributions to psychology became a major enterprise. Through the Women's Programs Office, we organized symposia at APA conventions that brought eminent women together to tell the stories of their lives that we later published in books of autobiographies (O'Connell & Russo, 1983, 1988). We also commissioned authors to write biographies about women psychologists. I hoped that by placing the women's stories in the larger context of psychology and society, students and colleagues would come to understand that psychology and the people in it (women and men) both reflect and shape the larger social context. As you will see, that principle—our lives reflect and shape the larger social context—is reflected in the issues I have had to address during my own retirement.

I cannot overemphasize the usefulness of understanding the past as a weapon to fight stereotypes and discrimination. My goal in studying women's history and participation in psychology was to change the circumstances of women in the field and to develop a psychology where men and women can work together on a mutual, equal basis. In addition to writing about women's status in psychology, I joined with women in other fields to work to change women's status across the disciplines. The passage of legislation to establish an NSF Committee on Women, Minorities, and the Handicapped in Science and Technology, was a particularly satisfying success. This work provided a foundation for subsequent development of programs aimed at diversifying the scientific and engineering workforce, including NSF's current ADVANCE program and my commitment to promoting the status of women in STEM fields is reflected in the *CareerWise* project.

Another big change in my intellectual development during this period was involvement in mental health issues. A large proportion of APA members are in clinical fields, and my social network became populated with feminist clinicians. In 1977, I was appointed to the Subpanel on the Mental Health of Women of the President's Commission on Mental Health, established by President Carter. There I became intensively involved in efforts to change the male-dominated mental health establishment, with a focus on the National Institute of Mental Health. I began to write and publish on the relationship between women's roles and status and mental health and roles for mental health professionals in dealing with women's issues.

In 1989, the Reagan White House launched an attempt to get then Surgeon General C. Everett Koop to portray abortion as a public health threat. This was the beginning of a campaign to construct a "postabortion syndrome" as a lever to deny women access to legal abortion that continues today and will be the basis for one of my major retirement book projects. I became a member of APA's "Blue Ribbon" Task Force to examine research findings on postabortion emotional responses to provide a report to the Surgeon General that has served as a basis for Congressional testimony. Although this campaign began in the U.S., it has become a worldwide movement. As a result I have been invited to present my work on the relation of abortion and mental health at a variety of international meetings in Canada, Chile, China, Guatemala, Mexico, and Scotland.

In 2001, one of my most exciting policy adventures occurred in conjunction with a referendum to restrict abortion in Switzerland. The mental health professionals in that country organized to refute the myths that were being used to argue for the referendum, and I was invited to an international symposium in Berne that examined the state of the art of research on abortion's mental health outcomes. It was exciting to meet so many researchers around the world (all with similar findings!) and I take great satisfaction in having helped contribute to the defeat of that referendum.

The fact that my work has become cited in amicus briefs and policy papers means that I have become a blip on the prolife radar screen. This means I have received pictures of dismembered fetus heads in the mail and have my work misrepresented and attacked on the web and in the media. Unfortunately, anyone can say anything on the web with little accountability, and the prolife forces have been quick to use cyberspace to avoid accountability in promoting their cause.

In the meantime, my efforts to understand the factors that promote a societal motherhood mandate and that undermine women's ability to control their childbearing led me to focus on women's work and family roles and the psychological impact of rape and violence against women. These concerns were reflected in my work for the President's Commission, the women's mental health agenda (Russo, 1990), and APA's Task Force on Violence Against Women. I became immersed in the literature on rape, battering, and sexual harassment. This work confirmed the importance of empowering women, promoting social and political equality, and enhancing mutual communication between women and men as strategies for prevention of a host of psychological and social problems. My subsequent work has focuses on links between intimate violence, unwanted pregnancy, and abortion (Russo, 2006). We have yet to appreciate fully the impact of physical and sexual violence on women and children over the life cycle. Given this context, it is not surprising that one of my big "retirement projects" is a book on reproductive issues that will focus on the outcomes of violence over the life cycle, including unintended pregnancy, and mental health effects.

I have also been particularly interested in how intersections of gender, ethnicity, and other aspects of culture affect women's experience. I had long been concerned with civil rights issues and had been a great admirer of Martin Luther King, Jr. during the 1960s. During graduate school I had worked as a psychological assistant in a Head Start Program, which included a center in Harlem, and included black women's issues in my work from its beginning. One of my most satisfying accomplishments has been preserving the autobiographies of black psychologists Mamie Phipps Clark, Ruth Howard, and Carolyn R. Payton. Despite their invisibility, I believe that psychology has been enriched by the contributions of ethnic minority women, and my work continues to explore intersections of gender and ethnicity (Landrine & Russo, 2010).

I was never actively involved in Hispanic women's issues until the day that Hortensia Amaro walked into my office at APA and asked me to join Division 35's Task Force on Hispanic Women, which she chaired. When I told her that I had never felt discrimination in my career because I was Hispanic, she responded, "But you are one of the few senior women role models we have and we need role models. Are you ashamed of being Hispanic?" Taken aback, I replied, "Of course not!" And I remembered my high school days in Santa Clara, which I hadn't thought about for years, when many of my friends were of Mexican ancestry and where a color line was drawn between "Mexicans" and "Spanish." I always thought that was ridiculous, for my Spanish ancestors could have just as easily gone to Mexico (several went to other countries in Latin America). Besides, I had thought, weren't we all Americans? I also remembered Danny and Anita, who had to date in secret because Anita's mother (who claimed Spanish ancestry) wouldn't let Anita date a Mexican (we covered for her). I also remembered an incident on Staten Island that I didn't mean much to me at the time, when someone asked me about my ancestry and I replied, "My father's Spanish and my mother's from Idaho—probably Irish." Their response: "Oh—just say you're Irish."

By the time Hortensia left my office, I was on the Task Force, and we began what has become a lifelong friendship forged in our work to enhance the status of Hispanic women in psychology and promote psychological knowledge about Hispanic women's lives. I have been particularly interested in how culture affects Hispanic women's experience of violence . I am also pleased that my work has preserved the autobiography of the first Chicana to obtain a Ph.D. in psychology, Martha Bernal, and that later I was successful in recruiting her to join the faculty at ASU where she worked until her retirement. In addition to conducting research related to Hispanic women's issues after relocating to ASU, I became involved in the community, serving a term on the Board of the Hispanic Women's Corporation.

Family Highlights

My father, Joseph Felipe, was the son of Spanish immigrants (Basque and Galician). My mother, Ruby, was the daughter of Mormons who immigrated to California from Idaho. The eldest of four children, I have two brothers, Joseph Jr. and Donald and a sister, Paula. My father, who attended the University of Santa Clara on a basketball scholarship, was the first person on either side of my family to obtain a college education. I was the first person in my family to obtain a Ph.D.

During my childhood, my mother, whose father died when she was 12, told me stories of living in a tent when their house burned and of working as a maid to earn money to attend secretarial school after high school graduation. She communicated what it was like to be poor, and emphasized the importance of being able to earn a living. Both parents also emphasized helping other people—for a time my mother worked as a social worker, and as a little girl I used to go with her mother to visit "her families." My father, who was a basketball and football coach until my sophomore year in high school when he went into business, was constantly doing something for "his boys." Watching them interact with others instilled a family ethic of service that has shaped my career goals and activities and that continues during my retirement.

In graduate school at Cornell University I married Thomas Russo, a student in Cornell's law school. After 7 years we divorced, and in 1975, I married Allen Meyer, my partner of nearly four decades. I tell students that marriage isn't for everyone, and it's better to have no marriage than an unhappy marriage—but there's absolutely nothing better than a happy marriage. Allen has been a wonderful source of support in good times and bad. When I crushed my ankle in a softball accident, he stayed by my side in the hospital and helped me adjust to the fact that I would have a permanent disability. After 6 months in a wheel chair and a year on crutches, I regained my ability to walk without a limp (usually). However, to this day the ankle is unstable and needs to be perpetually strengthened with exercise to maintain my balance and mobility.

Being able to have Allen by my side—before and after retirement—means that adversities are transformed into challenges to be overcome. Our closeness is both our greatest strength and greatest vulnerability however. It is difficult to prepare for the loss of a life long partner, and I regret I don't have any words of wisdom for doing so at the moment. We do not plan to die until our 90s, but recognize the need to expect the unexpected. Perhaps recognizing and accepting the inevitability of death is a productive first step. Meanwhile, living fully is the priority!

People sometimes ask me why I kept the name of my first husband (Russo) rather than go back to Felipe or take the name of Meyer. It's difficult to explain to young people how disruptive a change in name can be to one's professional (as well as personal) identity. I learned a lesson in disruption and invisibility when I changed my name to Russo after publishing under Felipe, and I was not about to go through that again. I do regret that I changed my name in the first place, but I wasn't aware that I had an option. Today's women do have an option, and need to be aware of it.

Honors and Awards

I have been fortunate in the many honors I have received, which include being elected to the Presidency of three APA divisions (Division 1—General Psychology; Division 34—Population and Environmental Psychology, and Division 35—Society for the Psychology of Women). Two honors are particularly special because they are named in honor of women I have loved and admired—Division 35's Carolyn Wood Sherif Award (1993) and the Denmark-Grunvald Award from the International Council of Psychologists (2009). Given I have devoted so much of my career trying to ensure that women's contributions to psychology do not become invisible, it was a kick to find myself on a list of the 100 most prominent living women in psychology in the English speaking world and to be considered a "Trailblazer" in Community Psychology by the Committee on Women of the Society for Research and Action. At the APA convention in 2011 I was surprised and moved by my second APA Presidential citation "for career-long dedication to the advancement of women's equality through psychological science,… tireless mentoring of other women in psychology, and service to the field of psychology… notable for both its enduring length and impressive breath."

Like anyone, I take pleasure in receiving such honors. The plaques on my office walls provided an important source of self-validation when times got rough—advocating change in one's field takes a certain amount of intestinal fortitude, for it is not always welcomed. I suspect they will retain their sustaining effects in retirement, particularly because they make me feel connected to an international feminist community. Accomplishments and deeds are never done by one person alone. All that I have accomplished reflects teamwork and connection. Whenever I have accepted an award, it's been on behalf of the team, and all of my colleagues and students who have worked with me share in the rewards and recognition that I achieve. I have been fortunate in being able to work with colleagues and students from diverse countries, cultures, and disciplines and I expect to continue that practice in retirement.

Reflections on Lessons Learned

I am often asked what I would do differently, but nothing really major comes to mind. I have had some miserable experiences, but all of my experiences, good and bad, have made me what I am, and I do enjoy life. For example, if I had spent more time networking with psychologists in graduate school rather than tutoring my law student husband, I might not have developed my interest in law and public policy. If I had concentrated on research in my first faculty position, I would have never gone to APA and been able to have such an impact on psychology. If I had stayed married to my first husband, I would never have experienced the joy of being married to someone who is a true partner. And so on.... now, in retirement, my new adventures will build on my previous experiences. My philosophy is Carpe diem! Learn from experience, but never look back. Nonetheless, I do have some suggestions for meeting the challenges of retirement.

Plan for retirement, but don't expect things to go as planned.

I sit at my computer amidst piles of books and papers that overflow on to the floor and stretch across my home office, each stack representing an item on a very long "to do" list. So many projects, so little time. This is not the retirement I imagined. But then that is the first lesson of my story—things will not go as planned, so the best plan is to expect the unexpected, be open to possibilities, be mindful, and have faith in your resilience and ability to adapt.

I am fond of saying that "retirement is like conception—it is a process, not a single event." I always expected to work until forced to retire, but my assumption was that the process would occur when I was in my late seventies. Mindful of research findings warning against relocating to a new environment after retirement, in 1985 my husband Allen Meyer and I moved to Arizona State University (ASU). Our plan was to ultimately retire in a place where we would have friends and connections to our community, and I could continue to have meaningful work if and when I desired it. Work has provided a substantial part of my meaning in life and to this day, I do not envision my life without some form of work—the big difference in retirement is lack of financial reward.

After a quarter of a century at ASU, The Plan, which was progressing nicely, went awry when I developed severe respiratory illness. After more than three years of deterioration, I could not function without cough suppressants. By that I mean I could not brush my teeth, talk for more than a few sentences, or walk at more than a snail's pace without coughing so hard I would uncontrollably vomit. Side effects from the anti-inflammatory drugs, lack of exercise, and an escalating body mass index, added to the toll. As my health deteriorated, so too did my work performance. I went to several doctors, took antibiotics along with my steroids, and tried herbal remedies, but nothing helped—until I visited the Oregon coast in June of 2007 and was cured after 9 days of breathing clean air. Unfortunately, after a week back in Phoenix the cough was back.

It turned out that over the years, the population exploded in Phoenix's metropolitan area, taking a toll on the environment in many ways, but particularly in erosion of air quality. My particular bête noire is particulate pollution—google the "brown cloud of Phoenix" if you want to know more. Suffice to say, despite the fact that I loved my job and had a wonderful community of friends in Phoenix, my priority in life became getting my health back. We now live in Corvallis, Oregon where the air is clean and environmental concerns are embedded in the local culture.

Make health a priority in life before and after retirement.

If you google "planning for retirement," you will receive a wealth of advice—most of it about financial planning. But what good is wealth without health? I am fortunate in having good genes and long-lived ancestors, so my major health problems during my youth, including chronic neck, knee, and ankle pain, have resulted from accidents. I am chagrined at how much I took my good health for granted. Indeed I took pride in working long hours, sitting at my computer for hours at a time, going days without sleep (my record: 37 hours), neglecting annual physical exams and dental check-ups, and eating fast food on the go. My major form of exercise was walking between the parking lot and my office. Some of this was an imbalanced focus on the values of working hard, helping people, and eschewing selfishness and vanity, while neglecting attention to the values of moderation, balance, and health. Ignorance of the risks I was taking was a factor as well. Fortunately, the first Surgeon General's Report on Smoking and Health came out in 1964 when I was a junior in college, so I never became a smoker.

I would make different choices today. In my youth, the medical profession considered nutrition a topic to be confined to Home Economics. Today, there is a multitude of research documenting the importance of nutrition, sleep, and exercise for good health, and reputable physicians such as Dr. Oz are translating the research findings for the public. We have gone from a limited focus on calories and minimum daily requirements of vitamins and minerals, to a broader vision of how a wide range of nutrients work synergistically to regulate bodily functioning. Although it will take a while to sort out truth from exaggeration for various claims, it's pretty clear to me that my grandmother was on to something when she told me to brush my teeth and eat my vegetables. I now appreciate the importance of eating salmon, olive oil, lentils, nuts, berries, and (dark) *chocolate* as well!

Although there is no "do-over" for the wayward health behaviors of my youth, I have taken health to heart during retirement. In addition to new developments in nutrition, toothpaste formulas, and skin cream, my health behaviors have been informed by new research on exercise. The health benefits of aerobic exercise have long been touted. However as one ages, loss of overall stamina, balance, muscle strength, and bone density become specific concerns, so other forms of exercise are needed as well. In particular, I have been bothered by stiff joints, hands numb from carpal tunnel syndrome, and inability to maintain balance due to ankle problems as a result of accidents. Physical therapy enabled me to avoid surgery for my wrists and ankles and led to the discovery of the benefits of a therapy pool, but insurance covered only a limited number of visits. The solution came in two parts. First, we built a home fitness center complete with a therapy pool where despite my bad ankles I can do water aerobics to my heart's content. Second, my husband and I now take a Gentle Yoga class together. How I wish I would have discovered Yoga when I was 20. I'm still a novice, but it has already made a big difference in my well-being. In addition to building stamina, strength, and flexibility, an unexpected benefit of taking a yoga class is that it provides some needed structure in my life—which brings me to another lesson.

Plan for some structure in your retirement.

A common retirement fantasy is that retirement is a time of being free and able to do whatever one wants to do whenever one wants to do it. Sleep in, take a trip on short notice, buy an RV and explore new vistas. The idea of freedom has always been appealing to me. One of the things I most liked about my career is that my jobs have a minimal amount of structure, particularly my job at ASU. There's always some structure in academic jobs—classes and deadlines must be met, for example. My surprise in retirement has been that I miss having some structure. I have learned new appreciation for the role that my environment has played in keeping me active and organized.

One effect of lack of routine and structure in retirement has been alteration of my time perception. At a stage in life when I would like time to slow down—after all, my remaining time on earth is limited—my perceived passage of time has accelerated. I cannot seem to accomplish half of the things I managed to do when I was working full time and active in the community. This became disturbing when I found myself losing track of what day it was, only being reminded when Friday came around and it was time for yoga class. I have now taken steps to remedy this problem by affiliating with the Department of Psychology at Oregon State University. Several new colleagues share my interests in women's health, particularly on the effects of violence on women's health, so I expect I will be able to structure an optimal balance between meaningful work and freedom to travel and pursue other interests. One of the great things about retirement is that I have enough financial security so I can choose to work at whatever I want. This brings me to yet another lesson.

■ **Put aside sufficient funds to ensure you have the life you want in retirement.**

Financial planning is typically high on any list of retirement tips, and deservedly so. My emphasis on health and other aspects of retirement that have yielded surprises for me does not mean that I deem financial resources as unimportant. Indeed, the ability to purchase organic food, construct a fitness center, pay for yoga classes, and work only when and where you wish requires financial resources that few will have without making saving for retirement part of a lifelong plan. This is one aspect of retirement that I got right. From my first full-time job, I have participated in TIAA-CREF which has meant regular saving for retirement. For many years I made supplemental contributions as well, and I participated in a deferred compensation program when I was head of the Women's Programs Office at the American Psychological Association.

One's wealth reflects both saving and spending, and my spending preferences and practices have served me well. I have never believed in wasting money on materialistic status indicators like fancy cars or jewelry. I was fond of saying that my clothes were never really in style—but never went out of style either. As I type this I am wearing jeans and a tee shirt that are more than 15 years old. After reading Ellen Langer's (2009) book, *Counterclockwise*, I decided that one of the reasons that I feel like I am in my 40s rather than my ripe old age of 68 is that I am still wearing the same clothes that I wore at that age! I highly recommend that book to all retirees, present and future.

Given we had no children and good health insurance, our major expenditures have involved our home. From the time I bought my first house, I viewed it as an investment, leading me to often describe myself as "living in my money." For the past 36 years of our marriage, Allen and I have lived in houses that were slightly more expensive than we could easily afford, and in the process we made substantial profits on our investment when the properties were sold. This meant we were financially prepared to deal with the unexpected, so when health problems meant I had to leave Phoenix, financial barriers were not a concern. We looked forward to our new adventures in Oregon. Six months after my miraculous recovery, we found a house in Corvallis, Oregon and I announced my intention to retire at the end of the academic year in 2009.

Things did not go as planned.

By July of 2008 we had moved into our new house in Oregon and put the Phoenix house on the market for $1.1 million. At this time Allen was teaching on-line courses part-time at Mesa College so could easily relocate. I had no teaching responsibilities in my last year with ASU so the plan was to stay in Oregon and commute when necessary. Two mortgages constituted a hefty burden, but I was still being paid by ASU and we had some savings as a cushion. It was estimated that it would take about six months for the house to sell. Unfortunately, at that point, the housing market went south. It took 18 months to sell our house. During that time, more than a half a million dollars of our previous equity had evaporated. I provide the figures so that you can understand the substantial hit taken by our retirement fund and appreciate the depth of the anxiety I was feeling as I faced losing my income from ASU at a time that I had two rather large mortgages. Fortunately, Keith Crnic, ASU's wonderful department chair, took me back, averting a severe family financial crisis.

So 2009-2010 was a time of belt-tightening and adaptation. We sold one of our cars and put a moratorium on all unnecessary expenses. I had an apartment in Phoenix and commuted to Oregon every other weekend. Once we had the double mortgage burden lifted, we were able to regain our financial footing and get back on track with our retirement plans. Although I did not go through life consciously saving for retirement, I am greatly appreciative of the fact that between our investments and social security income, despite losing so much of our money we still have enough savings to supplement our social security and live a comfortable life.

Nonetheless, the "expect the unexpected" principle still applies. Given the weakness of the economy and the downright treasonous determination of so many politicians to tear down the government and make Obama a one-term president, the strength of the American economy cannot be taken for granted. Although I have been involved in public policy and given substantial amounts of money to feminist causes all my life, I have had little involvement with partisan politics for nearly 40 years. That is about to become an unanticipated change in my retirement.

Build in time for friends and family.

The plan to move to a place early enough to establish connections to a community before retirement turned out to be wise even though I was unable to retire in Phoenix. The importance of building connections and making time for friends and family came home to me that last year when Allen lived in Oregon with our three dogs while I came back to teach at ASU. Although I didn't have a car, I got along fine because of tremendous support from friends who took me grocery shopping and helped with errands. They made sure I had company on the weekends I stayed in town, and when I had a medical emergency in the middle of the night, came to my aid and took me to the emergency room.

We have met a lot of interesting new acquaintances in Oregon and are on the way to making some of them real friends. One of the things about retirement is that there is more time to entertain, and we have had more people over for dinner in the past three months than we entertained in the last 5 years at ASU. Another benefit about being forced to leave Arizona is that family members, most of whom live in California, view us as more accessible and are more interested in visiting us. This surprising development led me to an insight that may help others with retirement planning.

When I left Washington, D.C. to move to Arizona, I thought I was moving closer to family and would consequently see more of them. As people used to lots of traveling, Allen and I didn't consider the 16 hour drive between Phoenix and my home town in Northern California particularly onerous, and after the move we spent various holidays with family for the first time in decades. But we did the driving. My family visited me once for Thanksgiving dinner in the 25 years we lived in Phoenix. Allen and I chose to move to Arizona partially to retire in a place closer to family. The flaw in the plan was that I didn't appreciate the great variation in psychological distance between Arizona and California among my family members. We might as well have moved to the other side of the moon. Knowing what I know now, I would have asked about the probability of them visiting various places I considered as possibilities for the move and included their preferences when weighing my options.

Be clear on your values.

Planning for retirement requires weighing a host of elements and effective planning requires clarifying values. Some people feel that retirement means they are "washed up" and lose self-worth because success in their career is what gave them value. For some, the amount of money they have defines their self-worth, so loss of income in retirement becomes a blow to self-esteem. But to me, success is the ability to do something meaningful with my life; to solve problems and to help people; to use my knowledge and skills to get people to work together and to build something lasting; to leave this earth just a bit better than when I came into it; to have an impact, to make a difference. I have achieved success on my terms and am grateful to have lived at a time when people were actually willing to pay me for doing the things I value. The difference in retirement is that I will no longer be paid for doing what I love to do. However, I have no doubt that I will continue to use my knowledge and skills to help people and work to make a difference for many years to come.

So my most important lesson to pass on is to live life in keeping with one's values regardless of life stage. Balancing diverse values requires mindfulness and self-reflection, and sometimes I have had to make sacrifices to maintain them. This has been reflected in my life in a variety of ways, including leaving a well-paid job with the National Institute of Child Health and Human Development because it was clear I would not get a promotion unless I violated my ethics, and making special efforts to seek out opportunities that would enable me to use my knowledge and skills on behalf of others. Living life in the service of your values will give you a sense of purpose and meaning—wherever your life path takes you in retirement, and whether or not you ever achieve what other people have defined as "success." From this perspective, retirement is not an end point, but one more stage in life's grand adventure.

References

Landrine, H. & Russo, N. F. (Eds.) (2010). *Handbook of diversity in feminist psychology*. New York: Springer.

Langer, E. (2009). *Counterclockwise: Mindful health and the power of possibility*. New York: Ballentine Books.

O'Connell, A. N. & Russo, N. F. (Eds.) (1983). *Models of achievement: Reflections of eminent women in psychology*. New York: Columbia University Press.

O'Connell, A. N. & Russo, N. F., (Eds.) (1988). *Models of achievement: Reflections of eminent women in psychology*, Volume II. New York: Lawrence Erlbaum.

Russo, N. F. (1990). Overview: Forging research priorities for women's mental health. *American Psychologist, 45*, 368 373.

Russo, N. F. (1994). The evolution of a feminist psychologist, advocate, and scholar. In P. Keller (Ed.) *Academic Careers: Career Decisions and Experiences of Psychologists* (pp.105-120). New York: Erlbaum.

Russo, N. F. (2006). Violence against women: A global health issue. In Q. Jing, M. R Rosenzweig, G. d'Ydewalle, H. Zhang, H. Chen, & K. Zhang (Eds.). *Progress in Psychological Science Around the World, Vol 2*: Social and Applied Issues. (pp. 181-198). Proceedings of the 28th International Congress of Psychology, Bejing, 2004. New York: Psychology Press (Taylor & Francis Group).

Creating A Lifetime of Possibilities:
A Look at Retirement

Nancy K. Schlossberg

*"Who of us can see, in its entirety...[the] path, whether
in life or art, and who can tell where it will end?"*
- Marc Chagall, artist -

After a retirement party for an elder stateswoman at the University of Maryland, two deans and I walked to our respective departments. They felt the retiree should have done so years before, despite the fact that she was a fantastic, active, productive woman. I knew right then that I would retire before I needed to—that I never wanted anyone to say that about me. And after many discussions with my dean and department chair, against their wishes, I retired at age 68. I was not worried; after all, I had studied transitions and had developed a model that serves as a lens for examining adult transitions. My professional experience led me to believe that I would ace retirement. But how wrong I was!

Soon after I retired, a newspaper reporter interviewed me about a project I had directed while at Maryland about grandparents raising grandchildren. He asked me a simple question: "How do you want to be identified in this story? What is your title?" I almost gagged and could not get out the words, "I am a retired professor." I fudged and said something like "I am a consultant." Several months later, my husband, already retired, asked me "Where are you going? When will you be back?" Another shock as I had worked all our married life and was not used to reporting to someone. In addition, friends asked, "Well, now that you are retired, what will you do?"

I was simultaneously confronting issues of identity—my tag, who I was; my changing relationships—how to renegotiate them;

and my purpose—how to develop a new reason to get up in the morning. I found that I was uncomfortable with this uncharted territory and realized I needed to learn more about the retirement transition. The more I struggled to define my own retirement, looking through both my personal and professional lenses, the more I realized that we are living in a period when the very definition of "retirement" is changing. In the past, we knew that retirement simply meant that you no longer went to work every day. Because people lived fewer years than they do now, retirees didn't feel the need to embark on new, long-term projects or commitments.

Now it's not so clear what constitutes retirement. Susan P. Robinson, former Vice President of the Center for Life Long Learning, and Mary Beth Lakin, Associate Director for Special Projects at the American Council on Education, are engaged in a research project funded by MetLife Foundation. They conclude that not only is retirement changing but so is the language used to describe it. *"Retirees and seniors are now rebounders, prime timers, or recareerers. In short, the term retirement is being retired, or at least redefined. Instead, increasing numbers of adults aged 55 to 79 are entering the third age of life"* (Robinson & Lakin, 2007). Columnist Ellen Goodman (2010) could not find the right term to use about her own retirement. Rather, she described her final column about her own retirement as a process of "letting go" and finding out what's next. She wrote: *"It involves a sense of future, a belief that every exit line is an entry, that we are moving on rather than out."*

It's tempting to equate retirement with aging, but not accurate. For people in some fields—pilots, professional athletes, dancers, or people with military careers—retirement comes at an early age. For them, retirement may imply a whole new career, or starting a new business. Homemakers also face retirement issues when their major role as CEO of a small family business ends. They too face the daunting task of constructing a new life.

I decided that my next project would be a personal one—I would study the retirement transition. My purpose was to understand more clearly what I was experiencing and then share my understanding with others in the same boat. Over the next five years, I conducted approximately 100 interviews and 20 focus groups as the foundation for writing two books, *Retire Smart, Retire Happy: Finding Your True Path in Life* (2004) and *Revitalizing Retirement: Reshaping Your Identity, Relationships, and Purpose* (2009). I learned that:

- There is no single retirement path—in fact, there are many ways to get a life;

- Retirees need to strengthen their Psychological Portfolios as well as their financial portfolios;

- Retirement is a series of transitions and not a date;

- Retirement happiness is feeling you "matter" and still count.

Six Ways to Get a Life After Retirement

I found that retirement was a very varied experience, that each person was unique, and that there is no way to categorize retirement. Despite that, I uncovered six major paths retirees followed. It is important to note: people change paths over time, combine paths, and pursue whichever path they choose in a unique way. A word about each path.

I am a Continuer. I continue writing and speaking, but no longer teach or work for an organization. As my daughter said, "The only thing retired about you is your paycheck." Continuers maintain their former identity, but in a modified way. Mort, a retired museum director, occasionally curates an art show; Larry, a retired roofer, will help out his old firm in an emergency. Continuers stay connected to their former work, their former identities, while developing on new fronts.

Adventurers find that retirement provides an opportunity to pursue an unrealized dream or try something new. Jane, a retired teacher, turned her hobby of raising goats into her new life. She bought a small farm and raises angora goats. She is making yarn and selling it at craft fares.

Easy Gliders declare that they have worked all their lives and retirement is the time to relax. They take each day as it comes. Sam, a retired bank teller, now plays golf, poker, and babysits for his grandchildren. For some, the joy of having no agenda and no pressure makes for a relaxed life.

Involved Spectators still care deeply about their previous work. However, they are no longer players, but stay involved. For example, Steve, a retired lobbyist, is no longer physically able to walk the halls of Congress. He still follows the news and stays on top of current events.

At some point, we will all be Searchers as we look for our niche. We might retire, then adventure into a new path, and then when that has played out, we might search again. Think of all the times you have said to yourself, "What's next?"

There are two kinds of Retreaters—those who are stepping back by using a moratorium to figure out what's next and those who are depressed and have become couch potatoes.

You can ask yourself which path do you want to be on at this time in your life? Do you want to Continue using existing skills and interests, but modifying them to fit retirement? Or become an Adventurer who sees retirement as an opportunity to start new endeavors? Or a Searcher exploring new options through trial and error? Are you an Easy Glider—who enjoys unscheduled time letting each day unfold? Or an Involved Spectator who cares deeply about the world, but engages in less active ways? Or a Retreater taking time out or disengaging from life? Whichever path you choose, you need to pay attention to your Psychological Portfolio.

The Importance of a Strong Psychological Portfolio

My story illustrates the importance of structuring your Psychological Portfolio, your Identity, Relationships, and Purpose, to protect against the bias and rejection sometimes encountered in retirement. I worked hard to craft a book proposal about retirement. Each rejection was accompanied by the same explanation: "She is the one to write a psychological book on retirement, but she no longer has a 'platform.'" I wondered what that meant. Finally, I realized that the rejections reflected an attitude about retirement. To publishers, as a retiree, I had less status, less ability to market sales, less importance. There is a happy ending to the story. Eventually, I found a professional publisher, and that became my platform.

Paying attention to your Psychological Portfolio will insure that you have a platform.

I coined the term Psychological Portfolio after studying many retirees who described the challenges of finding a new life (Schlossberg, 2009). Few of us realize we even have a Psychological Portfolio. As you think about retirement, it is important to consider your emerging Identity; ways to maximize your personal Relationships with friends and family; and approaches to help you figure out your Purpose in life. Ideally the three parts of the portfolio pie should be of equal strength.

Identity is key to your Psychological Portfolio. What do you put on a calling card? How do you identify yourself when you meet someone? Madge, a skilled journalist, could not wait to retire so that she could do some serious painting. She had her studio ready the day she retired. Yet it took her two years to say to herself and to others that she was an artist. Incorporating a new identity takes time. In between, though, it is important to remind yourself that you are more than your former job title. Modifying or changing you identity as circumstances change requires resilience.

Just as relationships play a part in your financial portfolio, as you provide for those you care about, Relationships play a critical role in your Psychological Portfolio. Replacing work relationships can take time and require effort. I heard the comment many times, "I don't miss work, I miss the schmoozing." It is critical to find a substitute for work relationships.

In addition, readjusting to family relationships can be challenging. I interviewed Cal, a retired executive. He was amazed that he screamed at his wife at the check out counter about the brand of cereal she had bought. Now that he was no longer working full time he went grocery shopping with her. Adjusting to being at home with her after 50 years of spending days apart takes time. And one couple felt guilty that they wanted to keep sailing and adventuring, but their daughter thought they should babysit for her since they were retired.

Having a Purpose is critical to well-being. Sociologists Phyllis Moen and Vivian Fields (2002) concluded that people's work provides social as well as financial capital. After retirement, participation in volunteer or part-time work is an effective way to build up your social capital. Many studies point to the relationship of volunteering and mental health and even longevity. But volunteering presents a conundrum for some women. They worked hard to be part of the workforce and now volunteering is being promoted again. According to a report, "The New Volunteer Workforce," nonprofits "desperately" need volunteers; yet every year volunteers are leaving their posts in growing numbers. To stem this tide, the report included as one of its suggestions a "hybrid" plan of providing stipends for volunteers (Eisner, Grimm, & Washburn, 2009).

I spent hours volunteering, doing many things I used to do as a professional, but receiving no pay. I began to resent volunteering. I felt guilty since after all, wasn't this the time to give back, to feel grateful for all that I had received over my life? Then something amazing happened that turned everything around. Robert Carter, CEO of the Senior Friendship Centers in Sarasota Florida, and Dennis Stover, former Vice President of the Centers, invited me to work on a short-term project as a "workateer." They offered me a small amount of money and coined the phrase. According to

Dennis Stover, "workateering" is a concept that bridges the experienced worker to the volunteer role and adds value and benefit to what volunteers are providing organizations. A small stipend is paid for the work the volunteer does. It provides a transition from paid work to volunteering. Hence—work with some dollars attached connects the person with past professional life, while beginning a life of mostly volunteering one's skills and talents. Stover expressed the hope that this 'hybrid' concept adds to the discussion of how we approach volunteerism as we look to Boomers retiring and wanting purpose in their next life phase.

So whether it is volunteering, paid employment, an internship—whatever—having a purpose is critical to well being. It is about everyone's need to make sense of their lives, to feel they have a life of meaning and purpose.

To summarize: You can ask yourself, "Is my portfolio as strong as it could be? Have I forged a retirement Identity, recharged my Relationships, and established a new sense of Purpose?"

Retirement is a Series of Transitions and Not a Date

Sociologist Phyllis Moen suggests that people spend more time planning a wedding than planning for retirement. And both have a great deal in common. There is a wedding date and a retirement date. What is ignored is what happens next. You plan for a wedding, but not the marriage; you plan for retirement but not for the years after. But both are major transitions and not events at one point in time.

In my studies of people in transition, it is clear that transitions do not happen at one point in time (Schlossberg, 2008).

They are a gradual process; time is the operative word. Transitions take time, and people's reactions to them change—for better or worse—while they are under way. At first, people think of nothing but being a new graduate, a new widow, a recent retiree. This is followed by a middle period of disruption—a period of great vulnerability. Although the onset of a transition may be linked to one identifiable event, they can take six months, a year, sometimes two years pass before one moves fully through a major transition. If, for example, you have just moved in with someone, it takes a while to know where the dishes and glasses are stored. But more important, it takes time to feel comfortable rearranging them. Finally, the change becomes integrated into your life, for better or worse. You've accommodated to your transition. Then, like Ellen Goodman, one begins to separate from the past and move toward a new role, new relationships, new routines, and emerging assumptions about themselves and the world.

Many who write about the transition process suggest that people go through sequentially specific stages from beginning to end. In fact, they give labels to each stage. My research and experience lead me to conclude that life is not that orderly. I interviewed a man who retired from the public school system. His first month was very difficult as he was accustomed to his routine, his relationships, and his professional identity. Now, a year later, he is comfortable with his new life. He is in an exercise program, serves as a volunteer for the court system as a guardian ad litem, and is becoming active with the League of Women Voters.

You can understand your retirement transition if you look at three major parts of the Transition Theory I describe in detail in

Overwhelmed: Coping with Life's Ups and Downs (2008):

- Examine the degree to which your life has been altered through changes in your roles, relationships, routines, assumptions;

- Locate where you are in the transition process (considering a change, beginning the change, two years after the change); and

- Identify the resources you can apply to making it a success –return to your Psychological Portfolio and strengthen your Identity, Relationships, and Purpose.

We have seen that planning ahead can sometimes be problematic, and negotiating transitions can be tricky. However, knowledge about the transition process can alleviate the confusing feelings that often go along with transitions.

Retirement Happiness is Feeling You "Matter" and Still Count

Morris Rosenberg, the late distinguished Sociologist from the University of Maryland, coined the phrase "mattering"—the need to feel noticed, appreciated, and depended upon—-as one that describes a universal, and often overlooked, motive that influences our thinking and behavior (Rosenberg & McCullough, 1981). It is critical to believe that we count in other's lives and feel we make a difference to them. Rosenberg found that teenagers who felt they mattered to teachers, peers, parents were less likely to engage in delinquent behavior than those who did not feel they mattered to others. He suggested, and I found, that retirees who no longer feel appreciated do not do as well as those who feel connected. Columnist David Brooks echoed this when he wrote, *Let me tell you what men want... Recognition. Men want others to recognize their significance. They want to feel important and part of something important."* (Brooks, 2006, p. 12). An example of this was the statement from the former head of a UN agency, *"I know who I was, but not who I am."* And Robert S. Weiss, Emeritus Professor of Sociology at the University of Massachusetts, found *"retirement perplexing...When I attend a professional conference... I tend to feel marginal."* (Weiss, 2005, pp. 3-5).

The concept, mattering, explains why some retirees are happier than others. *"It has been suggested that one problem of retirement is that one no longer matters; others no longer depend upon us...The reward of retirement, involving a surcease from labor, can be the punishment of not mattering. Existence loses its point and savor when one no longer makes a difference."* (Rosenberg & McCullough, 1981, pp. 179-180).

Mattering influences your behavior. I worked with Jill at a trade association. She decided she needed new skills and knowledge so that she could pursue a mid-career change. She wanted to move up the career ladder and knew without further education that would be impossible. She was informed that she had to come to the University between 8:30 a.m. and 4:30 p.m. to get the appropriate forms. She was forced to take a day off from work. When she arrived at the University, there was a notice on the door that the admissions office was closed. Finally she got the material and tried to make an appointment with a potential adviser to make sure this was the appropriate program for her. Again, the adviser's office hours were during the day. Finally in desperation she applied to a non-traditional program in another city. She was able to reach the adviser, go to classes one weekend a month and three weeks in the summer. It seemed ridiculous to her that she was forced to travel 1000 miles to get a school where adult learners mattered.

Another woman with whom I worked, Nora, retired from her administrative job in a community theatre at age sixty so that she could realize her dream to move to New York, find an agent and begin auditioning for plays. After a year, pounding the sidewalks with no luck, she returned home. She assumed that her lack of success related to her age. Then she read about two older women who were performing on Broadway. That added insult to injury. Now she could no longer blame her roadblocks solely on her age. Each time she reads about another 60-, 70-, or 80-year old man or woman starring in a Broadway production she feels sick inside, ashamed of herself for feeling envious, angry at herself for thinking she could do it, and upset that she was being sidelined. Now what can she do? Her loss of mattering was palpable.

What do people do when they no longer matter? The answer: get involved and stay involved. Develop your own mission statement. For example, one woman substituted exercise for work. She joined a health club, and was a regular in a water aerobics class that met three times a week. She realized that water aerobics was not the same as running a small company, but when she occasionally did not appear, people called her. Then, she knew she mattered.

Whether it is water aerobics, a book club, a luncheon group, a part-time job, a volunteer job—the specifics are irrelevant. What matters is that you matter to yourself, to others, to the community at large. A happy retirement depends heavily on these feelings. Remember, if it is not going the way you want it today, it is critical to turn your life around because the consequences of not mattering can lead to sadness, even depression.

And in Conclusion—Resilience is the Bottom Line

Now twelve years later, how does retirement look to me? As a Continuer I have tried to keep active professionally. I wrote two books on retirement and was fortunate to participate in a PBS special, "Retire Smart, Retire Happy" based on my book of the same name (Schlossberg, 2004). I speak about transitions and retirement. But over the years, opportunities to speak have diminished. Fortunately, I found other outlets for my interest in adult development and aging. I joined a board that recently launched a national Institute on the Ages in Sarasota, Florida.

Retirement, like the rest of life, is filled with ups and downs. The downs are the diminishing opportunities to contribute in meaningful ways and the ups are the opportunities to create a new life. Revitalizing your retirement requires resilience. According to the dictionary, resiliency refers to *"the power or ability to retreat to the original form…after being bent, compressed, or stretched… to spring back."* There are many examples of people who confronted major obstacles, but bounced back. With car dealerships closing at breakneck speed, Sue, a top salesperson I interviewed, realized that her financial survival depended on facing reality and making plans; she needed to work in an organization that would be there no matter what the economy. She applied for a job at a supermarket chain. She said, *"I have many years of management experience and plan on working to get back up to management level—even though I will start at the checkout counter."* And that is what she is doing—that's resilience.

There are many theories about resilience. Some suggest that it is a genetic predisposition, others that it is a combination of personal characteristics buffered by a supportive community providing a network of connections. This raises the question: What can we ourselves do to become resilient in times of stress? There's no magic pill, but there are resources you can utilize. One example: Psychologist Salvatore Maddi and his team studied the Illinois Bell Telephone (IBT) company over a period of ten years after the work force had been dramatically and drastically reduced. Some of the managers crumbled under the stress, while others embraced change and moved on. Dr. Maddi and his team developed the Hardiness Institute where people are trained to turn stressors into opportunities through "situational reconstruction" by imagining "alternative ways of thinking about the stressor." Specially designed workbooks take the participant through a step-by-step process teaching ways to look at adversity, deal with it, and even grow from it (Maddi, 2002). When I face the down times, I try to imagine alternative paths and ways to revitalize my life.

In conclusion, I learned that there is no single retirement path—that there are many possibilities in retirement. The knowledge—that options exist and we can choose—give me comfort as I struggle with my own retirement. Since transitions take time, I will continue to rebalance my Psychological Portfolio and figure out new ways to matter.

References

Brooks, D. (March 19, 2006). Run Barack, run. *New York Times*, p. 12.

Eisner, D., Grimm, Jr. R.T., Maynard, S. & Washburn, S. (2009). The new volunteer workforce. *Stanford Social Innovation Review*, Winter, (18), Retrieved from www.ssireview.org/articles/entry/the_new_volunteer_workforce

Goodman, E. (January 1, 2010). Letting Go. *The Washington Post*, Opinions.

Maddi, S.R. (2002). The story of hardiness: Twenty years of theorizing, research, and practice. *Consulting Psychology Journal, 54*, 173-185.

Moen, P. & Fields, V. (2002). Midcourse in the United States: Does unpaid community participation replace paid work? *Aging International, 27*, 21-48.

Robinson, S.P., & Lakin, M.B. (2007). *Framing new terrain: Older adults & higher education*. Washington, DC. American Council on Education.

Rosenberg, M. & McCullough, B.C. (1981). Mattering: Inferred significance to parents and mental health among adolescents. In R. Simmons (Ed.), *Research in community and mental health* (Vol. 2, pp. 163-182). Greenwich, CT: JAI Press.

Schlossberg, N.K. (2004). *Retire smart, retire happy: Finding your true path in life*. Washington, DC: American Psychological Association.

Schlossberg, N.K. (2008). *Overwhelmed: Coping with life's ups and downs*. Lanham, Md: M. Evans.

Schlossberg, N.K. (2009). *Revitalizing retirement: Reshaping your identity, relationships, and purpose.* Washington, DC: American Psychological Association.

Weiss, R.S. (2005). *The experience of retirement.* Ithaca, NY, and London: Cornell University Press.

Rethinking Retirement

Bonnie R. Strickland

When I started going to school in 1942, I immediately decided I wanted to be a school teacher and teach first graders. I never wavered from this goal, but I did continually change the grade I wanted to teach depending on which grade I was in. Fifth grade seemed perfect, so did tenth grade. In college, I received my teaching certificate and taught first, fifth, seventh and twelfth graders in a teaching practicum. Going on to graduate school, I thought teaching graduate students might be best of all. Then suddenly, having received as many degrees as I could muster, I found myself a teacher in a small, private university where I stayed for 11 years. I then moved to a larger, state university with even more diverse college students to teach—many first generation like me—as well as graduate students. I have enthusiastically returned to school every September for almost 70 years. So, why in the midst of a perfectly happy career as a professor did I take early retirement in 2003?

Most of the reason is that my University, along with so many others at that time, engaged in a buy out program to reduce the number of well paid senior faculty to save money and hire more junior people. The early buy out was attractive by giving me several more years credited toward my pension. My research program had wound down, my graduate students had graduated, and age 65 seemed an appropriate time. And, I thought about all the free time I would have and the opportunities that would open to me.

Unfortunately, I flunked retirement at first. Oh, I did all the "right" things. I became involved in local politics. I began some volunteer work; I stayed active in APA. I even took up golf. I enjoyed traveling at times other than school breaks. But, I missed

my job, my role as a teacher, and the company of like-minded colleagues. My university career had been perfect for me. I still have
a hard time believing that I was paid well for doing all I had ever
wanted to do, read and write and talk to people. I have now been
retired for 8 years. It's been quite a journey.

My first advice to those who are contemplating retirement:
Don't. If you are content and happy in your job why not stay? Of
course, I know many people who welcome retirement for all sorts
of reasons. They want more free time; they want to start a new
career; they want to rid themselves of arduous responsibilities;
they want to spend time enjoying other activities and any number
of other reasons. Go for it. But, let me give you at least one's
person's reactions to retirement knowing full well that all of us are
different and this may not resonate with anyone.

The Beginning

At first I savored my free time. I slept late. I booked international
travel where I had time to truly visit different countries than in
the summer or on school breaks. The most exciting trip I took
was an 18 day, 180 mile trek through Upper Mustang, a small
Kingdom in northern Nepal. The country had only been opened to
outside visitors since the early 1990s. There was no electricity, no
running water, and no roads. People still lived in very old, stone,
flat roofed houses and walked from village to village. Hiking in
hot weather and in snowfalls, we camped close to the villages
in empty animal corrals, the only flat space available. Some of
my other trips included Vietnam, Tibet, and Myanmar. They were
glorious. But, one can only do so much traveling. I soon found
that I really wanted to spend more time at home.

I threw myself into local politics and was elected to be on our Hampshire County Council of Government. For a while I was a member of my local Historical Society. Then, one day I found myself in a colonial cemetery trying to record names and dates from 18th century headstones that were worn through. It was November and snow was spitting in the air while I tried to write with frozen fingers. I decided to pass on this activity to our local Boy Scouts.

I did continue to teach an Honors seminar. It became the highlight of my week and the one place I felt content. In other activities, I was mostly bored. Having unpacked from one international trip before getting ready for another, I wandered around the house feeling frustrated and role less. I tried gardening and taking my dogs for long walks. I spent time in the South visiting family and old friends. I socialized. But, mostly I was bored. I had thought I would spend retirement time reading so I joined a book club. I enjoyed our meetings and read vociferously, but I still had too much time on my hands.

The Middle

The middle years of my so far eight year retirement are a blur. I really can't remember what I did except I continued to teach. The rest of my time seemed spent in aimless wandering. I did become more involved in APA activities and thoroughly enjoyed the social interactions with psychologists of every ilk. I realized that most of my dissatisfaction with retirement had to do with the fact that I was not longer as engaged with other people as I had been during my professional career.

The economic downturn also impacted me greatly. I had diversified my financial footing in terms of my pension, my equities portfolio, and real estate. For many years I have owned beach property on the Gulf in the panhandle of Florida. Well, we know what happened to Florida real estate. Because I still carry a mortgage on the unsold property and the expenses of insurance and taxes soared, I have been hard pressed to pay the bills. My investment portfolio also lost a considerable amount of its value. I began to live more frugally but was faced with the prospect of my partner having to return to work after our years of freedom. There went our international vacations and life of leisure. My partner is a school teacher and overcommitted to the Somali and Puerto Rican kindergartners who are just learning English in the inner city school in which she teaches. Because her school is woefully lacking in equipment and supplies, our private charity has become subsidizing her classroom. She is happy with her job to which she is committed from dawn to dusk, but I miss her terribly during the day.

The Present

One of the most telling aspects of retirement is that this is the age when many of us have to deal with both aging parents and unemployed children. My partner has two sons and two grandchildren. The oldest son has had continual difficulty in finding a job. He was working in construction until such work tapered off. He then went to work in an auto dealership which went bankrupt. My partner and I provide him a place to live, rent free when he is not working and, of course, this takes another toll on our limited financial resources. The second son and his wife have just moved in with us. He has just returned to the states after living abroad for some five years and is working at low paying jobs trying to amass enough money to begin a life here. My own parents are deceased as is my partner's mother, but there was both a financial and emotional burden caring for them when they were living. We want to insure that our parents are healthy and financially secure in their older years, but many of us are faced with their declining health and the need to support them as best we can.

So, my life in my retirement years has changed substantially. My time has become more family focused with my partner's family. (I never married nor had children). The expensive vacations are a thing of the past, and I feel lonely when my partner is away teaching. So, in many ways I have reverted to my pre-retirement days. I teach part-time at the University and do academic advising in our Honors College. I socialize with old friends. I still engage is some community activities, but more time is spent with family.

The marking of time through phases of my life such as transitioning into retirement leads me to think of my own mortality and to wonder about the years I have left. In my mind I feel young and fresh, but my physical body is succumbing to the vagaries of age. I struggle to find meaning in each moment.

Retirement is not what I dreamed it would be, but I believe I have come to some balance. I have basically involved myself in several different sets of activities. I realized that I do have enough free time to reengage myself in the physical activities that I have always loved—not the organized softball of early days, but tennis and down hill and cross country skiing. Although I have some health problems such as high blood pressure, high cholesterol and diabetes, they are all under control and physically, I can't remember a time when I've felt better.

I continue my volunteer work primarily with a survival center that offers food, clothing, social services and free health care to the consumers that come to the center. The staff thinks of me as their resident "shrink", and I practice a very different kind of psychological outreach. I am like an "executive coach" to the director and the staff. And, I am available to the consumers who come to the Center to talk about personal and emotional concerns. These are not the "worried well" issues of many of my previous clients, but are truly concerns about survival. And, the volunteer work gives me that social interaction that I so enjoy this time with a diverse and fascinating group of people.

For many years, with one long break away, I have been involved in the governance of the American Psychological Association (APA). I enjoy the excitement of grappling with the problems of a large organization. I truly believe that organized psychology is a major force in discovering knowledge that benefits individuals, in improving people's well being, and in advancing social justice. I have been a member of APA for over fifty years and think that I can sometimes bring a sense of history and seasoned judgment to the deliberations of the governance. On the other hand, I worry about taking a place in governance that could go to an early career psychologist.

My first involvement in APA was as the chair of one of the first committees considering equal opportunity and affirmative action. Sponsored by the Division of Clinical Psychology, our EOAA Committee, interestingly enough, was charged with recruiting and maintaining more women in governance positions. We, of course, also included ethnic minorities in our charge. But, looking back, these times seem quite quaint, especially now that women are a majority in APA and we have had a run of women presidents. I was president of the association in 1987, about the seventh or eighth woman in our up to then almost 100 year history. I tried to use the office to encourage more women and minorities to become more involved in APA. I miss those heady days, but I have stayed involved in APA through being president of three divisions and serving on the Council of Representative for several terms. I am currently on the Membership Committee which is charged with recruiting and maintaining members in APA. This includes two trips to Washington each year where I have a chance to interact with old and new colleagues. I also attend APA conventions, another source of great satisfaction in reconnecting with old friends and students.

The most enjoyable of my activities in retirement is the continued teaching that I do. I teach a small senior seminar for students who are completing a major project and contemplating their career plans. I teach in the fall semester, but one year the class wanted to continue meeting so we had lunch twice a week during this spring semester. In my early years of teaching, I was concerned with lecturing and covering material. Now, I'm much more likely to let the students do the talking. Almost all of my teaching now is by discussion, and I think we are all better for it. I also teach a one hour small seminar for first year students in which we simply talk about current events. As you can imagine, there are lively discussions and I feel privileged to be a part of their lives. It has been a joy to be with the students and especially at this time in their lives when they are making crucial career decisions. Students have been a vibrant and lively force in my life and give me the opportunity to continue my life's work.

Becoming older also means that I have a family of students throughout the world, many of whom I often hear from. A friend of mine, also a retired university professor, wrote:

The Old Teacher's Plea

Would the pupils come back, please,

to tell who I am by telling me who I was

to them once. Please. If only a few would

bear witness to a moment in their lives when

I reached them in a way that has lasted. You see,

I doubt my memory. Please pupils come back to me.

And, make it soon. Time erase time itself in time.

- D. Abramson -

I love hearing from students and old friends. One of my greatest joys is knowing I have made and continue to make a difference in people's lives and they in mine. I feel blessed that these opportunities are still available for me.

So, after flunking my early retirement, I have settled into a rewarding life in my older years. I treasure old friends and students. I am healthy and involved in a warm and loving relationship. I try to be content in these years I have left.

Concluding Remarks

There are things about retirement I wish I had known. I was surprised that I had difficulty at first finding things I truly enjoyed doing. It took me a long time to find myself involved in satisfying activities.

I wish I had known about the impending economic crisis (don't we all?). I had three financial pillows to depend on in my retirement years. One of these is my pension. Another is real estate and the third is investments in stocks and equities. So, even though I thought I had planned well and diversified, my losses in real estate and my portfolio have made it more difficult to feel financially secure.

Looking back, I believe I retired too soon. My research program had wound down and I was not taking any more students. And, my University was offering a generous buy out program. But, since I loved my job I wish I had stayed a bit longer.

In retirement, I'm happy that I have the option of continuing to teach part time. I didn't realize how important this was to me. As mentioned, I tried many other activities, some of which I still enjoy, but teaching is my first love. I am happy to have my health and do enjoy the physical activities in which I am involved. I play tennis almost every day. I wish I had taken lessons earlier.

My final words for those of you considering retirement are, follow your passion. As we age more gracefully, we may be surprised at the time we have left and how we might fill it with rewarding activities. Here's your chance to try something new, to pursue different paths, to enrich relationships and simply enjoy this next stage of your life. You may be surprised with what unfolds but likely you have been successful in your life so far and will continue to be. I wish you the best.

References

Abramson, Doris (2007). *Time will tell*. Athol, MA: Haley's.

Loss and Resilience through Change

Carolyn Saarni

Background

*R*etirement beckoned me like an illusory siren. I was looking forward to retirement: I had been department chair off and on for about 14 years, California's state budget was a disaster, and I found myself too often being the doomsayer to my colleagues (and especially our part-time adjunct faculty) that once again, budget shortages would create very difficult times for all. Students were upset with sometimes twice yearly fee hikes, and even paper clips were in short supply. Forget about copying—we emailed everything to the students for them to print out and use up their own ink cartridges. So, the timing seemed fitting; I'd leave before the really bad stuff hit the fan, so to speak. However, I made a very critical error: I did not ask my then-husband how he felt about my retirement. He had always prided himself as the "strong but silent type," and I had given up, in all candor, on his speaking from his heart, and so I neglected to inquire. To be sure, I announced my retirement to him months in advance; however, 6 days after filing my initial memo with my dean indicating my formal intention to retire, and also 6 days after our thirty-first anniversary, he announced his intention to leave. And leave he did, completely severing all ties to me and my extended family (but fortunately not with our grown children and grandchildren). At this writing, it has now been close to a year since we have spoken face-to-face, nor have we had any telephone conversations. He served me with the subpoena for divorce, I responded, and now it is a contested divorce that will run its expensive course.

*"Ships that pass in the night, and speak each other in passing,
Only a signal shone, a distant voice in the darkness;
So the ocean of life, we pass and speak one another,
Only a look and a voice, then darkness again and silence."*

- Henry Wadsworth Longfellow (1893; 1975) -

This poem captures elegantly what the passage of time and at first one-sided and then mutual withdrawal did to my marriage. A retirement that I thought would be a time to rejuvenate our relationship, to have enough time to do things together without my preoccupation with budgets, curriculum planning, personnel issues, and my own scholarship and teaching, proved to be anything but. Not surprisingly, after his decision also proved to be inflexible and unresponsive to my attempts at reconciliation and requests for couples counseling, I negotiated with my university administration to return to teaching half-time. Letting go of the chair position was definitely something I wanted to do. I willingly gave up my office and moved into a former storage room, sans window, so that one of our struggling assistant professors could have an office with a window. I have not regretted this at all. However, the theme of loss has been a recurrent one throughout my retirement (and, for that matter, during the last decade of my marriage), and in reading the research on who fares from best to worst in the last third of life, it seems that divorced women fare the poorest of all (e.g., Ozawa & Lum, 1998; Pienta, Hayward, & Jenkins, 2000; but compare with Price & Joo, 2005). This was downright scary to read, to say the least.

My narrative will be structured around the issues that commonly face retiring people; in terms of women psychologists who are retiring and/or retired, I will give special emphasis to those concerns that professional women face. I regret that I cannot speak knowledgeably for those psychologists in private practice or who are entrepreneurs; my experience does include a dozen years in private practice, but it was strictly adjunctive to my primary dedication to teaching and scholarship. At this time, I do not have a calling to resume a practice, and I'll elaborate on that below under the notion of freedom to explore new avenues, meanings, and ways of being.

Issues That Impact Retirement Freedom

"The freedom of retirement is not only a freedom from the need to respond to work's demands. It is also, notably, the freedom to engage in new activities, thoughts, and experiences." (Weiss, 2005, p. 74).

The options that retirement can bring are influenced by what Price and Nesteruk (2010) call human capital, which entails everything from educational attainment, financial wherewithal, health, and other material resources. If one has the good fortune to find oneself with considerable positive human capital at one's disposal, one is privileged to have more choices as to how one's retirement will unfold. Or perhaps I should frame this as one is privileged in being able to minimize some of the really unnerving aspects of retirement that include declining health, financial insecurity, and feeling trapped by not having or even seeing options. For the most part, women who hold professional degrees and have worked for at least a couple of decades will have moderate to good human capital available for retirement, i.e., more options and resources.

My challenge was the second part of this duality of freedom.

The predicted and the expected course of my retirement had suddenly evaporated when it came to what I would do next. There was no more life companion; I was alone. I was greatly relieved to reduce my commute time, to omit meetings and committees from my schedule, and I liked having a reduced teaching schedule (and with that, a reduced number of papers to grade, always my nemesis). Now that I was truly indeed free to explore novelty and adventure, I really was not sure what I wanted to do. I began with individual therapy for help with my grieving and later went on to a divorce therapy recovery group that also showed that I needed help with expressing my anger (see Hanauer's hard-hitting edited volume, *The Bitch in the House*, 2002). But these therapeutic engagements did not help me find closure about what would be my path for freedom to become the person who was probably more in charge of my destiny than I had ever been in my life. I had no one to account to, no minor children to worry about, and although I had an elderly mother, I was not the only adult who participated in her care. That much choice ended up confronting me with my aloneness. I had taken for granted a "we-ness" that proved to be an illusion, yet I am also aware that I had been emotionally lonely in my marriage. I have to take an ironic stance here: I have written extensively about children's developing skills of emotional competence, and even though I have always resolutely insisted in my writing that when we are in unfamiliar and challenging waters, we may well behave emotionally incompetently, I had been in familiar waters, namely, my emotional wasteland of a marriage, for so long that its very familiarity felt like a sufficient equilibrium, if not to flourish, at least to persevere. I had not demonstrated emotional competence, much less wisdom and emotional balance. I was like the proverbial ostrich with its head buried in the sand so that I would not see the spouse who had withdrawn so far that a vast chasm lay between us, and I acted as though there were still a little rickety wooden foot bridge spanning the chasm that would allow us to cross over to one another and connect once again.

Resuming a therapeutic practice was not something I wanted to do, not only because I was not finished with my own emotional turmoil, but I had over the years known a number of aging therapists who clung to their clients as a way to fill their own social and emotional needs. I was concerned that I could succumb to that need, given my current emotionally volatile situation. It felt unethical to me—in addition to being narcissistic. In any case, I am far more motivated to expand my writing repertoire, whether it be children's books or adult fiction. I was greatly humbled at how much I had to learn when I enrolled in an Introduction to Writing Fiction at the University of California (Berkeley) last fall, but I thoroughly enjoyed learning new ways to use language and structure in writing. I will continue to explore this avenue of new meaning-making and be open to what might ensue. I have no need to publish, but already I read fiction with a new and more keenly informed eye as to the craft of the writer. My journey in finding new meanings and new ways of being is a process that is unfolding, and I have discovered that I can tolerate the ambiguity of not having any answers.

Emotional Isolation Versus Social Isolation

Sociologists distinguish between the emotional isolation of not having a close intimate partner and the social isolation that comes with not having a sense of membership in a social network or community (e.g., Baarsen, Snijders, Smit, & Duijn, 2001; Weiss, 1998). That distinction felt very real to me, and I recognized that it was up to me to extend my social network further as a way to cope with the emotional isolation I experienced as a result of my marital break-down. In many ways, retirement (or half-time retirement) gave me the time I needed to extend my social network through nourishing what had been acquaintanceships into friendships. I am also very fortunate to have a highly engaged extended family—who would have thought that my cousins in mid-life are so delightful. In addition, a few years earlier I had provided an informal review for a sociologist friend, Kay Trimberger, who had published an excellent book titled *The New Single Woman* (2005). Through her focus groups and follow-up qualitative interviews 10 years later with a diverse group of women, she had found six key themes that seemed to differentiate the satisfied single mid-life women from those who felt caught in various quandaries and conflicts. These six themes that reliably provided satisfaction (in spite of there being no life partner) were as follows:

a. satisfying work,
b. relationships with the next generation,
c. a home or "nest,"
d. fulfilling engagement with friends and extended family members,
e. involvement in a community or neighborhood, and
f. an acceptance of one's sensuality/sexuality, whether it is experienced erotically with others or through sensory fulfillment as a celibate individual.

Trimberger's intention had been to create a "cultural narrative" that emphasized the resources to be cultivated by women who find themselves single as well as how to cultivate their own dignity as individuals—as opposed to being somehow deficient or incomplete because they are not coupled. What she has also outlined is a blue-print for individuals, regardless of gender, and who find themselves alone, to find their way toward maximizing life satisfaction. Note that she included satisfying work as one of her criteria, and I would suggest that the equivalent after retiring from one's work, is that one will need to find mission or purpose that minimizes feeling marginalized and maximizes opportunities for a social network. This can definitely be met by continuing one's professional identity but with a smaller foot-print so to speak. Indeed, this is what I have done, and so far it feels alright (although I still have that 100 mile round-trip commute, but it is 2 days a week instead of 4). Others become seriously committed to a volunteer effort or a political mission or caring for grandchildren. As for volunteering, I have participated in trail restoration (I am reliably the oldest person in the group) and helping with my local chapter of the California Native Plant Society. I look forward to expanding my volunteer efforts, but I want to make sure that I leave myself flexibility for continuing my writing, both of a scholarly sort as well as trying my hand at different genres.

In terms of Trimberger's other criteria, I do invest myself in my children and 3 grand-daughters (but see below), have a home that is modest but comfortable and in a liberal community that presents many opportunities for cultural venues as well as being a very 'walkable' community. I continue to work on developing my social network and sense of community, but I do feel stymied when it comes to the last criterion, acceptance of my sexuality. I believe I am both a sensual and sexual person, and the former I engage through my pleasure in gardening (I'm a bit of a 'flower floozie'), the world of nature, massage, and hot baths. But I very much miss a shared sexuality; remarriage has no appeal, but a "friend with benefits" definitely does.

Health

Considerable research on elders highlights the importance of health to retirement satisfaction (e.g., Wilson & Palha, 2007), and, indeed, there are also data that indicate early retirees exercise more than when they were full-time employed (Swenson, Marshall, Mikulich-Gilbertson, Baxter, & Morgenstern, 2005). Health crises, whether in oneself, a spouse, or another family member are more likely as one ages, and those who practice self-care and health-promoting activities may be more likely to enjoy a better quality of life until that point that one's genetic destiny expresses itself. I am definitely one of those part-time retirees who exercises more than when I worked full-time: aerobic dance twice a week, water aerobics twice a week, long hikes twice a month or more, gardening, walking when doing my errands as much as possible, occasional yoga, and most recently horse-back riding lessons. Whether it was due to grieving my marital break-up or increased exercise or both, I have lost about 25 pounds since retiring. The Social Security Administration has actuarially estimated that I will live another 20 years, and as a result, I have become more attentive to actively monitoring my health status, including getting all the various vaccines that should protect me from an unexpected malevolent illness. I am extraordinarily fortunate to have health coverage through my former employer, which functions as a supplement to Medicare (a bureaucratic nightmare). I now grow a lot of my own vegetables in my back yard, and I know they are organic and fresh from the earth to the pan or salad bowl. Lastly, I firmly believe in the benefits of massage, especially in the absence of a spouse's touch. I try to get a full body massage once a month, if I can afford to (for supportive evidence of the health value of massage, see Field's website for the Touch Research Institute at the University of Miami School of Medicine, 2011).

Finances

I begin this section with an extended quote from Daily and O'Brien, two women entrepreneurs (2003): *"As with your physical health, you cannot delegate your financial health. Develop a strong sense of personal responsibility for your finances, seek sound advice, but don't relinquish control... Regardless of how busy or tired we are, we must stay actively involved in all aspects of our financial health—saving, spending, investing, and protecting our future."* (p. 155).

Going from a two-income to a single-income household has been hard, and it was one of the reasons I returned to work half-time. Again, I am extremely fortunate to have a defined benefit pension, and I will be eligible for Social Security in the not distant future. However, the pending divorce means that if I keep the house, I also "inherit" all of the deferred capital repair and maintenance expenses associated with home ownership as an "off set" to the value of the house in the divorce settlement (California is a community property state, which means property is divided equally in a marital dissolution). We are not talking remodeling the kitchen here, it is more about the ancient roof, the cracked walk-ways, the twice annually overflowing lateral sewer line. At times I feel as though I have been caught broadsided by all of these deferred significant repairs, and then I remind myself of that image of the ostrich with her head in the sand. What was I thinking, or more likely, not thinking, not seeing? My car is 8 years old, and I will not be replacing it any time soon due to a felt sense of financial precariousness. I had hoped to travel internationally once a year after retiring, but that is now unlikely. I will have to set aside a budget for travel, for car replacement, for house repairs, for taxes and insurance, and so forth. I am very fortunate, however, when I compare my financial situation to the majority of divorced older women. I always worked through-out my adulthood, established my own pension, and earned my necessary Social Security 'quarters' and thus do not have to rely on another for financial support in my later years if I am prudent and stay knowledgeable about my financial situation. I also pay a sizable amount toward a long term care program that the State of California maintains for state employees, and although expensive, it gives me considerable peace of mind if something dire should happen to me and I need significant long-term care. I frequently remind myself how fortunate I am, and I am indeed so grateful for the relative financial security that I have. Other near-retirement or newly retired women psychologists absolutely must inform themselves about their financial situation. One may be in a marriage, but that spouse could require expensive care or die an untimely death, and one must plan for those possibilities financially, although one cannot plan for them emotionally.

Family Relationships

My ethnic heritage is mostly Finnish; my grandparents were immigrants, first settling in Astoria, Oregon, a town located at the mouth of the Columbia River; by 1920 or so they had moved to San Francisco. A politically liberal, non-religious, nature-appreciative set of beliefs and attitudes have come with that heritage. My siblings, my mother (my father is deceased), and my cousins form a collective, a clan almost, that is really remarkable. My mother is the 91-year-old matriarch and thrives on company, whether they are her neighbors coming over to visit, her grandchildren, her adult nieces and nephews, or her own children. Thanksgiving is probably the most special holiday in my extended family: About 30+ people show up, each bringing a dish to share, and thanks is truly given and genuinely felt for the kind of family that we are able to have. Last Thanksgiving was the first time in 31 years that my ex-husband was not present to carve one of the 2 turkeys; one of my brothers stepped up to the task, and it was noteworthy that my ex was not missed in an obvious way, although grief stung my eyes and heart for a while. Perhaps his emotional absence had been felt by my family prior to my willing to acknowledge it myself. As a non-religious family, our grace was a secular one, but to myself, I thanked my family for helping me to keep my head and heart steering in the direction of resilience.

My mother is an excellent role model for how to experience the last years of one's life, in spite of short-term memory and hearing deficits. Interestingly, a visit with her always includes her exclaiming how grateful she is for people in her life, whether it is her caregiver or her gardener. She has become more tolerant and flexible as she has aged, and to my surprise, she is my most ardent supporter when I have felt really mired down in the muck of the divorce process. My children are another matter. Although they are adults, they are caught in the middle of two parents who let their marriage wither. At this time, they are unable to hear my emotional experience, and I do not want to contribute to any loyalty conflict. I have noticed my son has lately been more demonstrative with his wife, and I wondered whether he had learned something about how a relationship is damaged when a husband ceases to be affectionate. My grand-daughters bring me much joy, and I regret very much that they live thousands of miles away and that I can see them only a couple of times a year (my son and his family live on the Big Island, Hawaii, and my daughter and her family live in upstate New York). We are experimenting with Skype and web cameras, although the two toddlers mainly make faces at their own camera reflections, but at least I get to see them and hear them being silly. I guess it is a good thing that I live in the San Francisco Bay Area, roughly half-way between both of them. I never realized how important it is to live near a major airport.

I recommend to other retiring or near-retirement women that you think ahead about repairing and nurturing family relationships, especially with your siblings and cousins, if you have any, for they are your peer-level kin as both of you go through the aging process. Just as my elderly mother has a kinship that encompasses 30+ people, consider how large or small you want your kinship circle to be. Perhaps your kinship consists more of an adopted family or dear friends, and again I emphasize, nourish that kinship, whatever form it takes. Do not wait to be nurtured yourself; take the initiative now to nourish those relationships.

Mastery and Control

"We are what we imagine ourselves to be, and we strive to moti-vate others to cooperate in this construction of the self." (p. 157, Singer & Salovey, 1993).

Although recent empirical research indicates that perceived high self-esteem and sense of mastery and control are positively correlated with retirement satisfaction for women (Price & Balaswamy, 2009), I think that we women psychologists are more likely inclined to look at that positive correlation through a more analytic lens. Granted, the recent emphasis on positive psychol-ogy and optimism indicate that positive biases in one's beliefs have individual benefits, but I am more intellectually intrigued by how the self devises these ego-serving attitudes. Yes, some of us might say such an ego-serving belief system has to do with having enjoyed a secure attachment in childhood, thereby internalizing a working model of an expectation of emotional security with oth-ers. Others of us might emphasize the scripts and schemata we have learned from peers, media, the work place, as well as from family, essentially a social learning model of attitudes and beliefs. As a social constructivist, I see humans as living in a complex sys-tem of dynamic feedback that involves how we impose our own constructions on our experience as well as the raw stuff of events that befall us (see Lewis' *Altering Fate: Why the Past does not Predict the Future*; 1997). From this perspective, both our history of attachments or relational history and our learned and reinforced scripts and schemata contribute to how we give meaning to our experience and define ourselves.

I am all too aware that as I write this semi-autobiographical narrative of my retirement experience, that I undoubtedly retrieve those memories and meanings that are congruent with my own self-concept construal and with how I would prefer to be seen by the reader. I have and will continue to have a professional identity as a developmental psychologist, and that identity and the collective experience that is associated with it provide me with considerable sense of mastery and self-esteem. I also endorse the perspective that self-esteem is domain-specific, and probably mastery and perceived control are as well. I chose to reduce my professional footprint by retiring and then returning to teach part-time; I exercised control over that domain of my life. The marital break-down came as a surprise; I was not prepared and obviously not in control of my ex-husband's decision to leave. Yet, I strive to master the aftermath, whether through therapy, exercise, the world of nature, and especially through cultivating my friendships and kinships.

For some time now psychologists have known that positive illusions are not an undesirable phenomena (e.g., Taylor & Brown, 1988). They are what sustain me in many ways—they persuade me that I am resilient in the face of emotional wounding. I know that I selectively disregard or minimize some of the negative feedback I receive (I can be controlling, judgmental, self-preoccupied, etc.), but I hope to catch myself before I stick my entire foot in my mouth and maybe just choke a bit over my figurative big toe and then proceed more intentionally in the ensuing interaction. As psychologists in the last third of our lives, we may be more aware than other professionals that we live dynamically dialectical lives: We are organisms of DNA that endlessly interact with a rich environment, yielding ever-changing organizations of a perceived identity that seeks continuity, even as we awaken each day a little bit different from who we were on the preceding day. Life is sure interesting.

Postscript

The original manuscript was finished about 9 months ago. My divorce is now final and thankfully behind me. I consider myself a "half-time retiree" because I teach full-time, but only for one semester of the year and I have the other semester free for travel, gardening, and spending time with friends and family. I continue to enjoy some degree of professional scholarly involvement, but on a much reduced level. My health is excellent (all that swimming, aerobic dance, hiking, and gardening must be doing some good), and even the financial picture is looking less scary than it did at first. I had to cope with a lot of significant transitions that came at me all at once, and I am thankful that my belief in my own resilience has been confirmed. Change is definitely not comfortable, but the results are enriching and heartening.

References

Baarsen, B., Snijders, T., Smit, J., & Duijn, M. (2001). Lonely but not alone: Emotional isolation and social isolation as two distinct dimensions of loneliness in older people. *Educational and Psychological Measurement, 61*, 119-135.

Daily, N. & O'Brien, K. (2003). Baby boom women: The generation of firsts. In N. Bauer-Maglin & A. Radosh (Eds.). *Women confronting retirement: A nontraditional guide*. (pp 150-158). New Brunswick, NJ: Rutgers University Press.

Field, T. (2011, January 18). The Touch Institute, University of Miami School of Medicine. Retrieved from http://www6. miami.edu/touch-research

Hanauer, C. (Ed.) (2002). *The bitch in the house*. New York: Harper Collins.

Lewis, M. (1997). *Altering fate: Why the past does not predict the future*. New York: Guilford.

Longfellow, H. W. (1893; 1975). *The poetical works of Henry Wadsworth Longfellow: Cambridge Edition*. Boston: Houghton-Mifflin.

Ozawa, M. N. & Lum, Y. S. (1998). Marital status and change in income status 10 years after retirement. *Social Work Research, 22*, 116-128.

Pienta, A., Hayward, M., & Jenkins, K. (2000). Health consequences of marriage for the retirement years. *Journal of Family Issues, 21*, 559-586.

Price, C. A. & Balaswamy, S. (2009). Beyond health and wealth: Predictors of women's retirement satisfaction. *International Journal of Aging and Human Development, 68*, 195-214.

Price, C. A. & Joo, E. (2005). Exploring the relationship between marital status and women's retirement satisfaction. *International Journal of Aging and Human Development, 61*, 37-55.

Price, C. A. & Nesteruk, O. (2010). Creating retirement paths: Examples from the lives of women. *Journal of Women and Aging, 22*, 136-149.

Singer, J. A. & Salovey, P. (1993). *The remembered self: Emotion and memory in personality.* New York: The Free Press.

Swenson, C.J., Marshall, J.A., Mikulich-Gilbertson, S.K., Baxter, J., & Morgenstern, N. (2005). Physical activity in older, rural, Hispanic, and non-Hispanic white adults. *Medicine & Science in Sports & Exercise, 37*, 995–1002.

Taylor, S. E. & Brown, J. D. (1988). Illusion and well-being: A social psychological perspective on mental health. *Psychological Bulletin, 103*, 193-210.

Trimberger, K. E. (1995). *The new single woman.* New York: Penguin Books.

Weiss, R. S. (1998). A taxonomy of relationships. *Journal of Personality and Social Relationships, 15*, 671-684.

Weiss, R. S. (2005). *The experience of retirement.* Ithaca, NY: Cornell University Press.

Wilson, D. M. & Palha, P. (2007). A systematic review of published research articles on health promotion at retirement. *Journal of Nursing Scholarship, 39*, 330–337.

Nearly Bionic, and Still Going

Martha E. Banks

"There's more than one way to skin a cat."
- Marjorie Adelle Stephens Banks-

I did not plan to retire. The way I retired is not the way I would recommend that anyone retire. It happened to me and I have tried to make the best of it.

How Retirement Came So Early

My retirement came early and unexpectedly, while I was in my 40s. I was ill, so ill that I was too tired to go to the doctor and actually cancelled an appointment. Even as I write this, I have trouble comprehending how I could have made such a decision. I am a total advocate for taking care of myself and others—at least, when I'm well enough to do so. When I came partially to my senses and rescheduled my appointment, I encountered a young male medical student who determined, with minimal examination and dogged refusal to listen to me, that there was "nothing wrong" with me. That bad diagnosis nearly cost me my life. The following week, I insisted on seeing my regular physician. As she entered the examining room, she took one look and asked, inelegantly, "What the hell happened to you?" I had no idea I looked that bad, but half an hour later, I was in the hospital.

When I entered the hospital, I called work and told the secretary that I was in the hospital and did not know when I would be discharged. The following morning, within 15 minutes of the start of the workday, my boss called to yell at me for not telling the secretary which hospital I was in. There were only three hospitals in town then and it was unlikely that I was in Children's. Clearly, it had not taken much for him to find me, but, frankly, I think my doctor kept me in the hospital an extra day so I would not have to return to work; she heard my boss yelling over the telephone as she tried to examine me and give me the bad news. The long and short of it is that I was bleeding internally, had become dangerously anemic, and needed emergency surgery. However, I had apparently been bleeding for a long time and was too weak for surgery.

So, when I left the hospital and returned home, I was referred to a surgeon and I tried to return to work. I think I went to work for two weeks, but I was just too weak to manage. The first surgeon who was caring and supportive was not on my insurance plan. She referred me to another surgeon who disrespected me and made my life even more miserable than it already was. Again, this is an indication of how sick I was. I never allow myself to be *that* mistreated. I like to think I am too good a self-advocate to stay in an abusive relationship. My contact with the surgeon was minimal, but I had to go to his office twice a week for liver and iron injections. Each month, I made a bit of progress at reducing the anemia, but then I would have a period and lose all of the progress. After two months, they gave me an injection to stop my period so I could fight the anemia. That night I wound up in the emergency room, hemorrhaging. They stopped the bleeding and told me that if I had another period, I would die. I wrote my will, informed my family of which funeral homes to patronize, which church to hold the funeral in, where to bury my body, and I scheduled the surgery.

The day before the surgery, the hospital called to let me know that I was too great a risk and I would need to sign a release relieving them of any responsibility if I insisted on having the surgery. I was prepared to die. It was that simple. I had lived a good life, accomplished more than I had ever dreamed I might. I was at peace. Then, my supervisor called to ask when I would be coming back to work because I had given them so many possible return dates and I had not gone back. I told him that it was highly probable that I would be dead within 24 hours, so not to worry about when I might return. I hung up on him. I'm not usually that rude, but if the hospital was afraid to risk having me as a patient, what did it matter if I chose not to listen to anything more from my boss or my supervisor?

Well, obviously, I survived the surgery or I would not be writing this chapter 17 years later. The surgeon treated my survival as a defeat rather than a triumph. Who knows, maybe I survived just to show him and my boss who was really in charge. I had gone into that surgery prayerfully and I came out the same way. As I slowly recovered, I found another surgeon to handle my post-operative care. She and my family physician were both shocked to discover that I had been badly butchered during the surgery. To this day, I'm not sure whether the surgeon or a student did the surgery.

I did return to work, but only on a part-time basis. It was half-time at first, and then quarter-time, and eventually, because I went back too soon and I was experiencing terrible problems with pain, weakness, and overwhelming fatigue, I had to stop. I was able to pursue retirement on disability, but even that process was inimical to recovery. For about a year and a half, I lived off my savings until my retirement was finally approved. I was finally able to get the kind of rest I needed to start improving. Progress was slow and when I was about ready to start looking at returning to work, I was in a devastating car accident.

Early Retirement: Misunderstood

So, for the past 17 years, I have had to put up with remarks that I don't look old enough to retire (hopefully, I will age out of that). The icing on the cake is the follow-up "You don't look disabled!" (I need to find a punctuation mark that expresses the combination of incredulity and disdain that accompanies these remarks.) Then, of course, there are the kindly advisors who tell me to use my cane, even under circumstances when I don't need it, so that other people will know that I have a disability.

Early retirement comes with social consequences. For me, retirement meant being added to another marginalized group. When I understood that I might die during surgery, I was ready, but I did not expect to find myself living with disability.

The negative reactions to visible disability are as difficult to manage as the reactions to my apparent age and the invisible aspects of the disability. Psychology colleagues have "diagnostically" informed me of my "improvement" over the years. A potential research collaborator with whom I had met several times with normal peer-to-peer communication, upon seeing me with a cane, refused to establish eye contact with me and prefaced every piece of conversation toward me with, "Can you tell her…?" addressed to another professional in the discussion. When, as division program co-chair, I refused to accept a late proposal, I was informed that "handicapped people have no business" being involved in convention programming. People who have seen me manage without a cane in accessible environments are visibly startled when they see me with a cane, trying to deal with mobility barriers; the most frequent question is "What's *that* for?" The need to educate people about disability was clear when a young boy informed me in a grocery store that I "can't walk"; I calmed his embarrassed mother and took advantage of the teachable moment.

I will never know to what extent the negative social consequences are magnified because I am a member of multiple marginalized groups. In a chapter in another book, I described the difficulty I had with the impunity with which some people feel free to engage in the "isms":

Early in my career, I had a boss who asked me if I would rather be discriminated against as a woman or as an African American. He was taken aback when I replied that I would rather not be discriminated against. Today, he would probably ask me if I would rather be discriminated against as a woman, an African American, or a Person with a Disability. My answer would still be the same. I am a Woman of Color with a Disability and I really do not want to be discriminated against. (Banks, in press)

Foundations for Retirement as I Know It

So, how do I explain the ensuing 17 years? These have been, literally, award-winning years. I say often that I am so glad I selected psychology as my career field. It allows me to move beyond a narrow definition of who I am as a professional.

I am also grateful for the liberal arts education I received at Brown University at the beginning of their New Curriculum which gave me, a person who has always been curious and willing to try new things, the opportunity to taste Greek classics, music, linguistics, the "hard" sciences of biology and physics, in addition to my major in psychology. My comfort with and experience with computers dated back to my first year of college; later, I owned, used, and taught health professionals how to use personal computers in clinical practice, even before the invention of the Macintosh©.

Brown University also encouraged me to mix and match, take a little from here and try it over there. I recall being the only student in my undergraduate statistics class who went from the classroom to the computer lab to program the formula and enter the numbers, so I had a paper trail in case I made a mistake (everyone else was fumbling with those new-fangled hand calculators). For my senior paper, I wrote about psychological responses to components of music, research that I continued in graduate school using music I had written as stimuli. After graduating from Brown, I worked in a research agency that provided guidance to women in midlife who were seeking education and/or careers; starting as a clerk, I moved up to computer programmer, working under the guidance of a research psychologist. Later, during my years as a clinician, I had conducted research evenings and weekends. What, you ask, does this have to do with retirement?

Psychology's Multiple Facets: Professional While Retired

Fatigue and pain are factors that seriously interfere with clinical work. When I retired, what I retired from was clinical work. I moved firmly into another area of psychology—research. Retirement gave me the freedom to approach research more leisurely, while adapting to schedules that allowed me much-needed rest. Prior to retirement, I was on the go all the time. I practiced clinical psychology during the weekdays and spent my evenings and weekends conducting research, writing, analyzing data, visiting libraries, and reading. The campus of the hospital where I practiced afforded me about 5 miles of walking a day, with clients in 3 buildings and the psychology administrative office located at the opposite end of the campus from my office. That level of activity was inimical to my post-surgical recovery. I dread to think how I would have managed if I had returned there after the automobile accident. Upon retirement, I took advantage of internet access to the psychology literature and reduced my library visits. I had used computers for my writing as a graduate student; that ability has served me well as a retiree.

In addition to research, I was able to contribute to the field through service in APA governance at both the division and association levels. With meetings scheduled sporadically during the year and the benefits of electronic asynchronous communication, I could pace myself, attend meetings, and carry out assignments and duties between meetings.

Prior to retirement, I was in a position to contribute perspectives of an African American woman with experience in several clinical areas, including neuropsychology, geriatric psychology, ethnic psychology, feminist psychology, consequences of interpersonal violence, and care giving. After retirement, it was particularly noteworthy that I had been on both sides of the proverbial rehabilitation desk; my perspectives were colored by my experiences as a service provider and a client. I found myself being called on to contribute to the literature on Women with Disabilities as a presenter, author, reviewer, and editor.

Since retiring, I had a brief stint in academia as a part-time leave replacement at a private college. The first year I was invited to reprise my role as an associate professor, teaching Black Psychology. Thirteen years earlier, I had taught full-time in the Psychology Department. I was invited to return when the Black Psychology course was dropped from the Psychology curriculum and picked up by the Black Studies department. A year later, I was promoted to full professor and asked to serve another year as a part-time leave replacement. Again, electronic asynchronous communication made it possible for me to pace myself and carry out my duties. All student assignments were submitted via e-mail. I scheduled my classes so that I only needed to be on campus two or three days each week; I could rest and recharge on the other days.

Still Going…or What Retirement Looks Like Behind the Scenes

Some people ask me why, when I am retired, I continue to make professional contributions when I could have just stopped years ago and taken to a rocking chair. I've never been built that way. As far back as I can remember, I've been on the go. At some level, I relate to the woman who said, *"You've just got to keep moving. If you get in a chair, you just stiffen up and end up staying there."* (Feldman & Tegart, 2003, p. 128).

This retirement has both a public face and a private face. Many people perceive me as always active, always thinking, full of history, someone who brings experiences that are different from others in the room. What they don't see is the woman who works in spurts and needs to rest often. Many would never imagine how much of this chapter is written from bed so that I can type for a while, rest, type some more, and rest again, until I finish. That approach makes much of my work take longer than it would have in the past. I have been blessed with the ability to organize (truthfully, this only works in some parts of my life).

Another piece of the private part involves bionics. I manage pain with a transcutaneous electrical nerve stimulation (TENS) unit. People who are not familiar with TENS units probably wonder why I carry a pager; the control box clips on the waistband of my skirt or slacks. The wires are hidden under my clothes. In recent years, I have been concerned about misunderstanding by airport security or fellow air travelers. Too few people are familiar with TENS units; that lack of familiarity combined with racism and fear of terrorism puts People of Color, *regardless of ethnicity*, at heightened risk for attack in lieu of questions.

Then, there is the fashion statement. I wear slacks, pant suits, and ankle length skirts. It's been a long time since my knees have been seen in public. I wear ankle braces and my wardrobe turns a visible disability (Cacciapaglia, Beauchamp, & Howells, 2004; Rohmer & Louvet, 2009) into an invisible one. My knees have also sported braces for extended periods of time. The braces have been replaced with synthetic cartilage that holds knee surgery or actual knee replacement at bay. There are times that I just stop and feel so grateful to have been born in this era. Without the miracles of modern health care, including technology, that so many take for granted, I am not sure how I would be able to manage.

Every once in a while, I have serious setbacks. For example, I tripped on a curb and broke both wrists. That led to a series of surgeries and more physical therapy. So, part of my experience of retirement involves a need for increased attention to how I move in space, as well as developing new ways to lift and carry personal and professional accoutrements.

Going in Other Directions

I have been religious all of my life, although I have not always attended religious services. One of the difficulties has been that I was affiliated with denominations that, despite their espoused theologies, were not accepting of educated people—especially "uppity" educated African American women. I frequently faced closed doors when I wanted to contribute in ways that I could because of my professional training and experience.

At the same time, I was trained in a graduate clinical psychology program that discouraged integration of my religion with psychology. During graduate school, I was active in worship, but the church was not a place where I shared much about psychology. As I completed graduate school, I was invited to deliver a sermon. I spoke on the need to show compassion for and provide support to people with mental illness; the pastor's comment was "I suppose you said those things because you're a psychologist."

Following my survival from surgery, I felt strongly that God had a purpose for keeping me here. I still had work to do. The nature of that work was not clear. With the exception of clinical practice, I continued most of the other work I had been doing. Then, people started to ask me to present and write in broader areas of disability than traumatic brain injury. They, more than I, recognized the value of the addition of my bilateral experiences of disability to my other expertise with marginalization.

I relate closely to Comas-Díaz' description that *"The goal of a feminist identity journey is to heal the self and to repair the world"* (2010, p. 433); my womanist identity is more inclusive than feminism has been to date. My professional work has always involved marginalized people. I had generally characterized this as working in the public interest. In recent years, I have been able to see that much of what I do is aptly described as social justice, providing some of the documentation that undergirds social action. As I read about others engaged in similar work, I recognize that my personal philosophy is similar to the Jewish concept of *tikkun olam*, engaging in activities designed for *"healing the pain of others and making the world a better place"* (Greene, 2010, p. 466) or *"accepting responsibility toward the Other"*(Comas-Díaz, 2010, p. 433). In recent years, I have moved beyond the relative safety of classroom teaching, professional presenting, and writing to advocacy and political activism.

For the past few years, I have worshiped in a denomination that is progressive in many areas, including inclusion of women as preachers and pastors, supporting diversity, objection to domestic violence, and removal of barriers that prevent full participation of People with Disabilities. In this denomination, I have been able to provide workshops based on Scripture, serve in administrative positions at the local church and district levels, receive training in preaching, and work nationally on issues of domestic violence and human trafficking. The training has provided me with solid religious underpinnings for my social justice work. I use my computer skills weekly to prepare PowerPoint announcement and worship slides for 2 churches. For the past three years, after a

30-year break following my first sermon, I have had numerous opportunities to preach in my local church and other churches. This has allowed me to join my religion and my social activism in the fellowship hall; guided by the Common Revised Lectionary, I can occasionally combine social activism with religion in the pulpit. My retirement has afforded me a sense of wholeness as others appreciate, support, and encourage me to pull together all the parts of myself for the benefit of others.

Retirement Is a Shift, Not an End

As I had not planned to retire when I did, I did not intentionally prepare for the type of retirement I have had so far. Given that I expected to die, I did not think I would reach this stage. I wish I had more reasonably anticipated the possibility of disability. After all, everyone who is temporarily abled is just one illness or one accident away from disability. However, I doubt that anticipation would have allowed me to consider the accomplishments I have had with limitations on my activity. In retirement, I am not yet post-career. I dare not predict the future path of my retirement (Watts, 2011).

I would recommend that retirement be considered a shift, rather than an end. So, I approach each day as if it were my last. I am guided by in depth worship and Bible study. It is important to me not to waste the talents and time with which I have been blessed. I continue to recognize that I live in a world that is in trouble and that I have something to contribute that might make that world a better place and that lives destined to loss, might be saved. Retirement, on a daily basis, is just the beginning.

References

Banks, M. E (in press). Women of Color with Disabilities. In L. Comas-Díaz & B. Greene (Eds.). *Women of Color's psychological health.* New York: Praeger.

Cacciapaglia, H. M., Beauchamp, K. L., & Howells, G. N. (2004). Visibility of disability: Effect on willingness to interact. *Rehabilitation Psychology, 49,* 180-182. doi:10.1037/0090-5550.49.2.180

Comas-Díaz, L. (2010). Healing the self, healing the world: A feminist journey. *Women & Therapy, 33(3-4),* 432-436. doi:10.1080/02703149.2010.484679

Feldman, S. I., & Tegart, G. (2003). Keep moving: Conceptions of illness and disability of middle-aged African-American women with arthritis. In M. E. Banks & E. Kaschak (Eds.), *Women with visible and invisible disabilities: Multiple intersections, multiple issues, multiple therapies.* (pp. 127-143). New York: Haworth Press. doi: 10.1300/J015v26n01_08

Greene, B. (2010). Intersectionality and the complexity of identities: How the personal shapes the professional psychotherapist. *Women & Therapy, 33(3-4),* 452-471. doi:10.1080/02703141003757547

Rohmer, O., & Louvet, E. (2009). Describing persons with disability: Salience of disability, gender, and ethnicity. *Rehabilitation Psychology, 54,* 76-82. doi:10.1037/a0014445

Watts, D. J. (2011). *Everything is obvious, once you know the answer: How common sense fails us.* New York: Crown Business/Random House.

Splash Down and Re-Entry

Not Retired From Life

Rachel Josefowitz Siegel

*I*t is March 2009. I wake up one morning to the sound of chainsaws outside my vacation condo in California. Instead of running away from the noise, I feel drawn to the window. I pull up a chair, sit down, and watch the skilled tree surgeon take down a magnificent tree. I am fascinated, totally engrossed, admiring his skill, his craftsmanship, his agility and risk-taking. He moves like an acrobat, swinging himself from one branch to another. I've been watching all morning, delaying my daily walk. I cheer him on; I rejoice in the emerging ocean view. I weep for the proud and gnarled old tree.

Is this a metaphor for my retirement? My old age? No, I have not been cut down before my time, but yes, I do more watching than doing, cheering and weeping from the sidelines. I am still deeply involved in the world around me, but far less inclined to take action. I worry about the ecological impact of destroying an old tree, and the wasteful energy consumed by the chainsaws. I worry about the state of the world and weep at the ever-present acts of violence against nature, against women and children, against the 'other'. I cheer our President and I cheer Hilary as she engages in her diplomatic journeys. I watch, I cheer, I weep, I worry, and I do less, much less. I have less energy at eighty-four than I did in my seventies when I retired, and much less than in my fifties when I was at the height of my creativity. I ask myself if this is OK.

Am I, like the tree, no longer needed, taking up too much space, blocking the view, standing in the way of improvement? Unlike the tree, my own retirement was not a sudden and arbitrary cutting down but a conscious and independent decision to change course while still able. But there are days or moments when the sky is gray, when my joints ache, when I'm tired or ill. There are times when I feel useless, unneeded, when doubts creep in and despondency is near. But then I question the concept of uselessness; I wonder what standards to apply to the current meaning of my life.

The Meanings of Productivity and Usefulness

What standards do we apply when we retire and look at our own retirement? "Productivity" and "usefulness" are buzzwords in our North American culture. Who are we when we are no longer usefully employed, when we can no longer measure our worth by what we produce or what we earn, when there's no product, no bottom line? As a therapist and as a mother, these questions are not new to me. My "product" has never been clearly defined, nor has my worth or self-esteem been measured by the product/s I produced. Before retirement, how did I as a therapist measure my product, or my success? Not by the number of "cures," not by the number of clients per day, not by the numbers in my bank account, though all of the above have at times made me feel successful, or at least useful. How did I as a mother do the same? In both roles, I sometimes learned, often the hard way, not to measure my own worth by my children's or my clients' success or happiness. Furthermore, I learned not to define their success or happiness by my own standards or by the prevailing standards of my own culture; I have at least tried to free myself of such ingrained assumptions. I have however felt a great deal of satisfaction, when things went well for both clients and offspring, and I have indulged in self-blame when things went badly. To put it another way, I have, on a daily basis, derived a sense of my own worth from both roles. Without these roles, that daily reminder of my usefulness or productivity is no longer available to me.

How do I measure my self-worth now, in retirement from these roles, without those daily reminders? I have no answers to those questions yet the absence of such answers does not trouble me. I am, on the whole, content with a profound sense of wellbeing that must, in itself, be part of the answer.

Not Retired from Life

It takes more creativity and imagination to recognize the ways in which I still have an impact on the world around me. I have retired from my primary occupations; I have not retired from life. I have slowed down, I have not stopped. I am not stagnant. My sphere of influence is more limited but not absent. The give and take of my casual encounters and the daily interactions with friends and family may even be more focused and more intense. Family visits are newly precious, imbued with an underlying awareness of my life's inevitable ending.

I now find seeds of usefulness in my own self-care. It is my job, my responsibility to myself and to my children, to remain well as long as I can, to avoid becoming a burden before my time. I swim, I exercise, and I try to keep my brain engaged. I visit doctors and physical therapists. I am protective of my aging body.

I nurture and enjoy the ever-evolving connections with my family of origin and with my children, my grandchildren, and their children. The pleasure I derive from my offspring and their

growing families fills me with a deep sense of wonder and grati-
tude. I am wiser now than I was while raising my children. I feel
that I can now reap the rewards of years in therapy and doing therapy, of consciousness raising and self-awareness. I apply a more
sophisticated knowledge of social and psychological forces. I feel
better informed and enriched by the years of having been a feminist therapist. In short, I have reason to believe that my feminist
training and practice have had a significant and positive impact on
my current family interactions, which have become less neurotic,
less anxious, less stressful, and more enjoyable. No longer active
in these roles, I have become a better mother, sister, grandmother,
and great-grandmother, responding to obvious needs and contributing from the sidelines in many subtle ways. I have also become
the grateful recipient of care from younger family members when
I needed help.

I have honed my skills as a teller of tales, a conveyor of family stories and genealogy, and a singer of the feminist history of
our time. Family members are now ready to hear the accounts
of our European wanderings and displacements during the Hitler
years. I talk with them of the excitement of our generation's feminist awakening and its central place in my own life journey. Being
perceived as an elder in my synagogue, I recently spoke there of
the changing roles of women in our congregation, as my daughter
and I had experienced them. I write short essays, musings and
memories, to be gathered into a volume for the family.

Life in a Retirement Community

I now live in a retirement community in Ithaca, NY, the college town that has been my home for over 60 years. Having lost my husband some twenty years ago, and lived alone since then, I was pleasantly surprised at how much I enjoy the company of others on a daily basis. Some of the residents had been part of my personal and professional world before I moved in; others are of similar educational and socio-economic background. It feels easy and relaxing to be myself among my age-mates, and refreshing to eat and visit together, after years of solitary meals at the kitchen table. We dawdle over dinner, schmooze and reminisce, go over current events and scientific discoveries. We socialize, we make connections.

The positive aspects of communal living far outweigh the negatives. I enjoy the company of a variety of people, both women and men. I like hearing their life stories, and am developing some dear new friendships. I am involved in the Resident's Council and in other activities that give me a feeling of belonging. I have been well cared for in the nursing unit following last year's hip replacement and heart surgery, and I feel secure about not becoming an undue burden on my family, should I need long-term care.

I could write an entire chapter about how much I keep learning in this environment. I have acquired a deeper awareness of the human ability to live fully in late life, in spite of the inevitable losses and the gradual or sudden diminution of capabilities. Here, we are not alone when we go through the painful transitions of our life stage, the surgeries and recoveries, the chronic and debilitating illnesses, and the deaths and losses that are more frequent in our population. The words that come to mind are courage, resilience, hope, determination, caring, and connection. There are times when painful feelings arise, when we feel the sadness of accumulated losses, the mixed feelings of survivorship. We count our own blessings and good fortune while we mourn the deaths and ordeals of others. At times we feel like family and help each other heal.

After Retirement and Into Old Age

In my experience, retirement and becoming old are intertwined. Shevy Healy and Theo Sonderegger said that successful aging and retirement depend in large part on overcoming our own ageist assumptions (private communications, 1990). This concept and the earlier exchange of ideas with my feminist therapist age cohort have helped prepare me for my own transition into retirement and into the final stage of life (my writings on these topics are listed at the end of this chapter). Since retirement I have occasionally been prompted to write more on old age and have continued to offer occasional lectures and workshops. I like to keep in touch with former colleagues and to stay active on some local human service boards.

In these more leisurely years, I not only look out the window, but I do a great deal of looking in and looking back. The memories of those parts of my life that have been well spent help me recapture my own sense of worth. The memories of my mistakes, and of periods of stagnation, indecisiveness, and depression are part of the package, but it is the knowledge that those were a necessary part of my development, and that I did get beyond them that usually lets me feel good about myself.

Old age, like any age, may be like a bed of roses, both beautiful and thorny. The rewards are many, so are the challenges and losses.

I occasionally experience periods of sadness and depression. At such times I may have bad dreams and ruminations, triggered no doubt by current life circumstances. I relive past traumas, unresolved tensions, and past events that I mishandled. Twinges of guilt emerge but do not last or dominate my days. At times of personal loss and funerals I feel acutely lonely and I mourn again the many loved ones who have preceded me in death. In my retirement community, death has become a normal part of living, making it easier to come to terms with my own inevitable mortality. I try to make the most of every day while I still can.

There is no formula for successful retirement. I have been fortunate in having few financial worries, though money management and estate planning take considerable time and energy. I have had several conversations with my children and healthcare providers about my wish to be able to die peacefully without extreme interventions. Having written a detailed medical directive and arranged for a legal healthcare proxy, I feel more at ease about the process of dying and thus can live my life more fully.

Concluding Thought

It is now 2011. I have just celebrated my eighty-seventh birthday. Usefulness and productivity are no longer the meaningful measures of my life. What I have come to value in retirement, and now in old age, are the acts of love and caring that I exchange with those around me. A smile, a hug, a listening ear, a friendly e-mail, a good laugh or some tears, or just plain being together and feeling connected. That is now what really matters.

Retirement agrees with me. I like the easing of responsibilities, the freedom of being able to come and go as I please, sleeping late on a weekday if I feel like it, making spontaneous decisions. I like having more time to write, to visit, to learn new skills, and to discover new pieces of truth. I like to watch the sunset, to daydream and be idle. I like having more time to feel the beauty all around me. The quiet enjoyment of daily life has become a precious privilege.

Old age also agrees with me. Being part of a large and loving extended family, life continues to bring me a full measure of 'naches ' and 'tzorres,' joys and sorrows. Individual relationships have become even more important and family gatherings more highly treasured. Each day feels like a gift. I am glad to be alive.

Coda

I wish I had known how much I would miss the discretionary income that allowed a certain level of charitable giving. Though I am financially comfortable and secure, I did not foresee the necessary cutbacks.

Having deliberately allowed my practice to dwindle, I wish I had realized a little sooner that the last few clients were beginning to feel like a burden, and that I had become more interested in writing and in spending time with my family and friends.

I am glad that I moved into a vibrant retirement community while still able to do it thoughtfully and comfortably. In this final and retirement stage of life, I am immensely grateful for the people skills, social skills, and feminist wisdom that I was able to develop during my years as a social worker and feminist therapist. Now that self-care takes up much of my time, each personal connection and encounter with loved ones brings me much joy and enhances my general sense of well-being.

In preparing for retirement it feels important to plan carefully, as well as to follow your gut feelings. Anticipate your financial needs as much as possible. Your social, emotional, and medical needs will keep changing. Your individual need for relaxation, stimulation and companionship will continue to be specific to who you are. Do some research into your options for a compatible late life environment. Above all, do not be afraid of change.

References

Siegel, R. J. (1990). Old women as Mother Figures. In E. Cole, & J. Knowles (Eds.), *Motherhood: A feminist perspective* (pp.89-97). New York: The Haworth Press.

Siegel, R.J. (1991). Love and work after 60: An integration of personal and professional growth within a long-term marriage, In E. Rosenthal (Ed.), *Women, aging and ageism* (pp. 69-79). New York: The Haworth Press.

Siegel, R.J. (1991). We are not your mothers: Report on two groups for women over sixty. In E. Rosenthal (Ed.), *Women, aging and ageism* (pp.81-89). New York: The Haworth Press.

Siegel, R. J. (1993). Between midlife and old age: Never too old to learn, In N. D. Davis, E. Cole, & E. D. Rothblum (Eds.), *Faces of women and aging* (pp. 173-185). New York: The Haworth Press.

Siegel, R. J. (1994, Spring). An immigrant again: This time in a country called Widowhood, *LILITH: The Independent Jewish Women's Magazine, 19,* 24-27.

Siegel, R. J. (1999). Silencing the voices of older women. In K. Judd, J. Ash de Pou, J. Tavares-Bucher, T. Sikoska, & J. Solomon (Eds.), *Ageing in a gendered world: Issues and identity for women* (pp.315-330). Santo Domingo/New York: INSTRAW/UN Publications.

Siegel, R. J. (2005). Ageism in psychiatric diagnosis. In P. Caplan, & L. Cosgrove (Eds.), *Bias in psychiatric diagnosis* (pp 89-96). New York, Rowman & Littlefield Inc.

Siegel, R. J., & Sonderegger, T. (1990). Ethical considerations in therapy with older women. In H. Lerman, & N. Porter (Eds.), *Feminist ethics in psychotherapy* (pp. 176-184). New York: Springer Publishing Company.

Siegel, R. J., & Sonderegger, T., (1995). Conflicts in care: later years in the life span. In C. Larsen, & E. Rave (Eds.), *Ethical decision making in therapy* (pp. 223-246). New York: The Guilford Press.

I'll Never Retire, She Said

Judith Worell

I am now in the ninth year of "retirement", meaning that for the most part, I no longer get paid for what I write or what I teach. When asked by any form I need to complete, what is my work status, I nevertheless indicate "retired." Clearly there is some contradiction here. The question of what we mean by the term "retired" lies at the heart of the problem. Does retired mean I no longer work for pay? Does it mean I no longer work anywhere? If I am retired, does it imply I am in a nursing home, a retirement village, or just sitting around my home reading or puttering in my garden?

Taking a look at my title here, this is the statement I gave my friends and colleagues for many years. "They will have to carry me out in a pine box" I was overheard to say over and again. By this statement I meant to deny the inevitable of termination from gainful employment teaching at a University. Unable to envision another role that would feed my interests so fully, I believed I would otherwise go hungry for lack of challenging things to engage my time and energies. To be honest, fear gripped me when I least expected, and I quickly moved to dispel that uncomfortable feeling through denial..

As with many academics who publish, I had been approached many times to write a text for some publishing company. I always demurred. But at this final point in my career, I said "yes" without much thought to several offers of book contracts. Thus, I ended up with three commitments to write texts on feminist and gender psychology. My retirement anxiety was reduced; I felt relieved and anxious to get started.

The first project was a revision of an earlier book I wrote on feminist therapy with coauthor Pam Remer, entitled

Feminist Perspectives in Therapy: An Empowerment Model for Women, in 1992. The new version emphasized diverse populations, and included case studies on selected minority clients, *Feminist Perspectives in Therapy: Empowering Diverse Women*, in 2003. I was pleased with that revision.

Then I agreed to develop and edit a two volume *Encyclopedia of Women and Gender* for Oxford University Press. This was a major project and would cover many areas for which I had limited knowledge. I had at the time a good acquaintance with many of the outstanding women psychologists in the field. Through this network I developed an "advisory board" of psychologists knowledgeable in seven different areas. In this manner, we were able to select experts who could write a chapter for each of our topics, which numbers over 100!

Finally, I agreed to edit a *Handbook of Girls' and Women's Psychological Health*. Considering all the topics that this latter volume would include, I was again aware that I knew little about some of the topics I would need to include. I approached Carol Goodheart, who had expertise in many of these topics, and she agreed, happily, to co-edit the text with me. In a whirlwind weekend, I flew down to Mexico, where Carol and her husband were on sabbatical for the year, and in two heavy days we drafted an outline of our projected encyclopedia. Deciding on a developmental approach, we began with mid-childhood, worked our way through midlife and beyond, and finally included a section on the ending stages of life. We called this section "Summing up and Winding down." We hoped to end in a positive, rather than a depressing note.

Who could be asked to write each of these chapters as an expert? Between Carol and myself, we knew many of the most outstanding experts in the field. For a few areas, we depended on the suggestions of the publisher representative from Oxford University Press. The result was a list of 90 distinguished authors whom we recruited, an amazing group of outstanding experts in the field of psychology and gender.

Reading and editing these chapters as they arrived took two years out of my "retirement" years (*Handbook of Girls' and Women's Psychological Health: Gender and Wellbeing across the Lifespan*, Oxford University Press, 2006). I enjoyed it all. One answer to satisfaction in retirement years, then, is to become involved in something you enjoy immensely, whether it be "work" or leisure.. I do not play golf and no longer play tennis (having recently broken my wrist playing that wonderful sport). Now that the editing was completed, another challenge faced me. What to do next?

As I began to write, an interesting thought occurred to me concerning what is meant to have a "feminist retirement"? Is this not an oxymoron? That is, if being a feminist calls upon one to be an activist in helping to change society toward a more egalitarian stance, then as a feminist can I ever retire? Today's communities, as we know them world-wide, are all stratified and inherently unequal in many ways. Then how can we ever rest or retire? Are we not called upon to resist and continue to help change the world? That is a hefty assignment to be sure. Perhaps in addition to redefining the concept of retirement, we need also to redefine the concept of change.

As I listen to the daily news reports, I could become immobilized by the enormity of problems facing individuals and communities around the globe. What could I possibly do as an individual? I have not resolved this question yet. Currently, I assuage my personal guilt by giving small amounts of money to this cause and that. Do I deceive myself by believing that I am changing the world one small bank check at a time? Part of your answer might be—why should I feel guilty about events for which I had no responsibility and that are not by any means under my control? The answer I give myself is that one person cannot achieve the impossible. I must forgive myself and all other individuals if we do not and cannot accomplish great changes in the world.

Where does this leave me in the feminist retirement story? I maintain my feminist identity, because that is who I am. I use the concept of a feminist story to suggest that all of our conscious experiences consist of a story we tell ourselves and others. Is the story true? Do I sound like a narrative psychologist? Labels are not important here, since again a label just encapsulates another story or another narrative.

The narrative that I give to comfort myself is that I can continue with my feminist activism one small step at a time. I give to large causes with small gifts. I volunteer for small community projects that are within my ability to complete. I joined several women's book clubs and I speak my mind in ways that perhaps may touch a spark of new understanding in another soul. Without using the term "feminist", I may question whether this book leads to a new view of women, or just a repeat of the conventional and traditional conceptions of traditional women's roles. In response to my remarks, some women may resist with closed minds, some women may agree with verbal support for my remarks, and some may wonder whether they too could consider other roles for women aside from what they believe.

Retirement does give us more unstructured time to fill with rewarding activities. The opportunity to read whatever journal or book attracts me is a prime reward of my current situation. Most communities have a public library with more appealing books than one could ever complete in a lifetime. I read the NY Times book reviews each Sunday to see what might look interesting. The "best seller" section gives the frequency with which each book is purchased, suggesting its relative popularity with the reading public. Along with the position in the frequency of sale column is a brief summary of the book's content. I avoid anything suggesting murder, violence, or mysticism.

Some of the more appealing books that I read recently include *The Help*, a book about "a white woman and two of her maids." The book is beautifully written and I loved it. After reading books I love, I send them on to whichever of my 3 daughters might also enjoy it. We have a family read-around going this way. Another book I enjoyed was *Best Friends Forever*. by Jennifer Weiner, about two girls who grow into womanhood together.

Although I usually read books written by women, there are some written by men that I have also enjoyed, one being *The Girl with the Dragon Tattoo* by Steig Larsson. Although I found this book fascinating, it was clearly not written by a woman, since the author does not seem to understand the soul of a woman. The main character is a young woman who never shows any emotion, positive or negative. But the author does show her as strong and determined, which I appreciate. Larsson followed that book with another, *The Girl who Played with Fire*, including the same main characters. Here, he goes into the woman's background in detail, explaining why she holds her emotions in check. This was very well done: I am looking forward to reading the final volume in this series.

Being alone at home has been a new experience for me. My spouse of 23 years developed Alzheimer's disease about 5 years ago, making him less of an ideal companion than he was previously. He was a true gentleman in an old-fashioned sense. He wanted to "take care of me" and at first had difficulty understanding why I did not need to be "taken care of." He was a widower and his former wife was also traditional in her personal and home life. We had some discussions about how he was going to live comfortably with the feminist side of me. We finally agreed we could take care of one another, and that seemed more egalitarian to me. I did not wish to play the part of the helpless woman. This was a good relationship for me. Certain behaviors remained for him that irked me, such as his insistence on holding my arm when we walk in public, as if to guide and protect. But it was clear that we cannot substantially change another person in a relationship and in that respect I did not try. Here, feminist activism remained dormant.

Once I was retired from the University, we had infinite time to travel. Bud enjoyed traveling as much as I did. Our first major trip was a safari in South Africa, Botswana, and Zimbabwe. These are all countries for which I had minimal information before we went. We signed on to a small group travel agency, Overseas

Adventures. Our group consisted of only 12 of us, several couples, and several singles, all of whom were seasoned travelers and
very compatible.

We traveled in a small van, with a window for everyone.
We drove through pristine landscapes, looking at herds of various animals, only a few of which I can detail: Bison, wildebeests,
elephants, and some kind of wild pigs. At one stop we were able
to climb up to a lookout ramp, where we could view herds of
elephants as they came down to a watering hole to drink. What
a thrill, families of elephants with small ones carefully protected
between two larger members of the group. I do love elephants,
they are social and group-minded and they protect one another.

Bud was a camera "nut"; his mantra was that one can never
have too many cameras. No sooner had he bought one than he was
ready for the next higher version. Unfortunately, older cameras are
worth nothing on the market. After Bud passed away 18 months
ago, I gave the most recent camera to one of my grandsons. The
rest remain in the hall cabinet: What to do with them? He also
neglected to select which pictures he wanted to keep: the result is
that I have cabinets and drawers filled with all of his photos, and
I am just immobilized when it comes down to selecting which to
keep and which to discard. I suppose that would make a perfect
retirement project, but somehow I resist.

Retirement also gave me more time for my dogs. I always
owned dogs, usually small ones. At that time I had two Shetland
Sheepdogs (Shelties), who spread hair all around the house and
needed constant brushing. Bud took to them immediately and
insisted on feeding and walking them, to which none of us, me or

the dogs, objected. But dogs have a limited lifespan, and one after the other, at age 15, each passed on to doggie heaven. I mourned for weeks. No more dogs, losing them was too painful.

But two years later I relented, and I now spend my retirement years walking and talking with a sweet and loving Bichon Frise, a small white and furry companion. This breed is super-attached, follows me every step in and out of the house. Do I believe that there is a feminist way to relate to a dog? One cannot be too egalitarian here, since I can love her but I have also to be the Alpha member of this family and take control in many situations. One way is to insist on a leash out side, not exactly egalitarian but effective in control.

At my advanced age, it is difficult to anticipate the future. While I was working, I made five-year plans for myself. What would I intend to accomplish in the next five years? But now a five-year plan seems unrealistic; I take life day by day. Do I have any sage advice for future generations? It seems important always to remember and treasure who you are. What is the core of your identity and how will you guard and treasure it. The feminist aspect of yourself may be one part of your core identity, intersecting with other valued parts of yourself: gender, nationality, race, culture, etc. At times it may be difficult to untangle these intersecting identities, but at the heart of it will be the feminist perspective that guides what you do with yourself and with others, and what you will become. Feminism may not tell you how to enjoy your every moment, so I will end with that advice. Life is a beautiful treasure, to live each day with zest and enjoyment is a privilege each of us can take as our own.

Revisions and Visions of Retirement: My Story

Mary Gergen

*O*nce upon a time, when I was in my fifties, I decided that I would retire from teaching when I was 68. It was an arbitrary number, but sounded pretty old to me at the time. Also, by then, my husband, four years older, might have retired, and I didn't want him to be having all the fun, while I was still slaving away at the office. During the last five years of my fulltime employment as a Professor of Psychology and Women's Studies, the tension of his being almost retired and my working schedule began to rise. He taught one class on Monday afternoons, and then he was free as a bird (with many nests beckoning him around the world), and I was pretty much shut in my birdcage for much of the week.

Another reason for choosing the number 68 was that I had had cancer when I was 48, and the possibility that I might not live to a ripe old age had influenced my thinking for some time. My father had died at 67; my mother had died at 60 and, most tragically, my sister at 50. I would have outlived them all by 68. And I was not fond of the idea of "dying with my boots on."

By the time I was nearing 67, I began to get cold feet about retiring. I didn't feel as old as I thought I would; in fact, I was feeling pretty sprightly. My medical exams were good, and I began to rethink my presumed early mortality. In addition, my salary was getting impressive to me, I enjoyed my students, and I loved working at my campus. Although I was part of the Penn State Department of Psychology, I worked at a regional campus, now called Brandywine, in a suburb of Philadelphia, about 15 minutes from my home. The campus was commuter-based, and the major expectations for faculty were first teaching, and second research, with service a very important necessity, given our small, very tightly knit community.

As I neared the magical age, I began to focus on the tedium of the school year routine. After 20 years, I realized the seasons of the schedule, which, like the outside world's, repeated themselves with regularity—weekly class schedule, midterms, finals, vacation, new semester class schedule, etc. I taught basic courses, with some variations, for first and second year students, primarily. Now and then I was able to do an honors course in introductory psychology, which I loved, and feminist theory, which was also a lively challenge. In these classes we engaged in free-form discussions, and the students experienced the thrill of developing their own ideas within the topic areas I created with and for them. In all my classes students did "action assignments"—which meant they went out in the world, tried out things related to their classroom work, and then wrote papers about their experiences. Those papers were fun to read, and I relished the adventures the students had and reported in nicely written prose.

My teaching was important to me, and I had a requirement that before I went into a class, I had to be excited about something I wanted to share with them. I recognized, however, that some of the crazy things I had done in my first five years of teaching, I no longer felt like doing. For example, I no longer was being filmed while I went through a bizarre routine to illustrate something about eyewitness testimony, and using the video as the proof of what they did and did not recall later. Each year, I was getting more routinized, and less "crazy." Although I was awarded a prestigious university wide teaching prize, I had begun to feel that my best days as a creative, innovative, and caring teacher were behind me.

When I thought about some of my major accomplishments at the university, I realized that I took special pleasure in unique, entrepreneurial activities, some that had a fairly lasting impact on the school. They were "extra-curricular" in important ways. In my second year, I naively took on the philosophy colloquium and produced an amazing conference, with outstanding speakers, discussing how feminist ideas had influenced their fields of study; these original papers became the basis of my first book (Gergen, 1988). I was innocent of the fact that at a commuter campus hardly anyone from the school would show up for the Saturday meetings; no one was expected to do something this grand at our humble campus. No one in University Relations bothered to create the publicity that would have made it a major event in the region. (I was very embarrassed by the lack of attendees, and I never forgave the person who was in charge of the PR for this fiasco.)

I also was successful in having the library, the most attractive building on campus, named for our founder, John Vairo. The man who failed on the PR front tried to block this effort, saying it was impossible to name a building after someone without several million dollars of contributions to the university; however, he hadn't read the fine print in the university's policy manual concerning who was eligible to be honored in this way; this time the goal was achieved, and Dr. Vairo was thrilled to have a building named after him.

With the help of my colleagues and friends, my third "personal best" was creating two major faculty prizes on behalf of my two favorite bosses, Madelyn Hanes and George Franz. I mention these "personal bests" because none of them had anything directly to do with my job, which had lost some of its luster as the years went by. (I guess if I had a 4th, which occurred after my retirement, it was donating a gift to Penn State, Brandywine, so that a statue of a lion, signed by President Bill Clinton during his visit to the campus, was kept in a prominent place as a mascot and a symbol of the campus' history, and not sold off at auction.)

I plunged ahead to my retirement, given my resolve, and I handed in my official letter of resignation in 2005. There could be no turning back once it was received. After this, I began to develop a special sensitivity to endings. The last "first day of school" and the last exams, the last students, the last day in my office, the last graduation, and so it went, until my last day and the farewell party. Sometimes I became very sentimental as I relished these Last Firsts and Last Endings. I took a photo of my last social psychology class, which I had especially relished; I felt I had been at my best for them, and it might have made a difference in some of their lives. Each time I pondered these endings, I felt a bittersweet sadness, which was, at the same time, a dramatic ritual, in which I had engaged at every ending since my high school graduation, when "We will have these moments to remember" was a hit song. I had also learned that this ritual of mine implanted a memory that I could treasure in the coming years.

One regret I had related to the friendships I had developed over the years. In one sense they were not intimate relationships because they depended on being together on the same faculty, sharing the same tasks, being privy to the same gossip, and caring about the same political power plays of the folks in Old Main at University Park, hours away from us. I knew it would never be the same again. Most of all, I knew that my close connection to my office mate would also change, although I really wanted our relationship to be an exception to my rule.

Although my teaching career at Penn State was officially over, I was asked to teach a course that summer, which I did, and then again in the spring semester of the following two years, as they wanted me to teach the capstone feminist theory course. The third year someone else wanted to teach it, and I agreed without much regret. Meanwhile, I often went back to parties and local events, met the new leadership team, and visited when I picked up my mail. The "life goes on" factor struck me little by little. I returned to my old office the first year I had retired, as I had been told I could use it during the days I was teaching, my desk had been taken over by an undergraduate research team. There was almost no desk space available, given the computer and other materials stacked there. It made perfect sense for this to happen, but the feeling of being displaced was heavy on my heart. Another sign that nothing stays the same was noticing that the rug I had left to decorate the office was rolled up and stashed in a corner. I took it home. Later the building was remodeled, and everyone who had an office there spent the year in a maze of cubicles in the library. I went to visit, and I had a good time, wandering up and down the aisles, hugging, greeting and saying "hi" to a wide variety of faculty. And then, as they all seemed to be very busy and active, I left.

I made a pledge to myself that I would only go back to campus if I had something special to do, and that I would not expect any special treatment. I also realized that I cared less and less about the concerns that were hot topics of the day. There was something repetitive about the issues. Some had been going on for 20 years, such as we needed dormitories to get the caliber of students that we deserved. I also realized, with guilt in my heart, that the phasing out that occurs when people retire, although to be expected and necessary, was something that I had been guilty of, when I thought back on times when my former office mate for almost 15 years would suddenly appear in my doorway. I was happy to see him, but then I needed to get things done, and I couldn't spend much time chatting. Over time we drifted apart, and today we meet, but the old casual intimacy is no longer there. It happens.

After the Fact

Unlike many faculty members whose lives are so circumscribed by their departments and their institutions that they hardly know there is life beyond the ivy covered walls, I had been living a double life in terms of academic worlds. My paid employment was Penn State, but my intellectual life flourished through my scholarly connections to my housemate-husband, Kenneth Gergen. Ken had moved from Harvard to Swarthmore College in the late 60s, when he became chair of the psychology department, and he has been connected to the college ever since. Although he retired at the same time I did, in 2006, he retains the title of Senior Research Professor, which he much prefers to Professor Emeritus.

During my academic development I spent the earliest part of my career as a psychologist working at Harvard in the Social Relations Department and then at the Business School; later I went to graduate school for my Ph.D., at Temple University in Philadelphia, and returned to work with Ken at Swarthmore College as a research assistant, and later as an associate. One of the things we recognized during that period was that if I was always working for him I was always going to be "in his shadow" without a separate identity or set of competencies. Getting my PhD had been a beginning on the road to my separate development, and working separately was another one. We made the decision that he would not seek further grants that would employ me, and we would see what might happen as a result. My career at Penn State was a significant step in that delineation process. Although we enforced a certain distance between us, the result was that we were in constant dialogue about our intellectual experiences. An important contribution to our development was a seminar I took in the Philosophy of the Behavioral Sciences, taught by Joseph Margolis at Temple. In many respects this course, and our conversations afterwards, paved the way for many of the ideas that developed later in our careers. We have never stopped this home seminar, and the result is that the academic stimulation that many people miss when they cut the ties to their primary institution was never diminished for me.

Because of our closely knit relationship, Ken and I continue to spend a great deal of time together, and have published many books, chapters and articles over the past 40 years. We also edit each other's papers, often attend each other's presentations, and perform together at many national and international venues. We have even been known to sing verses, act out skits, and read poetry in our presentations. In the last two years we have accepted invitations to India, Mexico, Brazil, Scandinavia, the Netherlands, Germany and England, as well as several places in the U. S. and Canada. One of our important projects is co-editing and writing the Positive Aging Newsletter, which goes out to thousands of subscribers as a free electronic resource. We now have five translators, who recreate the newsletter into Spanish, French, German, Portuguese, and Chinese. Our major focus is on shifting the view of aging from one of decline to one of rich development and happiness. We are aware that we have the responsibility to be "poster children" for our theme. If we feel old and crotchety, we have to go hide in a closet.

Ken's writings in social constructionism, have been a very fruitful resource for my work. As I have written about before, in particular in my book *Feminist Reconstructions in Psychology: Narrative, Gender and Performance* (2001), I work at the crossroads of social constructionism and feminist theory, and this is a particular mix of ideas and politics that require some stirring to get a good blend. Ken is a major creative force behind social constructionist ideas, and I bring a variety of feminist theories to the mix. As a constructionist/feminist, I have been in a minority position as a psychologist. As an advocate of qualitative inquiry I have advanced ideas that are marginal and controversial for many trained in traditional empirical studies. Despite the sometimes controversial reception I have received, overall, I have been recognized for my position, in part, because of its rarity. In addition I have been involved in doing performative work for twenty years, which is also an anomaly in the field. A sign of this long interest is shown by my most recent book, *Playing with Purpose: Adventures in Performative Social Science*, (2012), a culmination of performance work and theorizing, created with Ken Gergen. These interests have continued to evolve, without regard to my retirement. I appreciate the advantage of being able to continue to do scholarly work, without having an obligation to follow an academic schedule. Today, our major involvement is focused on relational theory, which is developed in Ken's last book, *Relational Being: Beyond Self and Community* (2009). I think this approach is an appealing one that especially resonates with feminist ideas. Certain core ideas have much in common with the feminist themes developed at the former Stone Center at Wellesley College, and Jean Baker Miller's relational ideas, particularly.

All of this is to say that my scholarly activities and interactions in the academic world are still alive and well, five years after my official retirement. In the last few years I have published 23 articles and book chapters, alone or collaboratively, which probably surpasses any other five year period in my career. I have participated in and presented at as many conferences, conventions, and other meetings as much as ever. I have kept up my professional work as a reviewer, editor, and program evaluator. As I have reflected on these years, I realize that the word "retirement" is what needs to be retired, as it does not reflect what people are doing after leaving their primary career activities. Rather than having nothing much to do, people seem to continue to be involved in committed, engaging, and sometimes far flung activities that may resemble a career change or development, rather than a retirement from one.

New Developments

In 1992, a group of our friends gathered in Taos, New Mexico at the home of Diana Whitney, an organization development consultant, during which we hatched a plan to have a conference there the following year, and at the end of that very successful endeavor, we decided to create an organization called the Taos Institute that was designed to promote social constructionist ideas in the world, especially in the practices we represented, mainly therapy, organization development, and communication. From that dinner party, and the ideas that flowered that evening, a very substantial non-profit organization grew into being. Today, the Institute is overseen by a Board, which consists of five of the seven founders, plus four others, with an executive director, 200 associates world-wide, a variety of educational activities and services, and a lively presence in the world. (Check out our website at www. TaosInstitute.net).

As one of the founders, I have discovered that I am now heavily engaged in the ongoing activities of the organization, both as a volunteer and as a paid provider. I work in the publishing wing, and also as an advisor in our PhD program, which we run under the auspices of Tilburg University, The Netherlands. At present I have eight graduate students, who are working on various projects relating social constructionist ideas to their specific field of interest. In Kansas, Greg is studying the narratives of farm organizations; Cara in Montreal is working on international collaborative educational programs; Siva in Mauritious is studying social policy and aging in his African nation; Alan in British Columbia, is working in education on a project related to aboriginal youth. Ann in Arizona is studying bereavement and recovery among Lesbian widows. Tricia's work is on environmental issues and literature; Rob's topic involves architecture; and Lisa's is on the notion of "careering." As one might imagine, I am continually enriched by the diversity of projects I oversee and hopefully bring to fruition.

So far, six of my other students have completed their dissertations and received their degrees. I'm very proud of my part in those success stories as well.

I've said little about my important family roles as wife, mother, stepmother, mother-in-law, and grandmother. (I refuse to be a step-grandmother.) Having grown up in the tidy fifties, radicalized in the "make love, not war" sixties, and then pacified in the disco seventies, I have many facets, many selves. Each of them has a "take" on the maternal, but basically, I have always been very committed to co-creating the best blended family possible, with the help of my husband and our kids. Having been the wicked stepmother for some years, I am so happy that my step children, now mature adults, and I are on very loving terms with one another, and have been for a long time. Ken was readily accepted as a father figure and "Daddy" by my biological children, who were five and six when we began living together. There are now few tensions in any familial direction.

Not much has changed due to my retirement in terms of being a mother. One of the habits I continue from my own mother's life is having a family Sunday dinner. When we are in town we invite our family members to dinner, and they come if they can. We have a jolly time, and we stay more in touch with each other's lives in this informal way. We celebrate birthdays at home, have a Thanksgiving feast, with extended family members, and always have a special Christmas Eve dinner together. One daughter is starting to host certain holidays at her house, and she organized our last birthday party (for Ken and me) at her table. Because one of my goals has been to keep the connections between our two sets of children strong, I am happy to see them cooperating to bring off a family celebration. One aspect of retiring is that I tend to think more of what life will be like when I am no longer here to "orchestrate" many of our occasions as a family. I fear, sometimes, that without the marital tie connecting Ken and me together, the children may drift apart. That is why I am glad that two of them, to celebrate their 50th birthdays, are going to New Orleans together with their spouses. They will be friends, forever, as well as siblings.

In terms of being a grandmother, I know that for many of my friends grandparenthood changed their lives, and included in this transition, for some of them, is a new occupation of baby-sitter, bottle washer, and chauffeur. I have been a grandmother for 16 years, with one granddaughter, followed by a grandson, 14. Although I love them and see them frequently, their other grandmother has been their primary one in terms of fulfilling the worker-grandmother role. My major involvement is with our bachelor son's child, now age 5. Although he lives with his mother and other grandparents, we see him often during his visiting time with his dad. For me, being with this child is very special, and I so look forward to time I can be with him. Being a grandmother has its advantages over being a mother, as my friends have often said, and it is not just about being able to "return" them at the end of the day. It is about being able to focus on the joys of childhood again, of sharing in the creativity of children's play, stoking the imagination, and presenting the child with new adventures, which always entails a form of learning (for me as well as him). Perhaps it is important to grandmother because it allows one to relive one's earlier life as a mother and to make up for some of the lapses one committed the first time around. I find it totally involving to engage deeply with a child, and that is one of the secrets to a satisfying life.

In terms of my retirement, I am happy to have the liberty to design my own days, and keeping a place for our grandson in that plan is always on my mind. There are times when I choose not to go on a trip because I would rather spend the time with him. One of my hopes is that I can live well and long enough to see him grow-up. At this point in his life, he is so talented, bright, and adorable that I fear how the world is going to cut him down to size, as it does to so many people. I hope that somehow my being alive will offer some protection from the potential dangers that can threaten him.

Besides my scholarly work, my travels with Ken, and my family roles, I love to play. Being retired allows me to have more time to play tennis with various groups of women and to play golf with Ken. One of my colleagues, who retired the same day I did, was motivated by one thing: to play golf every day. I am not like that, but I do enjoy the camaraderie of sports and the total involve-ment it entails. I remember, even when I was in chemotherapy, when I went to play tennis, I forgot my troubles and felt the light heartedness of playing the game. Playing a sport is a way to take a vacation from life. I don't think running on a treadmill for a half hour would be quite the same, and I never intend to find out. I do have some weights in my office and an article with exercises to do so that one can have arms like Michelle Obama's; I do them now and again, but so far no major results.

I'm also more involved in keeping up with political matters, and a member of Emily's List (a feminist group that supports pro-choice Democrat women candidates.) . Ken and I support many charitable organizations, mostly cultural and political, with an emphasis on social justice causes. I write letters to the editor, send emails to legislators, and generally get involved in mediated expressions of opinion. I spend more time reading the newspaper now than I did when I was working, and I feel as much a part of the national and local political world as I did when I was working at Penn State, maybe more so. I feel a bit guilty that I am not doing more in terms of demonstrations and volunteering. I am a Pennsylvania Official Prison Visitor, which gives me the right to go into prisons and keep a citizen's watch over them, but I haven't been called on to do any work there for some months, and I haven't gone out of my way to make it happen. The last effort I made involved writing against the sentence "Life without parole" which is, in effect, a prolonged death penalty, one that no one should have to suffer, in my view.

What is exciting on my agenda right now that I haven't already written about? Preparing for the holidays, with visitors and family members coming from afar; working on three book manuscripts as a co-author and co-editor; planning a surprise party for a dear friend, whose birthday is in March; dreaming about a Caribbean vacation over the New Year; pondering where I'll find the money to pay for the annual gift I give to Penn State; going to England in the summer to work on a project on performative social sciences with a colleague there. Traveling elsewhere in Europe for professional meetings and personal visits, going to New York for plays and museums;

speaking at a conference in California; attending APA, and being a part of a community of scholars in the Society for the Study of Women, Div. 35, where I have been a member since its inception in the 1970s, and active in the latter part of my career and thereafter.

Some Words of Wisdom for Those Contemplating Retirement

My narrative is quite one-sided, I realize, with very few mentions of tragedies, insurmountable difficulties, pain, or suffering. But it is also the manner in which I tend to view life. I try to focus on the rosy side, and I forget the bad. This is a general habit of being I find to be quite automatic. I remember once when I lost that feeling, when I felt simply exhausted and dead inside. It was shortly after that that I was diagnosed with cancer. For me, and this is totally my personal viewpoint, cancer is what can happen when you suffer from a loss or an emotional trauma that you cannot control. (It also helps to be going through hormonal changes and have a family history as long as your arm.) Overtime, I also found a way of being grateful for finding that cancerous lump in my breast. Because of that, my gynecologist discovered irregularities in my ovaries, and I was saved from dying of ovarian cancer.

I've discovered that the onion is a good metaphor for one's life. Within me are all the years of my life, wrapped one skin on top of another. My view resonates with the New Yorker cartoon in which a mother tells her daughter, "I understand you; I've been 15. You don't understand 45." Wisdom comes, I think, from having access to all those years, and being able to see things from many points of view. As I am writing this, I realize that I don't put much stock in the adage that old people are wise. As I look around at my fellow travelers on the age scale, there is a great deal of diversity. Our politics vary; our sympathies for immigrants; our views on peace and war; our tastes in music and food; our beliefs about religion and taxes; meat and potatoes; abortion and football teams; Pepsi and Coke. If we are all so wise, why do our conclusions differ so much?

Given this preamble in which I discredit my own right to be wise, what might I say about retiring well from one's career? First, be very intrigued by some things outside of work. Be excited and interested in joining a good cause, learning a new craft, honing a skill, starting a new job, growing a garden or an investment fund, playing a game, making a film, running for office, or falling in love. Research suggests that the most satisfied older people have strong social networks, are optimistic about life, are interested in the world around them, are emotionally stable, and tend to be nice. They rate their own health as good enough, adjust to their frailties; move around as much as possible on their own two feet, and don't have financial worries. That last one can be a very big problem, if one hasn't planned ahead or had the earning power to save. It is important to be realistic about what your income will be and how you are going to spend it. Talking to a knowledgeable and disinterested party that knows about the economics of retirement is a good idea. One expert recently suggested that in your first year of retirement you don't draw down more than 4% of your savings, in order for it to last for 30 years.

I wish I could say I understand where the money I spend comes from, where it goes, and how much I have left to spend. Ken and I have lived intuitively for more than 40 years, and whether we are up or down financially, we somehow sense it and either hunker down or expand. We are probably as well-off now as we were when we were working full-time, but we do have our limits and our perks. On the up-side, most of our travel is paid for by others, and that is how we see the world, except for some extra frills, such as spending a birthday night at a fabulous hotel over-looking the Taj Mahal. It is a memory we often recall with great relish. At the same time, we rarely buy designer clothes or expen-sive jewelry or watches. If we had to cut back, we could without much trouble. (Or so I say, given that I don't have to do so today.) When I was young and poor in my first marriage, my husband was called up into the air force as a reservist during the Cuban missile crisis, and I was pregnant with our second child. I figured out a budget for us of $275 a month, the salary of an airman first class. Fortunately we didn't really have to live on that money for long, but I am flexible and creative when it comes to money.

Younger people believe that health is something one takes for granted. Middle aged people worry as they start to see chinks in their armor, but older people learn to adjust. By and large, people manage to live well, even with major decrements in their youthful capacities. It is a good idea to eat well, sleep long, and laugh heart-ily in one's career days, as extra insurance against falling apart too soon. Keeping up good habits helps in retirement as well.

Overall, life is not that different for me today from what it was ten years ago; I don't envy people who have a full time job at all. I often wonder why some people are still carrying the burdens of fulltime employment when they don't really need to. It's snowing out right now, and the highway is packed with cars going about 10 miles an hour. In those cars are people going home from work, tense and tired, and eagerly awaiting the chance to kick off their shoes and relax with their loved ones. (At least that is my fantasy.) And here I am, writing up the joys of not being out there, struggling to get home. I'm already here.

References

Gergen, K. J. (2009). *Relational being: Beyond self and community*. New York: Oxford University Press.

Gergen, M. (Ed.) (1988). *Feminist thought and the structure of knowledge*. New York: New York University Press.

Gergen, M. (2001). *Feminist reconstructions in psychology: Narrative, gender and performance*. Thousand Oaks, CA: Sage.

Gergen, M., & Gergen, K. J. (2012). *Playing with purpose: Adventures in performative social science*, Walnut Creek, CA: Left Coast Press.

Co-housing in California: One Retirement Model

Ellen Kimmel

arly in 1979, life changed dramatically for me. My 18-year marriage was ending just as I was approaching 40. All the big questions from young adulthood were back again—what was I going to do with my personal life and what did the future hold including retirement? I had an established career as a tenured full professor at the University of South Florida in Tampa, but everything else was up for grabs. Prior to the demise of my marriage, I had never anticipated anything but being part of a couple. Other than living on my own during my senior year in college, which hardly counted, my adult life to that point was lived as a married person with children. Once, organizers of a state conference of Women in Communication asked me to speak on "The Woman Alone." I pointed out the irony of the invitation because at the time I was living with a husband, four daughters, a friend from Europe, two dogs and two cats— poor qualifications to pontificate on living alone. Of course a full house was not to last forever—children and friend would leave, pets would expire— but still there would be two. So I had always thought.

It was a time of intense reflection. One thing became clear to me in 1979. I would never marry again, not just because the statistics were against it, but because I saw no reason to do so. Childbearing was over for me, and the legal complications of marriage/divorce were significant deterrents. That's not to say I expected never to have another intimate relationship, though it did not seem certain I would, either. My feeling then was that men might come and go while women friends could be forever.

Another realization from this life review was that among my happiest memories were the many summers spent at girls' camps.

The camaraderie was priceless. Participation in the Women's Movement of the 60s and 70s replicated this experience in which shared women's company at work and play brought me great joy and a sense of belonging. Thus blossomed the idea of gathering some close women friends to plan an adult version of summer camp, group housing/living in retirement. Being alone without intense involvement in a career was not the only option for the last stage of my life. Obviously, the idea of communal living, intentional communities, co-housing, etc. was not new, just new to me. People had been doing this in one form or another since people were people, but no one in my circle actually was engaged in this lifestyle.

Financial realities also began to hit me. Although I had been a full professor for five years, my salary was modest, to say the least (salary discrimination remained to the end of the century on my campus [see Kimmel, 2007]), and I worried that I would never be able to afford a comfortable retirement. The divorce yielded a very small settlement, and there were college educations still to provide for (jointly). I had no expectation of a grand inheritance from my parents. As it turned out they actually gifted me with financial independence for themselves, but there was exactly one month's expenses left in their bank account when my mother died. My grandparents lived into their 90s (as did my parents) which left me with the further thought that I might have a long life to support in retirement. Sharing housing and other costs could address these concerns as well as provide a "family" for the later years.

With all these thoughts circulating in my head, I sat down to write out some advantages to co-housing and some various approaches to living with friends in retirement, raising as many questions along the way as I could think of. I immediately drove to Gainesville, Florida to visit my friend there to bounce off these loosely forming ideas with her. This led to our inviting a close friend of hers on the law school faculty at Florida State to help us chart a path that included addressing legal issues that would arise.

The period from the spring of 1979 to January 2, 2002 encompassed the long journey that culminated in three friends and myself purchasing a 4500-foot, 1887 Victorian house in Santa Cruz, CA. This story describes the journey as it has been lived by me to date. It's broken into stages of the process, namely, forming the group, finding and purchasing the property, and moving in and learning to live together. The last stage is ongoing so the story is incomplete. The narrative is limited to my personal vantage point, and I am not speaking for the other members of our group who have their own histories and thoughts about our project.

Forming the Group

In my case this critical task took several years. For my 40ish age mates in 1979, many of them also academics, retirement seemed a sort of fantasy. Many envisioned dropping in their tracks. Retire? Never! Nonetheless, my Gainesville friend was willing to look at this seriously (she was and still is married) as was another close married friend in Tampa. We had a number of rather concrete ideas, all of which involved including partners (female or male). Always, though, I saw the core of the group to be women friends, single or coupled. Interestingly, the responses to my suggesting the possibility of co-housing to women friends and acquaintances were and still are consistent. Actually there are two major reactions: Wow, what a great idea! or Not for me, I like my privacy too much! Over the years, numberless women of all ages have added that they had talked about sharing housing with good women friends. However, it's no surprise most if not all hadn't/won't act on it. It takes a lot of persistence and planning (and for younger women it also requires an admission that one is or will be getting older and might retire).

We love our friends, but can we live with them? This is an obvious question to ask. Exploring core values is critical. For example, how important is maintaining good health? Staying intellectually engaged? Keeping financially solvent, etc.? What are shared interests and habits? How do potential housemates deal with money, family, friends? How do they solve problems and deal with conflict? How much togetherness, aloneness do they feel most comfortable with, etc.?

By 1988 our group included three of the four women and their partners who eventually found and bought the property. Along the way, life changes precluded those in my original circle from participating. This is to be expected. The group was not closed to adding other members, and several considered joining us along the way, but only one made the commitment in the end. Thus, I would venture to say a group has to be acknowledged as fluid until they sign a contract (mortgage). In 2002, our final group included a single woman, two women with partners—one male and one female— and a married couple. There were 4 shares of 25% each with the 3 women holding 25% (their partners had no financial investment) and the married couple one 25% share.

Finding/Creating the Physical Plant

From 1979 until 1988, the thought of the original group was to buy land (one of that group had a gorgeous piece south of Gainesville) and build a sort of pod structure with a central space for communal living (dining, kitchen, library) and bedrooms/private space arranged around the central structure. Alternatively, we considered buying a condo or apartment building and reconfiguring it so there would be private bed-sitting areas and communal living areas. From 1988 on we expanded our search to include large plantation style homes in the south, buying an island off the coast of Florida or other warm spots, building or buying a mountain home in Colorado, renovating a New England mansion, exploring N. California (too expensive), and even buying land and building in Arkansas. We were talking about buying or building a conference center that would be converted into our retirement home as we began to reach that stage. Ours was a prolonged search that waxed and waned as we had time to travel in ones and twos to look at and think about various properties. We established a loose set of criteria for locating our home: a university nearby for a library and cultural stimulation, reasonable health facilities, good access to airports (we're a wandering bunch), reasonable climate, and enough space for us to live comfortably. Of course affordability was a factor, though we were vague about that since there was uncertainty how many, if any, would join us once we had a concrete prospect.

In the end, the fates conspired in our favor and the house "found" us. However, as Pavlov said, discoveries come to the prepared mind and ours after so many years certainly were prepared.

We were all in California a week before the 2001 APA meetings in San Francisco in order to hike together in the several state parks near the city. We were staying at one of our group's home in Santa Cruz, and her partner had been my realtor for this project in Massachusetts. She (the former realtor) mentioned over coffee one morning that the house we'd been looking for was for sale nearby and the price had just been lowered dramatically (the ".com bomb" recession hit Santa Cruz properties hard). We jumped into our rental van and drove the mile over to Mission Hill to view the long-sought-after house. My first thought was "Our house!" This opinion has never changed. I still think this was a perfect choice after living here for almost eight years. Of course it's not perfect, but given all the options we considered, this was as close as I think we could have come. And the town IS perfect, culturally rich, (among other things, home of UC Santa Cruz) friendly, geographically stunning and (for me) offers an ideal climate.

A word about the house itself seems in order. It sits on a corner lot one block from the city center facing a lovely, well-maintained park that fronts on the Mission of Santa Cruz. In fact the house was built on top of what had been a dormitory for the Indians who were kept (enslaved) here. If we dig deep enough, a roof tile from the dormitory will surface. The Willey House (Mr. Willey built it in 1887) is of Eastlake style with redwood construction. It is rather imposing with 3 stories and an attic stacked on top. The big blue "box's" appearance is softened by extensive porches on the first two floors, with columns and railings in contrasting white. No disputing that the first encounter with it produces a dramatic effect. It's not uncommon to note visitors (strangers) taking pictures of the house, and various local artists have painted it. I love the location, and the fact that people know and have a connection with the house. It made moving here for me, at least, less anonymous, linking us with the history of the town. It's been on two fund-raising tour of homes, and so many visitors entered with the comment that they've always wanted to see inside the house they pass by so often (it's long south side is on Mission Street, a main east-west artery).

The first floor consists of a large entryway, with a handsome walnut staircase and large stained glass window as the main features. The spacious living room has a fireplace and is filled with light due to many large windows. This room is open to the formal redwood-wainscoted dining room with a built-in redwood buffet and a fireplace. It has a south facing solarium that opens from inside to heat the room. The living and dining rooms have full sized pocket doors to enclose them so multiple activities can occur simultaneously. The kitchen is less grand, but has two ample pantries and a back enclosed porch. The ceilings are 12 feet high on the first floor, affording lots of high shelf space (ladders, please). The first floor begs for events, and so far we have obliged. On the second floor are 3 bedrooms of varying size and 1 and ½ baths (no bathroom on the first floor!). There is a large common room used as office, yoga and TV room. It's the warmest room in the house because it, too, has a solarium that produces great heat when the sun is shining. The third floor has three more bedrooms, two bathrooms and an open sitting space. The attic is an attic... properly full with two chimneys sticking out near its steeply pointed roof.

Another attractive feature is the semi-attached cottage and an enclosed courtyard where the hot tub resides (our addition).

The cottage can be used for housing renters (now) and live-in help when we begin to need assistance beyond daily help (later).

Over time we've decided to allocate one bedroom to each "co-housie" (our term for each other) with the smaller bed-rooms serving as office/sitting rooms that are mainly used by the person(s) whose bedroom is nearest, but the rooms are for every-one to sit in, practice music, or use for their guests. Each bedroom has its advantages: one is by far the largest with a bench in front of 3 dormer windows to look out on the park and the beautiful Mission Holy Cross Church, but it's on the 3rd floor, another has a half bath, and one is in the back, small but with fewer windows therefore more walls for hanging artwork, and less traffic noise.

As might be expected of a Victorian-era house, it is a bit shy on closet and storage space other than in the kitchen, and it's inconvenient not having a first-floor bath. We do have a large corrugated high ceiling garage that holds bicycles, surfboards, paints, suitcases, etc., and there is space under the entire house for storage, but it has a dirt floor and is damp. Still, it's good for storing some things such as Christmas decorations, glassware, etc. There is no air conditioning, though that's rarely needed given our cool coastal climate. But otherwise we received it in excep-tional condition for a 124-year-old structure. Subsequent to the earthquake of 1989, the previous owner updated and upgraded everything, floors, walls, wiring, plumbing, kitchen, baths, zoned gas hydronic central heating, internal vacuum cleaner, built-in speakers in the common rooms, steel reinforcements in all the railings, etc., and he made the house even more earthquake resis-tant and energy efficient. I worried about the street noise, but it ranges from not noticeable to tolerable even at peak traffic times (not past 9:30pm). We completely redid the garden to contain a formidable vegetative wall along a major street to diminish traffic noise and pollution.

We completed the purchase of the house January 2, 2002. Prior to that we worked hard with two lawyers to craft a 21-page legal document, a Memorandum of Agreement (MOA), which was recorded with the Santa Cruz County Clerk of Courts. Not recorded was a set of tentative House Rules that covered such things as guests, pets, smoking, etc. In the MOA we laid out all the considerations the lawyers and we could think of to live legally as tenants–in-common. One must work within individual state guidelines, in our case the often quirky California laws, to form an entity to own property jointly as unrelated adults. Because we did not have the cash to fund a legally more desirable Limited Liability Corporation (LLC), that could buy and hold title to the house, we had to go this route. Fortunately, in California there are many unrelated adults sharing ownership of housing, so that tenants-in-common is very common device. There also are plenty of lawyers expert in this field. Unfortunately, we were unaware of this latter fact and did not use such an expert to help us write the MOA and that led to difficulties when the composition of the group changed in 2008. We did hire one to help with this transition and subsequently to revise the MOA to address the deficiencies of the original document.

Moving In and Learning to Live Together

This process has been bumpy, very prolonged, and is still far from completion. Our first challenge was the immediate occupancy of the house in January 2002. None of the partners had yet retired, and the local partner was heading off to Washington, D. C. for 6 months. I was not due to retire until August, 2003 which meant we'd be leaving our new house empty for at least 6, more likely 18, months with no one onsite to oversee it. Because the original financing we'd counted on fell through at the last minute and delayed the closing, we could not advertise to rent the place until the fall quarter was almost over. Even so, something like 23 potential renters responded with interest to our ad. Our local owner had to hold a group interview to move quickly. We decided to accept the offer from a group of 10 male undergraduates who prepared a portfolio of bios and claimed to be members of a service organization. I flew out and helped with the follow up interview with a couple of the students' parents who assured us they would come over from San Jose and clean for their boys every weekend. Not. What a snow job! The students' 18-month tenancy was an unmitigated nightmare. They belonged to a party central fraternity, came and went noisily at all hours, held constant drunken parties, often leaning over our wraparound balconies to throw up or worse, and never disposed of their mountains of garbage. One party attendee put a fist or elbow into the original stained glass window in the entry causing a $3500 repair. (We insisted they pay immediately which they did—they were rich kids.)

We survived! My job during the first 6 months of this horror was to "make nice" via phone calls and e-mails to the upset neighbors, and, once our local partner got back into town, she made continuous trips over to the house to get the boys' raucous behavior under control. The aftermath of the renters' departure was some miffed if not hostile neighbors and a very costly cleanup both in labor and money. The up side of the renting fiasco was we were thousands of dollars richer, which enabled us to pay off a side loan made with the previous owner.

In June, 2003 we finally took possession of our house. The local co-owner rented her house in town and moved in with her partner lock, stock and barrel. I retired that August and my partner and I drove a Ryder truck, towing my car on a trailer behind, across country to start my new life. What an adventure! It was a very exciting time to see the long- held dream begin to materialize. Once in, we began to merge our possessions and engage in a decorating mania. My possessions were far fewer than my co-housie's because I had never lived in an old house and owned few pieces that would fit in our Victorian. Thus, most of my modern furnishings were distributed to children, students, friends, or the Salvation Army before I left Florida.

Moving is a two-part act. Going to California was the first act, but I did not complete the leaving part right away. I listed my Florida home for rent, thinking it would be nice to keep a warm place for the group to retreat to in the winter. But that did not pan out. No one was renting a house in 2003-4 when they could get cheap money to buy (remember?) Also, Florida is a jungle and will soon eat one's home if left alone. After a year of sitting empty under overhanging live oaks on the Hillsborough River gathering mildew, I abandoned Plan A and sold the house. Admittedly, it took me several more years to empty a storage unit with the last of my Florida treasures and break the final material ties to my home of 35 years. Emotional ties were something else. My partner remained behind, a big surprise. He never made the move west as we often had talked about after the Santa Cruz purchase. Happily, we have maintained our relationship (now in its 26th year), so that I get to Florida several times a year to see him and visit old friends.

Despite the disappointment of my sweetie's not joining me, the first years in Santa Cruz were busy and delightful. My co-housie and I and at times her partner stripped off all the frou frou wallpaper and painted every room in the house, ceilings, medallions, crown moldings and all, and tackled some outside painting as well (as mentioned previously, the house has many porches, railings and columns). After coffee and exercise first thing in the morning, I donned my paint clothes and started in. Frequent trips to the local hardware store made me a familiar figure, and the clerks often inquired about the pigeons I must be raising (I'm not the neatest painter...). My co-housie did a great deal of entertaining which enabled me to meet many people and join in the preparations and clean-up if I tired of painting. Santa Cruz is situated on the north side of Monterrey Bay and surrounded by redwood-covered low mountains. I joined the local Sierra Club and spent (still do) many Saturdays hiking the environs (we have 3 state parks in the town, plus county parks and beaches to walk). I love movies and there are 19 screens within 5-6 minutes walk from the house, with 8 of them showing independent and foreign films. Heaven. I joined the UCSC Women's Club and later UC Santa Cruz's chapter of Life Long Learners where I made many friends and enjoyed all sorts of activities and adventures. This has to sound like a Chamber of Commerce pitch, but not only are there outdoor and organizational activities, but this is one of the most culturally rich places in the country. And if one expands that to San Jose 40 minutes away and San Francisco 80 minutes away, it's almost overwhelming.

For 3 years (2003 -2006), there were 2 co-owners and one partner living in our house. Over that period, we rented the cottage and the entire 3rd floor plus one room on the second floor where our bedrooms were to a variety of undergraduate, graduate and non-student adults. I had expected we would always rent the cottage until we needed it in our declining years. But I never anticipated having renters inside our home as a permanent feature beyond the first transition year. However, the income was seductive. Rentals in this town are at a premium, and people pay as much for a room with kitchen privileges as they would for a house in other parts of the country.

With only 2 of the 5 co-owners living in the house, there was a natural tension around renters. The three people not enjoying the house wanted the income to offset the burden of supporting a place they could not yet enjoy full time. We living in the house were doing all the work and enduring all the hassle of living with a never-ending stream of strangers, some very nice, others quite difficult. Plus we were paying rent, albeit at a discounted rate (in addition to the monthly payment all co-owners paid.) When the rental market hit a slump, there was pressure for us to work harder to keep all the rooms filled. Advertising for, interviewing, vetting, settling in, cleaning up after renters was a constant chore, in addition to contending with the daily inconvenience of sharing kitchen and other (e.g., baths) space with strangers. No running around in bras and panties for us.

In the summer of 2006, our local partner placed her other home on the market just as the housing bubble was beginning its precipitous decline. She needed to sell her house because she had been renting it for 3 years to live with me and the tax law requires living in a home 2 of the last 5 years to escape paying capital gains taxes. No offers over the summer meant that in the fall she had to move back into her other house, leaving me as the only owner to occupy our home. This was a very stressful event for our whole group. Her partner had not enjoyed our tenure with all the renters and mourned her privacy. She earlier announced to the group that she had decided she did not want to continue the arrangement. Thus, she was happy that financial considerations had forced a departure. I was confronted with both the loss of my companions and few furnishings. Most of the furniture, carpets, artwork, kitchenware, etc. was theirs. I bought a few of their pieces, and they kindly left me a few pieces, but the place was pretty empty.

This situation continued for 3 long years. I spent thousands of dollars on re-furnishing and decorating once again to make the place home-like. However, I had to fill every bedroom but mine with renters, and I thus endured. Of course, life in Santa Cruz is so filled with activities and friends that it was still great, if not at all what I'd imagined on the housing front.

In the fall of 2008 the composition of our group changed. Three co-owners bought out the 4th partner. As early as January, 2006, that partner realized that she was not compatible with the rest of the group, a realization she had not shared with the other partners, in part out of concern for me. She tried to devise ways to buffer us all from the financial hit that would be caused by her departure, but no workable solution could be found. The tension was enormous because everyone stood to lose money and a lot of it. Further, the negotiations were made even more difficult due to the failings of our original MOA. The exit strategy for anything but death of a partner was vague and contradictory. Those staying had to find a way to let our partner off the hook and yet not box ourselves into a financial load we could not afford. Various attempts on both sides to find a replacement 4th partner were unsuccessful (why would anyone want to buy into a place with 3 close friends who could always out vote them?). Our settlement was a compromise that worked, but was not satisfactory to anyone in the group. This illustrates what is probably the main drawback to co-housing—life throws unexpected wrenches in our plans, and partnerships must adapt. However, the same holds for marital or business partnerships that dissolve and leave assets to deal with.

The summer of 2009 marked yet another phase of the moving in process. A member retired and began her gradual migration part time to Santa Cruz. However, she brought few possessions. In the summer of 2010 another owner retired with all her possessions to be integrated. To date she also is spending about 40-50% of her time in Santa Cruz, but it is her base since she sold her home back east.

Our moving-in phase has been about as awkward as it could be, but that is in part because of the differences in our ages and correlated times to retire as much as anything—a 10-year span from youngest to oldest can't be changed and in our case necessitates a much longer time to get settled. We are holding weekly house meetings via Skype to practice our group decision-making and to keep everyone apprised of the activities required to maintain a home. With only myself as the full time (10 of 12 months) person, it still falls on me to hold down the fort a lot of the time, while at the same time learning to share all decisions. We have discovered some unexpected differences in decorating tastes and various preferences, but that, too, is part of communal living. After 32 years since 1979, several realtors, 3 lawyers, 2 MOAs, and 4 mortgages (we have refinanced 3 times), I'm still hopeful that we'll eventually have a grand retirement and old age in our grand old Victorian.

Recommendations about forming the group.

As much as possible know well the people (owners' partners as well as the owners) you plan to live with. In our case, the owners, but less so the partners, knew each other for many years, worked together on APA committees and scholarly projects (all of us were academic psychologists, albeit from different universities located in the northeast and Florida), and played together. The playing included visiting each other's homes, rooming together at conferences, and domestic and foreign travel of the adventure variety (Nepal, Peru, Israel, Cambodia, Burma, N. Vietnam, Thailand, Trinidad, Tobago, Canada, Mexico, Patagonia, Switzerland, China, etc.). Travel especially affords opportunities to observe how people react under stress although it does not reveal how people live day to day. Knowing someone well does not guarantee that there will be no surprises when it comes to living together, but it helps to know enough to feel confident that one's future companions have good verbal and problem solving skills, are compatible, and enjoy many of the same activities.

Find group members who are planning retirements close in time, even if their ages vary, or, more to the point, whose expected move-in times are close together. I did not think this as important as it turned out to be, in part because my excitement that we could actually pull off the house purchase gave me tunnel vision.

Learn about each member's financial stability and ability to undertake this investment. This can be ascertained by holding frank discussions that include talking about financial planning for retirement. Share credit scores (they'll be revealed in the course of applying for the mortgage anyway).

Examine each potential member's money habits—from paying bills on time to seeing where they spend money.

Visit a person's home to see such things as how well things are maintained, organization, and tidiness, etc. as well as decorating tastes.

Test drive your group by sharing living quarters on vacations—rent a home and live together for some time.

I also recommend that each person obtain long-term care insurance unless s/he has assets that comfortably would cover any health problems.

About Criteria for Selecting the Property

The group must discuss this extensively. We explored all sorts of possibilities that met our general criteria. However, once I found what I thought was a great property that fulfilled them all and was a bit shocked at the reaction of some of those involved at the time: "Yuck, Arkansas! Who would even consider living there?" (Of course, I was born and raised in Tennessee…) We had never articulated that certain areas of the country were out of the question. I would strongly suggest that keeping an open mind and a willingness to keep the discussion ongoing are essential (true for finding any house). The greater the number of people involved, the more time and effort required is likely. Here's one area where majority rule cannot work—everyone must be happy.

Be persistent! That special place is there so don't give up! View it as a second home if the group does not intend to move in right away. This allows time to deal with currently owned property and to be very picky. If it is not necessary to rent immediately, here's a great opportunity to do a trial move in—check what possessions might work where. If the plan is to rent until the move in date, be careful! It helps in that case to select a location with a vigorous rental market. By any means do NOT rent to a gang of undergraduate boys, no matter how they go on about their service activities.

About Developing the MOA

There are experts out there to guide a group in drafting this document, so find one and use her or him. It's worth it. Look to the gay community for lawyers who specialize in the legalities of cohabitation and palimony because they have been owning property as unrelated adults forever.

Particularly attend to member exit strategies: death or withdrawal, default. etc. In the case of death, matters such as inheritance or possible replacement by a child or other family member of the deceased should be addressed. We have a "last person standing clause" in the MOA that stipulates that each of our wills decrees that the remaining partners have the right to stay in the house until the last one departs due to death or ill health. Only then will the house be sold and the proceeds distributed to heirs according to one's share. Further, the estate of the deceased partner is to pay off immediately its share of the mortgage and set aside funds to cover its share of any major expenses necessary to maintain the value of the house (new roof, flood repair, etc.). These are important measures to ensure remaining members will not be forced to leave their home. Of course, the mortgage will have to be refinanced, but for a lower amount.

Secondly, the MOA should be very clear about how a living partner may leave the group. The MOA should spell out unambig-uously the rights of both the departing and remaining owners. The first important fact to know is that a percent share is NOT worth as much as the percent of the assessed value of the house at the time the person wishes to leave. There is a discount for a share of a property that ranges from 20%–80%, depending on a variety of factors. The second fact is it's very difficult to sell a share—there is almost no market unless it is to a party who knows the remain-ing members well and there is a mutual desire to re-form the group with this new member. A stranger to the group would be foolish to buy into a situation where s/he potentially could be outvoted on any and every matter, depending on the MOA. Hypothetically, the original group could decide on such things as an expensive remodeling. In the unlikely event there is an interested buyer who is a stranger, the MOA should describe protections for the remaining owners from a person(s) who could lead to disruption of the communal life of the group. Owning collectively is like a marriage and the same concerns prevail. (See forming the group.)

The most likely buyer of the share is the remaining group. However, this might not be feasible financially, especially if there is a large mortgage and/ or large equity in the house. Be aware that any change in the ownership will necessitate re-financing and also may have property tax consequences (treated as a sale). Depending on the mortgage market, the remaining members might not qualify for a new mortgage, especially if they are retired and living on assets verses pensions. The departing owner may have to agree to have her/his name remain on the mortgage and, typically, be compensated (($1000-$2000 per year). The group in this case arranges to create a legal document that effectively absolves the departing member from any financial responsibility for the mortgage. Further, for credit purposes there is no debt attached to the name being left on the mortgage. Check with the lawyers on how to do this. We were able to refinance in part because 3 of the 4 of us were still employed and the other had a pension, plus we had a lot of equity in the house.

We failed to deal with the issue of renters in advance and that has led to various problems. If there are to be renters, the MOA should spell out such things as how many, for how long, etc., who is responsible to handle this, and if they would be compensated for this service.

About Moving in and Learning to Live Together

As mentioned earlier, the group should have a plan for moving in that aims to make this as simultaneous as possible. If that is not possible, then it's desirable to outline exactly how moving in at differing times will be accomplished and what the expectations are for all parties.

Allocation of individual and use of common space needs to be continuously deliberated. What seems a good plan may not work once the parties are living together. Our plans changed as time went on after the purchase. They are not yet fixed and can't be until the final moving in of everyone occurs. Even then, they must be flexible, responsive to changes in anyone's health or mobility. One specific suggestion about space is that if a member is living there, but not yet retired, her or his office should not be in the house, but at their place of employment.

Keep communicating, as painful as this sometimes can be. Smart people can figure out how to employ other than win-lose decision processes. Everyone has to feel valued and listened to. Everything about developing and maintaining good relationships goes for unrelated adults living together. There are plenty of advice books on this topic, so I won't belabor this point.

Final Word

I genuinely believe that my life is better for having close friends as living companions. That will become increasingly true as I age. If anyone asks should they live communally, I say, "Go for it!"

Reference

Kimmel, E.B. (2007). How did a nice girl like you...? In F.J. Crosby, M.S. Stockdale & S.A. Ropp (Eds.) *Sex discrimination in the workplace: Multidisciplinary perspectives.* (pp. 83-95).Malden, MA: Blackwell Publishing.

I Don't Knit, I'm No Gardener, but I Know How to Stay Busy

Florence L. Denmark

"Sooner or later I'm going to die, but I'm not going to retire."
- Margaret Mead -

In 1952, I began graduate work in psychology at the University of Pennsylvania. As a graduate assistant I was inspired by the words of the Department Chair, Robert A. Brotmarkle, who said, *"Remember the assistant of today is the professor of tomorrow."* I took his comment seriously, and following my doctorate in 1958, I began an academic career first at Hunter College and the Graduate School of the City University of New York (CUNY), and then was recruited by the Psychology Department at Pace University and officially retired in 2001 after serving 13 years as Chair of the department.

Was my life changed by an official retirement? Not really, except for major changes over the last year in my personal life, as noted below. I am actually busier than ever, with many friends and a larger than ever holiday card list. Fortunately, I am in good health and still have a lot of energy, even though not as much as I used to. In 2008, I had knee replacement surgery and while I was in pain at the time, I completely recovered and now I hardly ever remember I even had it.

Believe it or not, I am not, nor have I ever been a workaholic. I always find time to "play," taking advantage of all that New York has to offer, e.g., going to the theatre, the ballet, concerts, and enjoying many different restaurants with my friends and colleagues. I also do a lot of traveling.

My life, post-retirement, can be divided into four parts. One is my continuing involvement with psychology via Pace University;

another is my contributions to APA and other organizations; the third has to do with my work at the United Nations; and finally, my family relationships, including how I'm coping with recent, tragic events, the death of my daughter, Valerie, and then the loss of my dear husband, Bob. The fact that the section on my family is the last thing I will talk about here should not underscore their importance to me. While I may have officially retired from work, I will never retire from my family. Also, chronologically, the personal losses I have experienced came in the most recent period of my life.

Psychology via Pace University

When I officially retired from Pace, August 31st, 2001, I had been Chair of the department, as well as the Robert Scott Pace Distinguished Professor of Psychology. One year earlier I had decided to step down as Chair, but stayed on an extra year so that a search committee could find a new Chair from outside the department. I could have retired from Chair and gone back to the faculty, but I knew, in that case, no new position would be given to the department. Therefore, I believed that it was important for the department to recruit a Chair from outside. With the extra year, it gave the faculty time not only to recruit, but to get used to the idea that I would no longer be Chair, after 13 years. I was a good Chair, and could have continued after retirement, but felt that I had had enough.

I could have had nothing to do with any psychology related activities, but how many psychologists walk away completely from the field? Even those who were in full time positions at hospitals or clinics may "retire," but still have a part time practice. Ernest Hilgard was a prime example, a man who was still going into Stanford University every day, even when he was in his upper 90s.

At Pace, the department gave me an office and graduate assistants. In many ways they don't consider me retired. I have a mailbox alphabetically placed with the full time faculty, and a new title, Robert Scott Pace Distinguished Research Professor. Upon request, I agreed to teach a doctoral course in the history of psychology and agreed to continue to co-teach a Multicultural and Gender Issues class, with a colleague, June Chisholm, which we had been teaching for many years. In April 2002, I was presented with a Distinguished Faculty Achievement Award from Dyson College of Pace University. At Pace's commencement in 2010, I was given an Honorary Doctorate of Humane Letters.

My current schedule allows me to devote a fair amount of time to writing. I updated two of my textbooks in 2005, *Engendering Psychology: Women and Gender Revisited* (coauthored with Jeri Sechzer and Vita Rabinowitz), and a third edition of a women's studies text, *Women's Realities, Women's Choices*, which was written by the Hunter College Women's Studies Collective. The collective is now working on the 4th edition. In 2008, I published a second edition of *Psychology of Women: A Handbook of Issues and Theories* (coedited with Michelle Paludi). I also co-edited a book on international perceptions and experiences of violence, *International Perspectives on Violence*, and one on school violence, entitled *Violence in the Schools: A Cross-Cultural and Cross-National Perspective*.

I continue to travel, visiting far away children and going to many different countries, both for professional and personal reasons. I still take the time to work directly with students both as a professor and a mentor. Unlike my own graduate school years, many more women have entered the field of psychology, and I have been more than happy to assist them in their studies. I believe it is important that I serve as a role model and mentor for the coming generations.

APA and other Organizations

My involvement in the American Psychological Association (APA) as well as many other organizations has kept me connected to my colleagues throughout the world. I have not only long been an active participant in various APA divisions but I was President of APA's Division 35 (The Society for the Psychology of Women) in 1975, and in 1980 I was President of APA and National President of Psi Chi, so far the only President of both simultaneously. I have continued being active in APA's Division 35 and also Divisions 1 (Society for General Psychology) and 52 (International Psychology), two other divisions of which I served as President pre-retirement.

In 2001, I received an APA Presidential Citation for my contributions as a researcher, scholar, teacher, and leader. I received the 2004 American Psychological Foundation Gold Medal for Lifetime Achievement for Psychology in the Public Interest. The prestigious Ernest R. Hilgard Award for Career Contributions to General Psychology was also given to me in 2005 from the Society for General Psychology (Division 1). I also received the 2007 Raymond D. Fowler Award for Outstanding Member Contribution to APA, and other awards, as well.

I am very proud to have The Society for the Psychology of Women award for Contributions to Women and Aging named after me. Its purpose is to recognize scholarly or public policy accomplishments, or both, in the area of women and aging. This award was presented for the first time at the 2010 APA convention. The 2011 awardee is Mary Gergen, one of the co-editors of the book in which this chapter appears.

I have also been active in NYSPA (the New York State Psychological Association). Although I was a long-time member and past-president of NYSPA, I could not serve as a NYSPA division officer while I served on the New York State Board for Psychology. Once my term on the State Board ended in 2005, I made up for lost time and was elected President of DOWI (Division of Women's Issues), the Social Issues Division, and currently the Academic Division. I am active in all three of these divisions. This year, I received the Distinguished Service Award from NYSPA.

I am also active in the International Council of Psychologists (ICP), the International Association for Applied Psychology (IAAP), and the Eastern Psychological Association (EPA). I had served as President of ICP and EPA.

Psychology and the United Nations

I feel it is important to make psychologists from the United States aware of international psychology, to show that it is not just a US discipline. For that reason, I have become involved with the United Nations through the International Council of Psychologists and am one of the founders of Division 52 (International Psychology) of APA. Psychology is in a position to influence the work of the NGOs (Non Governmental Organizations), although at times, it is a slow incremental process. These NGOs are active in committee work with other NGOs and serve in a consultative status with the UN. I have also created international awareness through writing articles and basic texts that included perspectives from and information about international psychology.

I have made wonderful lifelong friends through my involvement in many organizations, including the International Council of Psychologists. I have made friends from Italy, Australia, India, England, Taiwan, and Japan, to name a few. My husband, Bob Wesner, an academic book publisher, used to call this our "travel club" because not only did we present scholarly papers at the meetings, but we had the opportunity to visit different countries where the annual meetings were held. The International Council of Psychologists is the group where we developed friendships, a small group where we had the chance to present papers together, to visit in each other's homes, to know one another's families—to really see what it is like to be a psychologist in their community.

I am currently the main International Council of Psychologists Non-governmental Organization (NGO) representative to the United Nations and am also an International Association of Applied Psychologists (IAAP) UN representative. I completed six years as chair of the United Nations Committee on Ageing and currently serve on the Executive Committees of Ageing, Family, and Mental Health. I chaired three very successful Psychology Days at the United Nations in October 2007. In 2007, I was elected to the National Academies of Practice as a distinguished scholar member. I received the Elder Award at the APA National Multicultural Conference in 2009. Then, in 2009 I was honored by St. Francis College as a pioneer in gender studies and international psychology. In 2011 at the APA convention, I received the Award for Outstanding Lifetime Contributions to Psychology.

Coping with Loss

Post retirement, I have dealt with many difficult experiences in my personal life, but none more terrible than the two experienced between July of 2009 and April of 2010. In 2009, I lost my daughter, Valerie, when she died following surgery for colorectal cancer. She was 50 when she died, but 49 when the cancer was discovered. Since there was no family history, and she had no symptoms, she had not undergone a colonoscopy, which is recommended beginning at age 50. (In 1998 I lost another daughter, Pamela, to Hepatitis C.) Losing a second daughter was a terrible tragedy, and less than a year later, in April 2010, I lost my husband, Bob. He passed away peacefully in his sleep in the early hours of April 13th. Although Bob suffered from Parkinson's Disease, and had a health aide to assist him for several years, when I awoke early that morning, Bob was gone—a result of heart failure, not a heart attack. His heart just stopped beating. Although his death was peaceful and painless, it was certainly a shock to me. I can't believe he is gone. I always remember the fortune that came along with my weight on a penny scale when I was 13 years old. It read "life with love is like a long, bright summer day. Such a love will be yours." How true. Bob really was my soul mate.

Until the day Bob died he was active at the UN, socialized with family and friends, traveled a great deal, read a lot, and was mentally alert. Bob appreciated and encouraged my achievements as I did his. Up to the time of his death, Bob was busy making future plans. According to his wishes, Bob was cremated and his remains were interred in the South Florida Military Cemetery on May 25th, 2010. While this past year had been extremely tough for me, I was comforted by the outpouring of love and support from family, friends, and colleagues from across the country and the world.

The pride I have felt in my children, step children, and grandchildren has eased the pain I have felt from these losses. My son, Richard, has a CPA and a Masters degree in Taxation and works for the Internal Revenue Service in Washington D.C. My oldest step daughter, Kathy, also has a CPA and works for the State of Washington in Seattle. Kathy has two children. Chandra, the oldest, is an actuary, and Matt finished a six year stint in the Navy and will be going back to college in the fall. My stepson Michael is an Associate Professor of Psychology, as is his wife Josephine Tan, on the faculty at Lakehead University, in Thunder Bay, Canada. Wendy, my younger step daughter, is a Registered Nurse in Chicago and has two school aged children, Bradley and Jackie. I am very proud of all of them but I only wish they all lived closer geographically.

Concluding Thoughts on Retirement

What do you wish you had known before you reached this stage in your career, in terms of retirement?

Something I didn't expect early on was how much I would still be working while I was considered "retired." Although I did officially retire in 2001, since that time I have been just as active in the Pace University Psychology department, teaching graduate students, at the United Nations and at other organizations such as ICP, IAAP, and various APA divisions. I have continued to take on new responsibilities and am working just as much as I did prior to my "retirement." I do this because I enjoy what I do.

Although I have many friends in New York City, I didn't realize that my close relatives would live so far away and how much I would wish they were nearer. My sister and nieces are in Florida; my sister and brother-in-law are in Milwaukee; and children and step children range from Washington, D.C., to Chicago, Seattle, and Canada. This past year has been very tough and I wish that my family were closer. I never visualized being without my husband and the one daughter who lived in the New York area.

Additionally, as I have gotten older, some people have begun to treat me as if I am frail and delicate, showing excessive concern for my well being. While this level of care is appreciated, I wish those people would understand that age is only a number. I still feel young and energetic and ready to work hard and take on new adventures. I did not expect to be treated in such a manner. This is very important to me as the attitudes toward older women are something which I have focused on for much of my career.

What do you wish you had done differently in terms of retirement?
There is nothing I can think of that I wish I had done differently and I am very happy with where I am in retirement. I have continued to work, learn, mentor, and enjoy the benefits of being con-

nected to so many interesting people in the field. I have traveled and gone to conferences throughout the world. I have continued to write papers, present, and publish, ensuring the growth of the field. At the same time, I have balanced this with taking time for myself to travel for pleasure, enjoy the company of family and friends, and do other things I enjoy such as going to the theatre and the ballet. I am not required to go to department or University meetings, which gives me more time and flexibility to do other things I enjoy doing.

What are you happy about in terms of what you anticipated and did (or are doing) to prepare for retirement?

I was very happy that I took out long-term healthcare insurance for both Bob and me, which covers care at home, as well as in a nursing home if needed. This was very useful when my husband was diagnosed with Parkinson's Disease and long term care paid for his health aide. I also ensured that I was still involved in many different activities that I enjoy doing and maintaining activity in areas that would allow me to travel. Keeping busy is a lifeline for me.

Additionally, I have stayed active in my mentoring activities to keep a connection with younger generations of psychologists/ professionals. As an academic, one of the greatest satisfactions I get is mentoring students and new faculty members and other newcomers to the field of psychology. As a feminist, I feel it is particularly important to mentor young women entering the field, who are often unaware of how to maneuver through the politically charged atmosphere of graduate level psychology departments, as well as how to succeed in the job market once they complete their degrees. I have also mentored those who were interested in how to get their papers published, including writing and publishing papers with my graduate assistants, and those who wished to be involved in organizations. The importance of collaboration, whether in publishing papers or protesting against social injustice, cannot be overstated. I believe it is the job of the older generations to guide younger generations to continue the great work that has been done in the field and ensure the prosperity of the field for the future.

Words of wisdom for others envisioning their post-career futures: There is no right or wrong answer as to what one should do upon retirement. Some of you won't retire, others will partially retire, and some will completely leave the discipline of psychology. The main thing is to do what is right for you, not what is right for someone else. Regardless of your choice, I hope you will take time to mentor others and help them on the road to success. Above all, make happy memories so that when you look back at your life, you won't feel regret.

On Vacation Until Further Notice

Lillie Weiss

"Twenty years from now you will be more disappointed by the things you didn't do than the ones you did. So throw off the bowlines. Sail away from the safe harbor. Catch the trade winds in your sail. Explore. Dream. Discover."
- Mark Twain -

In May 2006 my husband and I closed down our psychology practice of many years. If people had told me a couple of years earlier that I would be retiring soon, I would have said that they were crazy. I felt we had an ideal situation: we owned a lovely office condo that was like our second home, we had gradually cut back our work hours to only three days a week, we set our own schedule and we chose whom we worked with very carefully. We loved what we did and knew what a meaningful undertaking and privilege our work was. We had the best of both worlds—working only a few days a week and having plenty of leisure time, being our own bosses in an environment we loved. Why retire? What would we do? We certainly could make a much better contribution using our skills and talents as psychologists than doing any type of volunteer job. What else would we do? And what could be more rewarding than what we did? Not only did I like being a therapist, I also enjoyed my other activities: teaching, writing, research, and the whole gamut of options available to psychologists.

This is the story of my transition from being a psychologist for nearly four decades to a new life. Like most major life decisions, it doesn't have a clean beginning, middle, or end, and like other life changes, it involves several phases: the decision process, the in-between zone, and the new beginning.

▍The Decision Process

"If you don't know where you are going, any road will get you there." - Lewis Carroll

It began with a sudden urge to purge. We found ourselves cleaning out everything in the house, starting with the garage and tackling every room after that, borrowing our neighbors' trash bins to throw out stuff we hadn't used for years and donating two roomfuls of boxes to charity. Next we attacked the office, again tossing, shredding, donating, simplifying. We knew a big change was coming, that behavior often precedes conscious thought. We were clearing space—for what? I learned many lessons from our purging experience, mainly that we need to empty space first before deciding what to put into it, a good metaphor for what was to follow. Before I retired, a client gave me this advice from a retiree: "Don't do anything for a year until you decide what you want to do. Don't make any commitments." That has proved very helpful, and I would recommend it to others. After our clearing out process, there followed a series of synchronistic events that helped me make the decision to retire.

At different points in my career whenever I reached a plateau, I would search for new things to do within my field. It was with this in mind that I walked into Border's Bookstore a few weeks following the major cleaning spree. Retirement was certainly not on my mind then. I walked out with two books—one by Julia Cameron on writing and the other on simplifying your life. I had already read Julia Cameron's *The Artist's Way* (1992) years ago and for months had used the basic ingredients of her program to stimulate creativity—"morning pages," three pages of daily handwritten stream-of-consciousness writing every morning and a weekly "artist date," a visit to a gallery, museum, or any other art venue—but had given up the practice long ago. I started writing again every morning and waited for the Muse to make her appearance. She arrived in the form of an old college friend whom I hadn't seen in years and who took me on an artist date that changed my life.

Chaja, an avid art lover, had the Scottsdale Museum of Contemporary Art as the first stop on her itinerary. We first went to a photography exhibit of people on the fringes of life shot in the "bowels of the earth," those dark places you don't want to enter. I was both entranced and horrified by some of the images. "Would you want these in your home?" she asked. "No," I said. I liked the pictures but didn't want them in my home. I wanted—what? "You want serenity," she said, as though reading my thoughts, reflecting what I was feeling. Yes, I loved people and was curious about them and their behavior, but I wanted to deal with their beauty and creativity, not their depression and distress.

After viewing several exhibits, we wandered into the gift shop where the most beautiful Italian music was playing, and I felt tears come to my eyes. I immediately bought the CD and realized how many more things I enjoyed besides studying people and how much more there was to explore. A sign immediately caught my eye: *"Twenty years from now, you will be more disappointed by the things you didn't do than by the ones you did."* It encouraged you to "Explore. Dream. Discover." Looking at the words and being with Chaja, I saw nearly four decades of my life pass by in a flash. There were so many memories of when we attended the university together. I had two majors then—Psychology and English Literature. I had focused on one: might it be time to spend more time on the other? I had been fortunate to have been in a career I loved for nearly 40 years, but there was so much more to learn— so many other worlds to explore! I was ready to let go. I picked up a yellow luggage tag: *"On vacation until further notice."* "One day soon I'll put this on my office door," I said, which I did when I retired a year later.

After the "artist date," I used the exercises in my last book, *Therapist's Guide to Self-Care* (2004), to redesign my life and decide what to keep and what to discard. I wanted to keep all my options open, to maintain my license but have the freedom to explore other venues. I also didn't want to spend any more 110 degree heat summers. To do that I would give up the clinical work but not the other aspects of psychology. I would still be a psychologist but no longer a therapist, not if I wanted to pursue new projects—vocational or leisure—and not if I wanted to be gone for long periods. Looking back, doing the exercises from my own book was my goodbye to therapy. I was transitioning from patient-care to self-care, and retirement was the ultimate self-care. "Retirement" had such negative connotations: retire from what? –the world? –life? "Retirement" meant I'd never work again, a "sabbatical" meant I would, and "on vacation until further notice" was the most open-ended and freeing.

Other synchronistic events helped with the decision. We were staying at a B&B where I was enjoying the beautiful scenery and my husband was taking pictures. "I know what we can do," I said. "We can travel to beautiful places. I can write about them, and you can take pictures." When we went in for breakfast, seated by us was a famous travel writer couple—he was talking pixels and mega pixels, and she was taking notes. They were *working* while we were....enjoying our breakfast! It took several of these events to make me realize I didn't want a new career—I just didn't want to *work*—at least for now!

Planning for Retirement

> *"Tell me, what is it you plan to do with your one wild and precious life?"*   - Mary Oliver

The next step was to develop a timetable for easing out of one role into another. After talking to our financial advisor, we chose a date we wanted to be celebratory and memorable—falling on the week of my husband's 64th birthday and our 40th wedding anniversary. Coming up with a financial plan was very difficult. A synchronistic event at that time was being asked to give a talk on money and psychologists. It forced me to make a plan even though I had no idea what our expenses would be, what a summer home would cost, whether we would work in the future or what exactly we would be doing. We wanted enough funds to have the freedom to travel, attend workshops, and live comfortably. The only advice I can give is to talk to a financial planner and to overestimate what you will need. I am glad we did both as this has been a more frugal retirement than we had anticipated. We couldn't foresee the recession that followed.

We had a full year to close down our practice, sell our office condo, find a summer home, and think about what we would do when we retired. We found a few articles helpful in providing guidelines on professional practice transitions (Koocher, 2003; McGee, 2003). We had to make many decisions: when to tell clients, when to stop accepting new ones, when and how to inform others, how to make a living while phasing out, and so on. And of course there was grief work involved. Although there are some hard-and-fast rules, almost everything required judgment, and everyone says goodbye in his or her own way. I made no commitments for what I would do immediately after I retired, but I explored some ideas and put them in an envelope titled "Ideas to Explore" into which I still put notes of paper whenever I think of anything to do—career or leisure-wise. There were moments of anxiety, but I trusted I would figure it out later.

I had always relied on "right brain" phenomena as much as my analytical skills to make important decisions. Besides synchronistic events, my nightly dreams came in handy, and two of my books have been on their usefulness. When I was trying to figure out what to do after retirement, I dreamt that my friend, a talented homemaker, arranged a meeting for me to assess my domestic interests. There were some Scrabble tiles on the floor. At the end, she looks at me kindly, affectionately, and tells me I'm hopeless. I wake up realizing I have no real hobbies besides psychology—psychology and words. When I received an offer to conduct some training workshops when I retired, all night long I kept hearing the song "My Nightmare" in my dreams.

Post Retirement

"All changes, even the most longed for, have their melancholy; for what we leave behind us is part of ourselves; we must die to one life before we can enter another." - Anatole France

No matter how carefully you plan, life is full of surprises. I vowed to put nothing on my calendar for a year—and immediately got called for jury duty. Everything had gone smoothly in our plans so far. We sold our office and were building a summer place in Flagstaff, which was supposed to be ready months before our retirement date and where we were going to move our office condo furniture. The date for completion kept getting postponed, and we found ourselves with an office load of furniture and no place to store it—so we moved everything to our home in Scottsdale. Meanwhile our son and a friend moved in with us temporarily, and it was—to put it mildly—crowded. We had chairs and boxes everywhere. I call this period "Living in the Land of Temporary and the House of Chairs" or "Not Quite What I Was Planning." Finding ourselves with a houseful of chairs, 110 degree heat outside, discovering roof rats in our yard, and no place to escape, we did what any two mature adults would do—we ran away from home! We spent as much time as we could in Flagstaff watching our summer house being—or more accurately, *not* being—built. This was living in limbo, and "one day at a time" took very concrete meaning. Others have described a similar period of retirement transition, whether it is the chaos of moving, going on "The Trip" or any activity that engrosses you so completely that you don't have time to think about the life you left behind. This phase has been described as "the narrows" (Davidson, 2008) or "the fertile void" (Levine, 2005), that seeming emptiness where a great deal happens under the surface. The physical upheaval simply reflected what was underneath. "One day we'll have a routine, and things will get back to normal,"

I told a retired friend. "In retirement, this is normal," she countered. "There is no routine."

Maybe things have to get more complicated before they get simpler, but our summer home was finally ready, our Scottsdale home was free of chairs, and we started living in the "House of Now." As I look back over the past five years, every day has been different. My day usually consists of an early morning swim, "morning pages," reading the paper, and a walk sometime later that day. I try to limit errands and chores to only a few hours a week (not always successfully), and each day I decide what I want to do that day—unless I have made specific plans to be somewhere. I jokingly refer to my "Drop In University," where I can "drop in" (or drop out) without any consequences: formal and informal classes, lectures, exhibits, and other events, most of which are free or at a minimal cost, short-term, and do not have the rain-or-shine requirements of the working world. I put these on my calendar—with a question mark. I read a great deal, visit friends and family, see movies and shows, and do many of the leisure activities I did prior to retirement. I continue to explore, though most of my exploration is local and regional rather than traveling to far-off places.

For the first three years of retirement, I left my old life almost completely and did not do anything of a professional nature. However, I have since reconnected with long-time friends and colleagues and have rejoined our local psychological association as well as some new ones, as much for social reasons as for learning. The only professional activities I have engaged in since I retired have been reviewing an author's book proposal for my publisher, preparing a PowerPoint workshop for our local association, teaching a seminar on journaling to psychiatry residents, and writing this chapter.

Some Lessons I have Learned—and am Still Learning

"We must be willing to get rid of the life we've planned, so as to have the life that is waiting for us." - Joseph Campbell

Get a life before you retire. One of the most helpful books I read prior to retiring was Ralph Warner's *Get a Life* (2000). He suggests several "commodities" besides money to invest in before taking the big step: curiosity, health, friends, family, and meaningful interests. If your entire life revolves around work, then your life stops when your work does. I am glad I did much of my traveling and other items on my "bucket list" then and did not wait for "some day." Plan for the future but live in the present. Life is short: I look at the obituaries in the paper daily and see names of people my age and younger.

Design the life you want and figure out a way to make it happen. The best way to predict the future is to create it. Focus on "making a life" versus "making a living." Use your "right brain" as well as analytical thinking in your retirement planning: dreams, writing, intuition, meditation, poetry, art—those languages of the soul—to help you. Make a collage of your new life. Have an "Idea Box" of what you might want to do. What else do you want to retire from besides work? Make a list of "Things I Don't Do Anymore."

Be prepared for transitions. Transition has been described as jumping from one trapeze bar to another. Allow yourself to leap if the old life no longer fits—but leave a safety net. Transitions, though stressful, are some of the most growth-filled experiences.

Make no major commitments for at least a year. Leave your calendar open as much as possible if you are undecided what you want to do next and use the time to explore. Be careful what you say yes to. Put activities on the calendar in pencil—and with a question mark. Change "What will I do for the rest of my life?" to "What will I do today?'

Be open to new experiences. Approach everything you can with an open mind. Explore as much as you can. Much of this stage—as any other—is learning and enjoying.

Expect surprises, good and bad. If there is a constant to life, it's change. Surprises can be good—the nice card from your friend, the unexpected gift, the wedding or birth announcement—or the dreaded phone call.

Approach the negative surprises from a higher or spiritual perspective. Carrie Fisher, in her act *Wishful Drinking*, said she tries to distinguish between "problems"—death, divorce, illness, and "inconveniences." I remember standing in my living room during the first few months of upheaval when I was living in the "Land of Temporary and the House of Chairs," looking at the mess that was my home, when the thought quickly entered my mind: "It's all material," and just as quickly, "and it's immaterial." Gerotranscendence, a shift from the material to the spiritual, is one of the characteristics of this stage of life when faced with minor and major "inconveniences." I frequently have to remind myself that life has its ups and downs, that some days you are the pigeon and others the statue, and that this too shall pass. For the "problems"—I have personally lost some very good friends at this time—it is a poignant reminder that life is short and to cherish what we have.

Retirement is a process and not an end stage. Retirement doesn't mean a life of leisure or a stress-free life. There is stress in working, stress in retirement, and stress in being alive. Retirement is simply another stage of life. Every stage has its pluses and minuses, and this one is no exception. What I like about being retired is the freedom to live life on my own schedule, to leave many of the "shoulds" and obligations behind and to discover each day anew. I am much more rested and can usually do what I want whenever I want to. The good news about retirement is that if some major inconvenience comes up, I have the time to deal with it. The bad news is I have the time to worry about it. One of the blessings of work is that regardless of what else is going on in your life, you can fully put it aside—at least that was true in my case.

I enjoy this stage of life now—but I also enjoyed my working years. Retirement is not better or worse, just different. I can honestly say that the only time in these five years that I questioned if I had made a mistake by closing my practice was the day when the stock marked dropped to less than half of what it was before and I woke up anxiously wondering, "Did we retire too soon?" We have a more frugal lifestyle than we did before the recession but so does just about everyone else we know. And if we hadn't retired, we would still be living a more frugal lifestyle—and working.

Not all is rosy, however. After the dust had settled, I remember one morning looking at the long day and years ahead. I called my sister and a friend, both of whom had been retired. "Do you ever get bored?" I asked. The answer was no. That gave me hope. I changed "What do I *do*?" to "What do I do *today*?" and whenever that anxious feeling hits again (very seldom), I ask, "What do I do today?" and concentrate on the present.

Develop and maintain positive relationships. Spending time with friends and family has been one of the most meaningful experiences for me. Although there is "a pruning of relationships" as we get older, adding new relationships is also essential. I never thought I would have to "work" at making friends since they were always a part of my life. Then suddenly our two best friends died, others got ill, and we were spending the summer in a community where we hardly knew anyone. I also realized how important being in a community was and appreciate the one we have in our present home.

Have a space you can call your own. One of the first things I missed when I retired was an office. I had always kept strict boundaries between my home and work life, and after I retired, there was no place to call my own. I looked around our home and didn't know where I would put a desk. I finally ended up partitioning a closet and using that space for a little work area, although whenever the choice is between sitting outdoors and reading and entering the dark room, I go outside.

Let there be spaces in your togetherness. Although my husband and I had worked in the same office condo, we each had our own space, did our work and came back together at the end of the day. Being together all the time was an adjustment, and we have learned to put space between us. Fortunately, we can each be in different parts of the house without getting in each other's way.

Headphones also come in handy if one likes to listen to music or watch TV while the other likes quiet. The research finds that marriage gets better at this stage of life as Maggie Scarf describes in her book *September Song: The Good News about Marriage in the Later Years* (2008) as couples have more freedom and time to appreciate each other and don't focus so much on the small stuff.

Don't worry about what you tell others. "I don't know what I'd say if anyone asked me what I do if I retired," is something I often hear from working psychologists. (The answer is "whatever I want.") Nobody can take away your accomplishments, your friends and family love you for who you are, and to most younger people you are already invisible—so it doesn't matter. Patrick Fanning's tongue-in-cheek book *Not Dead Yet ... and One or Two Other Good Things About Retirement* (2008) helps in not taking oneself too seriously.

Make certain that you matter. Although you may not care what others think, what matters is that you are important to yourself, that *you* matter. Nancy Schlossberg describes *mattering* in her book *Revitalizing Retirement* (2009) which she finds is at the heart of a successful retirement: to have a purpose, to feel useful and not marginal.

Appreciate life in the third chapter. This time of life has been described as "late adulthood," "the bonus years," "being neither young nor old." Sarah Lawrence-Lightfoot (2009) refers to the 25 years after age 50 as the "third chapter," a period of recapturing dreams following the "venturing forth" and "cocooning" stages of earlier years. There are many books on the advantages of this stage of life, some of which I have already referred to (Davidson,

2008; Levine, 2005; Scarf, 2008). Besides relationships getting sweeter, people are generally happier in spite of diminishment of capacities. The "aging paradox" is that despite declining abilities, we become happier as we age. I find it helpful to remind myself of this whenever I see the losses in people not much older than I.

Plan for the future—and then let go. Although, like wine, we may get better with age, I am deeply aware that wine turns into vinegar if kept too long. Try to control what you can—most people I know at this stage of life have their living wills, their long-term health insurance, and even their "stash" of medications should they become incapacitated—and then let go. Probably the best advice comes from my good friend, a psychologist in San Francisco: "I have done everything I can within my control but I can't control the rest so I am not going to worry about it." I also find it helpful to ask myself, "What am I *not* thinking of?"—one of many suggestions from a book by another dear friend and colleague (Palladino, 2007) of what to do when your mind wanders off into unpleasant territory.

You never stop being a psychologist. "Do you miss being a therapist?" a friend asked. "We never stopped," my husband replied, jokingly. Like parenting, it is part of your DNA even when you are no longer involved in the daily caretaking. And just for practice, we have had some challenging situations where we have had to use our clinical skills to the max. I miss it—but not the responsibility and commitment that accompanies it. I am indebted to my good friend Roberta, a therapist in New York, for providing me with the magic words whenever I am tempted to get into that role: "I am confident that you can figure it out." You can still listen to people and be caring without taking care of them.

There is a strong need for direction—but no road map—for post-career female psychologists. I attended the roundtable meeting on "retiring but not shy" women (Cole & Gergen, 2010) at the annual American Psychological Association to learn what other female psychologists were doing, and I saw women at different stages taking different paths. It is still uncharted territory, and there is a strong need but very little guidance at this stage. Of the very thick APA program, there were only a handful of programs that addressed this very important topic.

What I have missed most is a peer group, a group of like-minded retired women psychologists with whom I can meet on a regular basis. For years, I have been meeting monthly with a group of mental health professionals, and I also see other psychologists at lunch or at workshops. I realize when I do so how much I enjoy the companionship as well as the sharing. I also enjoy the intellectual stimulation of psychology workshops and lectures, and nothing excites me as much as learning something new about people and their behavior. These all meet different needs, but there is no one group that is specifically designed for post-career female psychologists—or even retired psychologists in general—that addresses all these needs.

Psychology has been my first—and maybe my only—true career passion, and I'm never so excited, engrossed, or absorbed as when I'm learning something new about people's behavior which I can apply. I still enjoy that—but not the responsibility and caretaking that goes with it. I am still open to new projects in my field if they are brief, require minimal commitment, are new or different and pay well.

There are likely many psychologists in my position (or who will be soon) who are taking the time to smell the flowers and are still interested in psychology and belonging to a community of psychologists. What I would like to see is a niche for them—an ongoing community of post-career women psychologists that combines the built-in structure of the working world with the "drop in" freedom of the retirement world, one that makes allowances for summer and winter escapes, where women can congregate, share ideas, and utilize the synergy from these encounters. "Project Renewment" is the closest I have seen for a model, a new word replacing the "tired" with the "new" in "retirement," whose aim is *"to provide a forum for career women fifty-five years and older to use their strategic thinking, curiosity and vision to forge new directions for their future that are equally, if not more, satisfying than their working years"* (Bratter & Dennis, 2008, p.186). As more and more women psychologists enter their 60s and 70s and want to leave the frenzy of the work world for a more relaxed pace—but are not yet ready for the nursing home—there is a strong need for a niche for women who are retiring—but not shy.

References

Bratter, B., & Dennis, H. (2008). *Project renewment: The first retirement model for career women.* New York: Scribner.

Cameron, J. (1992). *The artist's way.* New York: Jeremy P. Tarcher.

Cole, E., & Gergen, M. (2010). *Retiring, but not shy—Post-career planning among feminist psychologists.* Roundtable discussion, American Psychological Association Annual Convention, San Diego.

Davidson, S. (2008). *Leap! What will we do with the rest of our lives?* New York: Ballantine.

Fanning, P. (2008). *Not dead yet...and one or two other good things about retirement.* Oakland, CA: New Harbinger.

Koocher, G. (2003). Ethical and legal issues in professional practice transitions. *Professional Psychology: Research and Practice*, 34(4), 383-387.

Lawrence-Lightfoot, S. (2009). *The third chapter: Passion, risk and adventure in the 25 years after 50.* New York: Crichton Books.

Levine, S. (2005). *Inventing the second half of our lives: Women in second adulthood.* New York: Penguin.

McGee, T. (2005). Observations on the retirement of professional psychologists. *Professional Psychology: Research and Practice*, 34(4), 388-395.

Palladino, L.J. (2007). *Find your focus zone: An effective new plan to defeat distraction and overload.* New York: Simon & Schuster.

Scarf, M. (2008). *September song: The good news about marriage in the later years.* New York: Penguin.

Schlossberg, N.K. (2009). *Revitalizing retirement: Reshaping your identity, relationships, and purpose.* Washington, DC: American Psychological Association.

Warner, R. (2000). *Get a life.* Berkeley, CA: Nolo.

Weiss, L. (2004). *Therapist's guide to self-care.* New York: Brunner-Routledge.

Change Occurs

Mary T. Howard

*O*ur editor suggested we make our accounts rather personal, and this feels very much so for me. I hope my readers find useful nuggets here in looking at their own careers.

On May 3, 2010, I began what felt to me a rather abrupt retirement, though I had been contemplating it for several years and had been eligible for several more. Of course, one is never financially ready, though it has, in fact, worked out for me as it does for most in my profession. I did experience a range of emotions, from duress to pleasure, when, as a result of federal budget cuts, I was among the most senior and highest paid employees who were dismissed from their jobs. I worked for a veterans' affairs medical center for 30 years.

Suddenly, at retirement, I had minimally 40 hours a week for which I had to plan, rather than it being planned for me by the demands necessary for earning the dollars for necessities and my fancies. A little background can add prospective of this noted unease.

My first job was the summer after my 14th birthday. It was as an assistant housemaid to my mother who was employed as a housekeeper. And from then until I retired, I was either working or in school, with the exception of a three month long road trip with my mother, my first year out of college, from Kansas City, MO, to Vancouver, Canada, to Mexico, and back to Kansas City. We visited her friends across the country and went sightseeing. Our arrangement was that she would finance room and board, and I, the gas and car maintenance. We made it all the way into Arizona on the return trip before I, sheepishly, told her the last gas fill up had taken the last of my money saved up from my year of teaching the

prior year. She, fortunately, smiled as she said she had been awaiting such an announcement and then provided the needed funds
for the completion of the ride home. My only other work hiatus
was the nine months used to find my way out of Philadelphia.
This city, known as the city of brotherly love, is the only place
where I fearfully locked my car doors and grew eyes in the back
of my head. This occurred after having the car of a visiting friend,
and later my car, vandalized in a long term paid parking lot in
the "good neighborhood" where I lived. And soon after I read of
the police calmly walking by a woman sprawled on the floor of
the Market and Broad Street downtown transit exchange, with her
briefcase beside her and dressed in a suit. This occurred two hours
before the police approached her to investigate. They said they
thought she was drunk. In fact, she had been assaulted and left
unconscious. And I'm not easily scared. Before Philadelphia I had
happily lived in the Bronx, New York, in an area known as the
Fort Apache neighborhood and also ridden in a police car there. I
have also hitchhiked across Europe and North Africa, as well as
traveled alone in India. In New York, if someone is found lying in
a gutter, the police politely inquire immediately as to the problem.
My feelings about Philadelphia are such that I don't even change
planes there if I can avoid it.

So, after many years of having at least 40 hours of a 168 hour
week automatically accounted for, I suddenly, after retirement, had
to organize those hours on my own. This was a complete disruption of my comfortable, familiar, lifestyle. What to do? My biggest planned task was to read and discard and/or organize my huge
accumulation of journals, magazines, books, and papers including
presentations, correspondence, and professional information.

My most recent employment and residence had been, as I mentioned, for 30 years. Previously, and from birth, I had never lived in any one place for more than five years. It is amazing what one can accumulate in one place in 30 years. And add to that what I brought home from the office. It took 40 hours of devoted attention to clear out the office. I finally understood the defeated look on the face of my beloved professor, Dr. Donald G. Patterson, when I visited his office which he was clearing out upon his retirement, from the University of Minnesota, and his generous bestowal of several of his many books to the students who visited him.

Are there things to do other than clearing papers? Oh, my, yes. Committee meetings, presentations, conferences, luncheons and dinners out, and travel. But I did all those things while working. My retired friends tell me they are busier than ever. And those with some length to their retirement say it took three to four years to get organized. As a year has just gone by, it becomes more and more evident that it will take at least that for me. Oh dear!

One of the things that, no doubt, affected my working life as well as my more recent years, is knowing that I am one of the first 100 African Americans to earn a doctoral degree in psychology. And that I had a most prominent and supportive advisor, Dr. Ralph Berdie, then Director of the Counseling Center at the University of Minnesota, as well as the support of Dr. E.G. Williamson, then Dean of Student Services, and the friendship of Dr. Theda Heganah, a counselor who became the first woman Director of Counseling at that university. All of these mentors nudged me about my performance, encouraged me to become active in professional associations, provided references, and arranged professional connections. My post-doctoral activities, various social and cultural changes in society, and my current age have led to my recently receiving recognition for elders, as well as general professional recognition.

What have I learned along the way? First, the validity of the truism, change occurs. I have grown from the only child of a widow who, at age five, wanted to be a nurse, to earn a PhD and become president of a then 10,000 member national professional organization, The American College Personnel Association. Second, life is exciting if you will let it be. Take some calculated risks and evaluate the positive aspects of any experience and don't dwell on the negatives. Try out new options that are offered in both personal and professional life. Failure can occur, but stay open to new possibilities. Third, enjoy new friendships and hang on to the old and proven ones. Some of mine are dying off, but I have good memories. Fourth, respond to the overtures of the young people you know, and show your appreciation by responding—hopefully without intruding with uninvited advice. Fifth, happily learn also from your younger friends, including technology such as I-pads, cell phones, and computer intricacies.

A bit of background may help one, including me, to better understand the current adjustment I am making. I was brought up by a single mother. My father died of a heart condition three months before I was born. He was a business man who owned the largest barbershop in San Francisco, with 18 chairs. My mother, who married late, after many trips across the United States including driving a T-Model Ford on such a trip, had only me and never married again. Her own family was entrepreneurially inclined including ownership of a small farm in Kansas, a taxicab company in Kansas City, MO, and rental property as well as a range outside Janesville, CA. At one time they owned a hotel in Independence, MO. Knowledge of this background led to similar ventures along with my educational ventures.

The special lesson I learned was that one is responsible for one's own support. This attitude was, no doubt, in part, responsible for my divorce after more than 12 years of a compatible marriage. After our marriage my husband established a solid dental practice in Birmingham, AL, and I taught for five years at Miles College there. But I only had a Master's degree and while that was acceptable there, I felt insecure. Unfortunately, since I was African American, I was not admissible to the University of Alabama. My husband could not move his practice on a whim. Thus, when I was offered a Fellowship at the University of Minnesota, I left to work on my doctoral degree, hoping that our marriage was strong enough to survive three years of my being away with only intermittent visiting home. It, unfortunately, did not survive.

It was unfair of me to expect him to seriously consider moving his practice to California where I could have attended graduate school, as well as fulfill my need to have financial independence as might need to be. My mother had provided that model of independence and it seems to have stuck with me.

Now, as to my "post career life" or retirement. I mentioned that during our lives together, my mother taught me to be both independent and adventurous. And my professional life provided resources for me to enjoy both. My first trip overseas was to a professional conference in Russia and included a visit to a graduate school friend in Turkey. We are still friends and she visited me here this year. Another graduate school friend, with whom I am still friends, arranged consultations for me in India where I also spoke at a conference. Other trips followed including a hitch-hiking one mentioned above, from Scotland to North Africa; an education one to China; a consultation one to South Africa; and a family visiting one, most recently to Thailand, courtesy of prior entertaining of foreign exchange students. I've also made two trips to South America. I also follow the every two year Senior Olympic competitions around the United States, courtesy of a now-retired-to-Hawaii former student of mine who, in her recent competition in Houston, TX, won seven medals and three ribbons in track and field events.

Along the way I have also fostered some teenagers, all now at least 30 years old and four of whom stay close and are my "family." So I now enjoy the pleasures of being grandmother to seven.

Lessons to be learned I have mentioned above. Hopefully a brief review of my life will trigger memories and concerns in my readers for their own review and valuations.

Finding Meaning in Retirement

Diane J. Willis

*"A people is not defeated until the hearts of its
women are on the ground..."*
(Traditional Cheyenne Proverb)

This chapter focuses on retirement as a continuation and maturation of my life's work rather than a conclusion or marked change from my earlier work. Having said that, there are also aspects of retirement that involve both negative and positive transitions—all of which have been a great learning experience. Writing this chapter helped to crystallize those aspects of my personal and professional identity that are most meaningful to me, and hopefully will offer some insight to others. My ruminations are offered as one person's experience on this journey through retirement.

Many thanks to my good friend, Jan L. Culbertson, Ph.D., for critiquing this chapter and for her very helpful comments.

Pre-Retirement Activities

Before taking early retirement on July 1, 1999, I had a long, and I think productive, career as a professor at the University of Oklahoma Health Sciences Center (OUHSC)—a university teaching hospital that provided both my early learning experiences in pediatric and clinical child psychology as well as my career focus for 30+ years. My path to this professional role was circuitous, given that my first profession was medical technology, followed by a stint as a student at a Baptist seminary, followed by graduate studies in psychology. I graduated from Northeastern State University in Tahlequah, Oklahoma with a B.A. in biology, and considered applying to medical school. Because I was undecided about career directions, I entered Medical Technology training at

St. John's Hospital in Tulsa, Oklahoma and worked briefly in this field after graduation. However, I was still undecided about a career path. I had been very active in the Baptist Church youth activities while growing up, and I had a dream of attending Seminary. Thus, I applied to the Southern Baptist Theological Seminary in Louisville, Kentucky and was accepted in 1962. I took various religious education courses and made lifelong friendships with fellow seminary students that I have maintained to this day. Although I did not complete a degree in religious education, the experience of working with theologian Dr. Wayne Oates and others helped me decide on a career path and field of study—psychology.

I was accepted in the psychology graduate program at George Peabody College of Vanderbilt University in Nashville, and completed my Master of Arts degree there in 1964. Although I could have continued my doctoral training there, I wanted to return to my native Oklahoma and be nearer my family. I applied to the University of Oklahoma, and was accepted in their doctoral program in psychology, from which I graduated in 1970. My training as a medical technologist actually helped provide support for my graduate training, and my love of biology has remained strong over the years. It led to my interest in working in a medical setting upon graduation from OU, and I was fortunate to do a 2-year internship from 1969-1971 at OU Health Sciences Center with Dr. Logan Wright in the Department of Pediatrics and Dr. Oscar Parsons in the Department of Psychiatry and Behavioral Sciences. With Logan as my mentor, I was fortunate enough to be on the ground floor of the development of the field of pediatric psychology in the late 1960s and early 1970s, and learn from his innovative ideas for practice of psychology within a hospital medical environment.

In 1971, I received my first faculty appointment at OUHSC as Assistant Professor of Medical Psychology in the Departments of Pediatrics and Psychiatry and Behavioral Sciences, as well as Chief Psychologist in the Department of Communication Disorders. In 1975, I moved to the Child Study Center, where I assumed the role of Chief of Psychological Services and Associate Director of the Child Study Center. Over the next 25 years, I devoted my energies to developing new programs for children with developmental disabilities in the Oklahoma City area and around the state. In 1975, new Federal and State laws had been passed that would guarantee a free and appropriate public education to all children, regardless of disability. With this as an impetus, I developed one of the first programs for diagnosing and teaching children with Specific Learning Disabilities in Oklahoma, and was also active in developing special education services for children with hearing impairment and speech/language problems. I was a strong advocate for development of special education programs for children with all types of disabilities.

In the early 70s, I worked with many children who were hospitalized at Oklahoma Children's Hospital due to injuries suffered from abuse and neglect. I became concerned that there was no systematic way to train medical personnel to detect signs of abuse and neglect, and train them on ways to protect these children from further harm. I worked with a fellow physician to initiate the first Child Protection Committee at OU Children's Hospital, where pediatricians, radiologists, social workers, and psychologists met regularly to review cases of suspected abuse/neglect and assure that children received Protective Services from the Oklahoma Department of Human Services (DHS). OU Children's Hospital became one of the leading hospitals in the state for careful assessment of potential abuse and neglect injuries in children and referral of children to protective services. All medical students and residents who train in the Department of Pediatrics now obtain state-of-the-art training in the area of abuse/neglect, thanks to our advocacy and program development efforts.

Despite these advances, I was not satisfied with just detecting abuse and neglect and treating the child victims. I also wanted to develop a treatment program for parents who were committing the abuse, and this advocacy led to co-founding the Parents' Assistance Center (PAC) in Oklahoma City, which is still in existence today. Through advocacy efforts with the Child Protection Committee and Parents' Assistance Center, literally thousands of abusive parents and abused children have received services in the State of Oklahoma. I believed strongly in advocating for the needs of children who were maltreated, through serving on the Board of PAC, serving on the Governor's Committee on Children and Youth, serving as Chair of the Legislative Committee on the Region VII Child Abuse Prevention Task Force, making countless speeches to various local and regional organizations concerned with prevention of maltreatment, and providing direct treatment to the children and their families.

At the Child Study Center, I coordinated the child abuse program and all psychological services in general; supervised assessment and treatment of children and families; and made court appearances on behalf of patients who were abused or neglected. At the Child Study Center, I initiated the first comprehensive assessment and treatment program for children who were abused and neglected, and provided training for psychology interns to work with these children and to co-lead group treatment for their parents at PAC. Yet we had some difficulty getting abused children seen in treatment because no one would pay for their treatment. At that time, Logan Wright and I met with the Medical Director of DHS. When we explained the plight of these children and how their therapy could be covered through Medicaid, the Director initiated the ruling that therapy and assessment of children in DHS care could be covered under Medicaid. Thus, Oklahoma became one of the first States to reimburse mental health services under Medicaid.

In reflecting back on my work at the Child Study Center, I realized that my talents and passion revolved around program development, advocating for new policies and new legislation to protect children and provide for their needs, providing training for students from psychology and other disciplines, and providing mentoring for young professionals. In establishing new treatment programs at Child Study Center, I enjoyed conceptualizing and planning the new services, but I also took great pleasure in recruiting talented young psychologists with expertise in the areas of learning disabilities, neuropsychology, ADHD and behavior disorders, infant assessment and treatment, and other developmental disabilities to come in on the ground floor and bring the programs to fruition. These clinics, and the psychologists who direct them, have provided cutting-edge training opportunities for pediatric residents, medical students, trainees from all the allied health professions (i.e., psychology, OT, PT, speech/language pathology, and social work), as well as professionals around the State and region (e.g., Indian Health professionals, foster parents, Head Start). Though an active clinician and academician, my role increasingly became one of mentor and supporter of these young psychologists as they created their respective programs and also established research and advocacy programs in their respective specialty areas. One of my greatest pleasures over the years is to see talented young professionals mature and achieve such amazing goals in their own careers. Mentoring these professionals was, and continues to be, a priority for me.

Yet another theme in my professional career has been concern for mental health services for individuals from minority groups who did not have access to good health and mental health services. Throughout my career, I have been proud of being a voting member of the Kiowa Tribe, and an advocate for better mental health services for American Indian children and families. I have devoted time and energy to helping American Indian families locally, as well as working at a national level to bring attention to their needs. I established the first Psychology Clinic at the Cheyenne-Arapaho Indian Health Service Clinics in El Reno and Concho, Oklahoma and at Clinton Indian Hospital in Clinton, Oklahoma. I continue to provide services to these clinics to this day. Psychology interns and postdoctoral fellows from OUHSC sign up to accompany me to these clinics each month; thus, I am helping to mentor the next generation of psychologists who will know how to serve American Indian families. I also was active in consulting, teaching, and providing clinical services to American Indian children and families from the Chickasaw Tribe (at Ada Indian Hospital, Human Services Branch) and Carter Seminary (Boarding School for ages 6 years through High School). I have written and taught extensively at a national level, helped to encourage better research on mental health services to American Indians, and have testified before the US Congress on several occasions about the mental health needs of American Indians.

As a member of the Kiowa tribe, I had both a personal and professional interest in working on behalf of American Indian children and families. My identity as an American Indian and an advocate was shaped by my father, William P. Willis, who served as a member of the Oklahoma House of Representatives for 30 years. He was Chair of Appropriations for many years and served as Speaker of the House for three terms. He was a strong advocate for the less fortunate and a strong spokesperson for education. Through his example and tutelage, I learned how to present my "causes" to legislators in a way that would be likely to influence their thinking and their development of new legislation. I realized that there were few psychology colleagues who felt comfortable translating their psychology knowledge into advocacy efforts, but I felt this was an important use of my skills and professional expertise. Now it is much more commonplace to have psychologists working in the public policy arena through the wonderful efforts of the APA Public Policy Office, the Practice Directorate, and other professional advocacy groups. However, in the 1970s and 1980s, there were few others to serve as mentors in policy and advocacy work within the profession. Over the years, I have tried to use my expertise in testifying before the Oklahoma legislature and the US Congress regarding needs of children with disabilities, those who have been maltreated, as well as the mental health needs of American Indian children and families. I was honored to be appointed to the US Advisory Board on Child Abuse and Neglect and was able to take my advocacy efforts to a national level through development of policy statements that we hoped would influence legislation on behalf of maltreated children. I have attempted to mentor other psychologists to help them put their knowledge to work through policy and advocacy efforts in their communities and states as well as the national level.

During my tenure as a faculty member, I was also active in the American Psychological Association (APA) and its divisions, having served as President of Divisions 12, 29, 37, and Divisions 53 and 54 when they were Sections under Division 12. When I was editor of the Society of Pediatric Psychology Newsletter, I gained approval to convert the newsletter into a journal. Thus, I became the Founding Editor of the *Journal of Pediatric Psychology (JPP)*. Later, having resigned as editor of *JPP* to become President of the Section on Pediatric Psychology, I was asked to assume the editorship of the *Journal of Clinical Child Psychology*. I was able to develop this journal into a peer-reviewed, scholarly publication.

I have been fortunate to serve on several APA boards and committees, later serving on the Committee on Rural Health, where I focused the committee on "telehealth." I am a member of the Section on Ethnic Minorities under Division 12, a member of Division 35 and 45, as well as a member of the Society of Indian Psychologists. I wrote the initial bylaws for Section 6 (American

Indian/Alaska Natives/ Indigenous Peoples) under Division 35, and now serve as President-Elect of this section (2009-2011).

Movement Toward Retirement

Having worked hard for 34 years and having been privileged to initiate numerous first time programs in the State of Oklahoma, I began to get restless, somewhat bored, and burned out at the Child Study Center. I had contemplated early retirement (early in terms of age and years of employment that qualified me for retirement by the State of Oklahoma), and I began to seriously consider what I might do if I retired. In 1998, I was approached by the Director of Three Feathers Associates—a private agency that obtained grants to provide a variety of services to American Indian families—regarding a possible work opportunity. The Director asked if I would assume a position with them to help set up the Wave I Early Head Start (birth to 3) programs in Indian country. I met with the Chair of the Department of Pediatrics to ask if Three Feathers could contract with the Department for one half of my time and salary. With his approval, I took the position and was both invigorated and excited to be on the ground floor of establishing the first Early Head Start (EHS) programs for Indian country. After a wonderful year working with Pine Ridge, Standing Rock Sioux, Eastern and Western Band Cherokees in North Carolina and Oklahoma, Spirit Lake Sioux, and other tribes, I felt as if this was a new area where all of us working to help establish these programs could make worthwhile contributions. President and Mrs. Clinton, along with the *Zero to Three* organization in D.C., were committed to early intervention efforts and to passing legislation to establish this new program nationally.

By the end of 1998, the American Indian Institute at University of Oklahoma was awarded the new grant to consult with tribes as they continued to establish Wave II EHS programs. This meant that Three Feathers Associates was no longer providing the support for EHS programs in Indian country, and thus, I returned full time to OUHSC until May/ June 1999. At that time, the head of the American Indian Programs Branch, Head Start Bureau, in the US Department of Health and Human Services (DHHS) suggested to the Director of the American Indian Institute that she hire me to run the EHS Wave II consultation and training services. When I received the invitation from the Director of the Institute, I was ready to retire from the Health Sciences Center, and immediately wrote a letter of retirement to the Department Chair in Pediatrics effective July 1, 1999. Thus, when I took early retirement at the age of 62 years I felt like a bird freed from its cage. I then moved from one busy position to another, in which I was on the road immediately consulting all over the US to various Indian tribes. The psychology faculty and staff at the Child Study Center had wanted to host a retirement party for me, but there was no time due to my busy schedule until November 1999. At the wonderful retirement party, the Chair of Pediatrics surprised me by awarding me the prestigious title of "Professor Emeritus" of Pediatrics and Medical Psychology—an honor I had not applied for or requested. The citation states that this title was given in recognition of 30+ years of significant contributions to the mission of the department in the areas of program development, teaching, research, publication, and clinical service.

So, after 34 years as a faculty member in the Department of Pediatrics, and Director of Psychological Services and Training at the Child Study Center, my office emptied, my garage at home filled with boxes, books, and journals, I embarked on a journey that had me rejuvenated and re-energized. Why? Was I unhappy at the Child Study Center? Absolutely not! The programs I had the good fortune to develop and the psychology faculty we recruited to direct these programs were far exceeding my expectations. I was proud of their work, but there seemed to be no further challenges that excited me in that setting. On the other hand, I was excited by the idea of being on the ground floor of creating something new, like EHS, where one can aid tribes in their recruitment of pregnant women, working with low income families of newborn infants and toddlers, and seeing that EHS criteria are followed to provide good health care, good nutrition, early stimulation with infants, and teaching tribal staff the multitude of ways they can enhance the growth and development of the whole family. As an American Indian psychologist who had spent her career working with families and children who were disadvantaged, low income, maltreated, or had disabilities, I saw an opportunity to help tribes establish health programs that would provide pregnant women good nutrition, free them if possible from substance abuse and smoking, and provide them the kind of educational and emotional support many had not previously received. The three years I spent working with tribal staff and EHS directors, and working with staff in the Head Start Bureau in Washington, DC, convinced me that this is a government program of great value to our low income populations.

◼ Post Retirement?

The freedom to CHOOSE what one wants to do after retirement has been the most rewarding to me. Post retirement freed me up to do more APA Accreditation Site Visits to wonderful internship and postdoctoral fellowship programs across the United States, and to take on extra teaching jobs and consultations both in and out of state. I was even invited to become the Chair of the BODs of Jacobson House, A Native Art Center and Museum in Norman. This challenge I accepted and have loved working with professional Native women and men on the board.

Also, in post-retirement, I was most fortunate to be asked to teach an American Indian Health course by the Director of the Native American Studies Program at the University of Oklahoma. It appealed to me because I would be meeting with young undergraduates and some graduate students enrolled in the course. It was a way to keep up on the latest literature, and to invite experts from the medical center to speak on topics like diabetes, cardiac disease, and cancer among American Indians. This would allow the class to learn about the various ways in which these diseases present themselves, as well as information about their etiology and treatment. Because there is a proven link between behavior and health problems, one half of the course focused on behavioral health practices and the ways that behavior contributes to health issues such as obesity, diabetes, heart problems, etc. In this area, I could call on my many years of professional work as a psychologist in a medical center and my work as a consultant to tribes for the American Indian Institute. I also could feel young working with such a diverse and interesting group of students. So future retirees, oftentimes the contacts you have pre-retirement can offer fun, stimulating, and exciting new opportunities for you should you decide you want to continue to stay abreast, keep young, or just not be bored.

Another valued opportunity came when I was invited to teach courses internationally through the University of Oklahoma's Advanced Programs on behalf of the Department of Human Relations. I was once again challenged intellectually as I developed graduate courses on "Introduction to Human Relations," "Child Abuse and Neglect," and "Basic Counseling Skills." Teaching these courses provided an opportunity for my first trip to Europe, and this was very exciting to me. I taught at Air Force, Navy, and Army bases in Germany, Iceland, Japan, Spain, England, and Italy, and gained great appreciation for our men and women in uniform. Given that I had never traveled abroad until my 60s, it felt as if my education had just begun. I felt so very fortunate to meet these men and women, many of whom were planning career service in the American Armed Forces. And it was fun immersing myself in the history, culture and sights of each country visited, often renting a car and touring for a week after teaching my course. This wonderful experience provided an opportunity to take a friend and two of my three sisters with me.

Having worked hard all my life, and certainly getting older, retirement has not slowed me down yet. Part of this "push" to keep on working and being productive comes under the heading of "workaholic." Sometimes, perhaps oftentimes, we retirees cannot give ourselves permission to just sit and smell the flowers or read a good book or travel to some destination we would love to see. But at least in retirement one has the freedom to choose what one wants to do and I want to continue to contribute to others in some meaningful way.

Post retirement has also afforded me more time to spend with my brothers and sisters. As stated, two of my sisters and a friend accompanied me on various trips to Europe, especially when I taught in Germany. My three sisters and I took our very first trip together in May, 2011 and had a great time. This is an activity we plan to do yearly. And nieces and nephews are in and out of my home several times a year, especially for OU football games. Several of my nieces and nephews consider me their 'mother' away from home and I have taken several of them with me on trips in the U.S.

What I wish I had known before I reached this stage in my retirement and what I wish I had done differently.

Hindsight is terrific! It has only been in recent years that researchers began looking at retirees' adjustment profiles, or publishing articles on "what is retirement" so those looking for a research idea while you are young might research this area (Wang, 2007; Fehr, 2012) But on to more concrete suggestions. As a faculty member in the Department of Pediatrics, OUHSC, under the TIAA/CREF and any other retirement plans of choice, I would have put down the maximum amount, affordable additional savings (mutual funds, Treasury bills, more real estate, etc) in savings. I did invest in rental properties plus a lakehouse, but these do not provide ready cash unless sold. So, early career psychologists, put back as much in savings on a monthly basis as you can afford (money managers recommend 10-15%of salary) because it will come in handy when you retire. It will free you up to travel, spend time (and money) with family, and any other activity you wish to do.

Second, take your first trips abroad when you are young because this broadens your perspective and opens your mind to so many other people, cultures, history, politics and policies, and wonderful scenery and experiences. Some people go to just sightsee but I challenge you to read about each country, about the historical figures and their lives, about their system of government. If you plan ahead you might even make contact with other professionals in the country where you are traveling, visit their centers or universities, and maybe even guest lecture.

Third, I realized after my retirement that my education was just beginning. Rarely was there time to read novels, biographies, history, so my knowledge and education expanded after retirement. Prior to retirement, time at work and home (speaking as a single, unmarried woman with no children or multiple children if one considers the closeness I have with nieces and nephews) was spent writing grants, reviewing articles, preparing publications for articles and professional books, preparing lectures, writing reports, etc. It was as though my days at Peabody College and University of Oklahoma were spent in a tunnel, devoid of extra-curricular activities where I was finally 'processed' (spit out) with a PhD, internship, faculty position, etc.

In summary, I fear I may continue to be a very busy and happy retiree in the State of Oklahoma! I continue to teach courses through the OU Native American Studies Program, the OU Advanced Programs (which offers graduate courses to

American military personnel stationed around the world), and provide various seminars and lectures to the psychology training program at OUHSC. I continue to teach and serve on professional committees nationally within the American Psychological Association, and have recently served as President of the American Orthopsychiatric Association. Never one to let grass grow under my feet, I actively keep up with my large extended family and my national family of friends and associates—always, as my friends and families say, the one to pick up the phone and stay in touch. I am very devoted to my 9 cats, am an avid fan of OU football, and enjoy my hobbies of gardening, genealogy, collecting American Indian art, walking near an ocean, reading, and traveling nationally and internationally.

References:

Wang, M. (2007) Profiling retirees in the retirement transition and adjustment process: Examining the longitudinal change patterns of retirees' psychological well-being. *Journal of Applied Psychology, 92*, 455-474.

Fehr, R. (2012). Is retirement always stressful? The potential impact of creativity. *American Psychologist, 67*, 76-77.

AUTHOR BIOS

Asuncion Miteria Austria

Asuncion Miteria Austria, Ph.D., founded the Graduate Program in Clinical Psychology at Cardinal Stritch University and currently serves as its Chair, Director of Clinical Training, and Professor. She received her BA in psychology (Magna Cum Laude) from the University of the Philippines, her MA from Columbia University, her Ph.D. from Northwestern University and her post-doctoral training from the Neuropsychiatric Institute, Abraham School of Medicine, University of Illinois at the Medical Center. A licensed psychologist, she is fellow of APA. She has served as president for the Division of Clinical Psychology's Sections on the Clinical Psychology of Women and the Clinical Psychology of Ethnic Minorities. She has served on several APA Governance Boards and currently serves on the Board for the Advancement of Psychology in the Public Interest. She has received numerous national awards from APA on mentoring, education, distinguished leadership, community service and outstanding contributions to the clinical psychology of ethnic minorities as well as women. She received the 2006 Distinguished Leadership for Women in Psychology Award and the 2007 Distinguished Elder Psychologist Award. She also received the Cardinal Stritch 2007 Teaching Excellence and Campus Leadership Award and the 2010 Cardinal Stritch University Distinguished Scholar Award.

Her recent publications include: "Spirituality and Resilience of Filipinos" in Rayburn and Comas-Diaz, *WomanSoul: The inner life of women's spirituality* (Praeger, 2008.) "Enhancing Capabilities of Women and Ethnic minorities" with A. Marie M. Austria in Rayburn, Denmark, Reuder and Austria, (Eds.), *Handbook for women mentors: Transcending barriers of stereotype, race and ethnicity.* (Praeger, 2010).

Martha E. Banks

Martha E. Banks, Ph.D., is a research neuropsychologist in the Research & Development Division of ABackans DCP, Inc., in Akron, Ohio and a former professor of Black Studies at The College of Wooster. Prior to her retirement from the Brecksville Veterans Administration Medical Center, she served as a clinical psychologist. She is a codeveloper of the *Ackerman-Banks Neuropsychological Rehabilitation Battery©*. Her research focuses on traumatic brain injury sustained by victims of intimate partner violence. Dr. Banks has extensive governance experience in the American Psychological Association, including service as 2008-2009 President of the Society for the Psychology of Women. Dr. Banks' recent publications include:

Banks, M. E. & Kaschak, E. (Eds.) (2003). *Women with Visible and Invisible Disabilities: Multiple Intersections, Multiple Issues, Multiple Therapies*. New York: Haworth Press.

Marshall, C. A., Kendall, E., Banks, M. E., & Gover, R. M. S. (Eds.) (2009). *Disability: Insights from Across Fields and Around the World, Volumes I, II, and III*. Westport, CT: Praeger. [Choice journal's Outstanding Academic Title 2009]

Banks, M. E. (2008). Women with disabilities: Cultural competence in rehabilitation psychology. *Disability and Rehabilitation: An International, Multidisciplinary Journal, 30*(3), 184-190. doi:10.1080/09638280701532243

Banks, M. E., & Ackerman, R. J. (2009). Disability from interpersonal violence: Culturally relevant assessment and treatment. In J. L. Chin (Ed.), *Diversity in Mind and in Action*. (pp. 113-136). Westport, CT: Greenwood Publishing.

Banks, M. E. (2010). Special Issues for Women with Disabilities. In M. A. Paludi (Ed.) *Feminism and Women's Rights Worldwide*. (pp. 149-160). Santa Barbara, CA: ABC-CLIO.

Janis S. Bohan and Glenda Russell

Janis Bohan received her Ph.D. in Developmental Psychology from the University of Rochester, New York and immediately began a teaching career at Metropolitan State College of Denver that would span 30 years. Her teaching, writing, and research focused on several topic areas, most notably feminist psychology (especially feminist perspectives on women's place in the history of psychology), the psychology of sexual orientation, and social constructionist approaches to those topics. Janis has also published and presented widely. Her publications include two books on women's place in psychology (*Replacing Women: Readings toward a more Inclusive Psychology* and *Seldom Seen, Rarely Heard: Women's Place in Psychology*) and two books on the psychology of sexual orientation (*Psychology and Sexual Orientation: Coming to Terms* and, with Glenda Russell, *Conversations about Psychology and Sexual Orientation*) as well as numerous journal articles and book chapters.

Janis retired from her professional role in 2000, and subsequent years have been spent with some professional writing and presentations and a changing assortment of volunteer community and political activities. In recent years, she has added a part-time job as a contract editor, editing work written by professionals whose first language is not English. One happy challenge of her retirement has been sharing her personal and some of her professional life with a partner who is not retired.

Glenda Russell was drawn to psychology in part because the field provided so many career options. She has taken advantage of the variety of professional roles offered by psychology, having worked as a therapist, researcher, teacher, and consultant. Glenda's primary research and scholarly interests have been the psychological consequences of anti-LGBT politics, processes of undoing internalized oppression, out-group activism, and liberation psychology. In addition to journal articles and chapters on these and other topics, she wrote *Voted Out: Psychological Consequences of Antigay Politics* and, with Janis Bohan, *Conversations about Psychology and Sexual Orientation*. Her research has also served as the basis for a choral oratorio and a PBS video.

Glenda currently works as a clinician and research coordinator at Counseling and Psychological Services at the University of

Colorado, Boulder where she also teaches a research seminar to first-generation students; she has a private psychotherapy practice on the side. Glenda is working on two books, one on the relationship between LGBT people and heterosexual allies, and the other a psychological and political survival kit for LGBT people. Before and during her career in psychology, she has engaged in many community and political ventures. At this point, she can barely imagine retiring. However, she hopes that when she does, her retirement looks a lot like Janis Bohan's.

Ellen Cole

Ellen Cole is Professor of Psychology Emerita at Alaska Pacific University (APU) in Anchorage, where she directed the Master of Science in Counseling Psychology program. She is past-president of the Alaska Psychological Association and the Society for the Psychology of Women, Division 35 of the American Psychological Association, as well as an AASECT-certified Sex Therapist Diplomate and a Fellow of APA. For 12 years Ellen co-edited the journal *Women & Therapy* and the Haworth Press book program, "Innovations in Feminist Studies." She is author and editor of many publications, including *Featuring Females: Feminist Analyses of Media*, co-edited with Jessica Henderson Daniel, *Refugee Women and their Mental Health*, co-edited with Oliva Espin and Esther Rothblum, and *Wilderness Therapy for Women*, co-edited with Eve Erdman and Esther Rothblum. She has received a variety of professional awards, including a Distinguished Publication Award and two awards for Jewish scholarship from the Association for Women in Psychology, two Faculty Merit Awards for research from APU, a Woman of Achievement award from Anchorage's YWCA, and perhaps most meaningful, an award for Outstanding Contribution to Students from the students at APU. At age 70 she went back to school and earned a Master of Arts degree in Positive Psychology from the University of Pennsylvania. Ellen is currently Visiting Professor at the College of St. Rose in Albany, NY, teaches psychology to high school seniors at the Albany Academies, and with Jane Giddan conducts "70Candles" conversation groups for women in various locations throughout the U.S. (visit their blog www.70candles.com).

Eileen L. Cooley

Eileen L. Cooley is a professor of psychology at Agnes Scott College, a liberal arts college for women in metropolitan Atlanta, and a licensed psychologist in Georgia. She earned her Ph.D. in Clinical Psychology from Emory University and has worked as a faculty member and a private practitioner for over 20 years. She has taught courses in Abnormal Psychology, Psychological Assessment, and Introduction to Counseling, along with mentoring undergraduate women pursuing careers in psychology. She has published studies on attachment styles and depression in women and is co-editor of a book highlighting careers of 20th century neuropsychologists. As a private practitioner, her work has focused on adults presenting with depression, anxiety, and relationship concerns. She is currently developing a qualitative research project focused on working women with retired partners, and is anticipating her own retirement from teaching within the next several years.

Jessica Henderson Daniel

Jessica Henderson Daniel, Ph.D., ABPP, is Associate Professor of Psychology in the Department of Psychiatry at Harvard Medical School. At Children's Hospital, Boston, she is Director of Training in Psychology in the Department of Psychiatry and Associate Director of the LEAH (Leadership Education in Adolescent Health) Training Program in the Division of Adolescent Medicine.

In 1993 as chair of the Massachusetts Board of Registration of Psychologists, she proposed that the Board consider passing regulations requiring both instruction and training about people of color in order to be licensed as a private practitioner in Massachusetts. Massachusetts continues to be the only state with such regulations.

In the American Psychological Association (APA), she has served as president of the Society for the Psychology of Women (SWP-Division 35). From 2005-2007, she was the first African American to serve as member-at-large on the APA Board of Directors.

In 1999, she founded *Next Generation Program*, an ethnically based mentoring program for early career women of color who are committed to research careers that focus on adolescents. The NG Women's achievements include: three are recipients of K Career Awards, three are associate professors and two are employed at research-related agencies (Institute of Medicine and Centers for Disease Control).

In APA, she is a founding faculty member of both the LIWP (Leadership Institute for Women in Psychology) and the Diversity

Leadership Development Workshop. Her career has primarily focused on instruction, training and mentoring. She has received numerous awards for all three areas. She is an APA fellow.

Florence L. Denmark

Florence L. Denmark is an internationally recognized scholar, researcher and policy maker. She received her Ph.D. from the University of Pennsylvania in social psychology and has 6 honorary degrees. Denmark is the Robert Scott Pace Distinguished Research Professor of Psychology at Pace University in New York.

A past president of the American Psychological Association (APA) and the International Council of Psychologists (ICP), she holds fellowship status in the APA and the Association for Psychological Science. She is also a Fellow of the Society for Experimental Social Psychology (SESP) and the New York Academy of Sciences. She has received numerous national and international awards for her contributions to psychology. She received the 2004 American Psychological Foundation Gold Medal for Lifetime Achievement for Psychology in the Public Interest. In 2005, she received the Ernest R. Hilgard Award for her Career Contribution to General Psychology. She is the recipient in 2007 of the Raymond Fowler Award for Outstanding Service to APA. Also in 2007, Denmark was elected to the National Academies of Practice as a distinguished scholar member. She received the Elder Award at the APA National Multicultural Conference in 2009. In 2011 at the APA convention, Denmark received the Award for Outstanding Lifetime Contributions to Psychology.

Denmark's most significant research and extensive publications have emphasized women's leadership and leadership styles, the interaction of status and gender, ageing women in cross-cultural perspective, and the history of women in psychology. Denmark was the main NGO representative to the United Nations for the American Psychological Association and is currently the main NGO representative for the International Council of Psychologists. She is the immediate past Chair of the United Nations/New York NGO Committee on Ageing and serves on the Executive Committee of the UN NGO Committees on Ageing, Mental Health, and Family.

Mary Gergen

Mary Gergen is Professor Emerita of Psychology and Women's Studies at Penn State University, Brandywine, as well as a board member of the Taos Institute, a non-profit organization dedicated to the integration of social constructionist ideas with diverse professional practices throughout the world. She serves as an advisor to doctoral candidates in a joint international program in the Social Sciences with Tilburg University, The Netherlands. With a strong interest in feminist gerontology, she is a co-editor of the Positive Aging newsletter, an online publication, which is available in six languages. Her major works are involved at the intersection of feminist theory and social constructionist ideas. In 2001 she published *Feminist Reconstructions in Psychology: Narrative, Gender and Performance*. She has also been author or editor of seven other books, as well as over one hundred articles and chapters for scholarly books. She has published pieces on aging, dialogue, gender, narratives, collaborative practices, performance, and qualitative inquiry. Most recently she has written *Playing with Purpose: Adventures in Performative Social Science,* with Kenneth J. Gergen. Mary is a fellow of the Society for the Psychology of Women, American Psychological Association.

Marcia Hill

Dr. Marcia Hill is a psychologist in private practice in Montpelier, VT. She has edited or co-edited eleven books about various topics in psychotherapy, and is the author of *Diary of a Country Therapist.* In addition, Marcia is a former editor of the journal *Women & Therapy* and has served as Chair of the Feminist Therapy Institute. She has been working as a psychologist for over 35 years. Doesn't that seem long enough? In her moving-toward-retirement life, Marcia is also an artist, and you can see her work at: www.marciahillart.wordpress.com

Mary Tatum Howard

Mary Tatum Howard, Ph.D. received her B. A. in Sociology and English from West Virginia State College, her M.A. in Personnel and Guidance from the University of Missouri at Kansas City, and her Ph.D. in Counseling Psychology from the University of Minnesota. Her lifetime of contributions include activities ranging from the presidency of the American College Personnel Association (ACPA) to service in the Peace Corps and Volunteers in Service to America (VISTA). She worked for many years as a psychologist with the Veteran's Administration in St. Cloud, MN, where she focused on trauma, addiction and women's issues as core areas of interest.

The breadth of Dr. Howard's accomplishments and contributions was recognized with a Wellstone Lifetime Achievement Award in October 2009 and the 2011 National Multicultural Conference honored her with a Presidential Citation from the American Psychological Association. Dr. Howard served for many years as a member of the Governing Council of the Minnesota Psychological Association, representing the interests of rural communities. She is a Distinguished Elder of MPA, a recipient of MPA's Community Service Awards, and a founding member and Elder of the Minnesota Association of Black Psychologists. She is a Fellow of the American Psychological Association and the American Psychological Society. Dr. Howard is an ACPA Diamond Honoree.

Janis Sanchez-Hucles

Janis Sanchez-Hucles is a Professor of Psychology at Old Dominion University in Norfolk, Virginia and a Clinical Psychologist in part time private practice in Virginia Beach, Virginia. She has been involved in developing and teaching courses in: The Psychology of Women, The Psychology of African Americans, and Psychodynamic Therapy. Her research has focused on clinical training, the recruitment, retention and inclusion of women and minorities in the sciences, diversity, feminism, and issues pertaining to trauma and violence. She has become a national speaker and trainer of professionals in the health and mental health applications of cultural competency. Dr. Sanchez is the author of numerous book chapters and journal articles including: Racism as a form of Emotional Abuse and Trauma, Racial and

Cultural Factors in Domestic Violence for Families of Color, and two books, *The First Session with African Americans: A Step by Step guide*, and she is a co-editor of: *Women and Leadership: Transforming Visions and Diverse Voices*. Dr. Sanchez is a fellow of the American Psychological Association (APA) and she has served on a variety of APA advisory boards, committees and task forces.

Ellen B. Kimmel

Ellen B. Kimmel is Professor Emerita of the University of South Florida, Tampa, Florida and currently resides in Santa Cruz in a communal home. As a psychologist, her research interests were in feminist pedagogy and feminist research methods (e.g., *Innovative Methods for Feminist Psychological Research*, with Mary Crawford, 1999). She was active in the Society for the Psychology of Women, serving as its President (1987 – 1988) and in the Southeastern Psychological Association. Among many organizational involvements in her 42-year career, she treasures participation in the Nags Heart feminist retreats/conferences, where she still attends and leads sessions despite being retired since 2003.

Bernice Lott

Bernice Lott is Professor Emerita of Psychology and Women's Studies at the University of Rhode Island and is a former Dean of its University College. She has taught at the University of Colorado and Kentucky State College and was a visiting scholar/professor at Brown University's Center for Research and Teaching on

Women, Stanford University's Institute for Research on Women and Gender, the Department of Psychology in Waikato University, New Zealand, and the University of Hawaii at Manoa. She received her university's Excellence Award for scholarly achievement, served as president of APA's Division 35 (The Psychology of Women), and has been honored for scholarly, teaching, mentoring and social policy contributions by APA's Committee on Women, Division 35, the Association for Women in Psychology, and the National Multicultural Conference and Summit. In 1999, The University of Rhode Island awarded her the honorary degree of Doctor of Humane Letters. She is the author of numerous theoretical and empirical articles, chapters and books in the areas of social learning, gender, poverty and other social issues and is a Fellow of APA and of Divisions 1, 8, 9, and 35. Her areas of interest are interpersonal discrimination; the intersections among gender, ethnicity, and social class; multicultural issues; the social psychology of poverty; and the social psychology of dissent. She represented Division 9 (SPSSI) on APA's Council of Representatives from 2001 to 2007; is a member of an Interdivisional Minority Pipeline Project working on strategies to increase the recruitment and retention of graduate students of color; and has represented Divisions 9 and 35 on the coalition of Divisions for Social Justice. A 2007 book on economic injustice (co-authored with Heather Bullock) was honored by the National Library Association and the Association for Women in Psychology. Her newest book (2010) is on multiculturalism and diversity.

Nancy Felipe Russo

Nancy Felipe Russo, Ph.D., Courtesy Professor in Psychology, Oregon State University and Regents Professor of Psychology and Women and Gender Studies - Emeritus, Arizona State University, is author or editor of more than 225 publications related to the psychology of women and gender. Her leadership roles include founding Director, APA's Women's Programs Office; President and Council Representative, APA's Division of the Psychology of Women; and President, APA's Division of General Psychology. She was a member of APA's Committee on Nonsexist Research, Task Force on Male Violence Against Women, Task Force on Women and Depression, Task Force on Post Abortion Emotional Responses, and Task Force on Abortion and Mental Health. Former editor of the *Psychology of Women Quarterly* and the *American Journal of Orthopsychiatry*, and a Fellow of APA, APS, and the New York Academy of Sciences, Russo's many awards and honors include APA's Award for Distinguished Contributions to Psychology in the Public Interest, the Distinguished International Psychologist Award from APA's Division of International Psychology, and the Denmark-Gunvald Award for significant contributions to the psychology of women and gender from the International Council of Psychologists. Other honors include a Carolyn Wood Sherif Award and a Heritage Award for Contributions to Public Policy from APA's Division 35. Identified as a "Trailblazing Woman in Community Psychology" by APA Division 27's Committee on Women, she received a Distinguished Career Award from the Association for Women in Psychology, and was recognized by

APA's Board of Ethnic Minority Affairs for contributions to ethnic minority issues.

Carolyn Saarni

Dr. Carolyn Saarni received her Ph.D. from the University of California at Berkeley, specializing in developmental psychology. She began her academic career at New York University, and her post-doctoral training in clinical psychology was acquired in New York as well; she has been a licensed psychologist in California since 1979 (currently inactive status). In 1980 she joined the Graduate Department of Counseling at Sonoma State University (California) where she trains prospective marriage and family therapists and school counselors. She was also Department Chair for many years.

Professor Saarni's research has focused on children's emotional development. Her co-edited volumes include *Lying and Deception in Everyday Life*, *The Socialization of Emotion*, and *Children's Understanding of Emotion*. Her book, *The Development of Emotional Competence* (Guilford Press), describes the development of specific skills of emotional competence that are contextualized by cultural values, beliefs about emotion, and assumptions about the nature of the relationship between the individual and the larger society.

Her work has been published in many periodicals as well as in other edited volumes. In the last few years she has had chapters on emotional development published in the *Handbook of Child Psychology*, *The Handbook of Personality Development*, *The Handbook of Emotions*, and additional chapters for several other edited books on emotional intelligence; most recently her chapter on emotional competence and effective negotiation strategies appeared in *Psychological and Political Strategies for Peace Negotiation.*

Nancy K. Schlossberg

Nancy K Schlossberg spent most of her career as a professor of counseling psychology. She taught at Howard University, Wayne State, and 26 years at the University of Maryland, College Park. She is the author of nine books, copresident of TransitionWorks, a consulting firm; Professor Emerita at the College of Education, University of Maryland, College Park; and served as president of the National Career Development Association. She has been honored for her work by the American Psychological Association and the American Counseling Association and the University of Maryland. A frequent guest on radio and TV, Dr. Schlossberg's work was showcased on page one of *USA Today*, and quoted in the *New York Times, the St. Petersburg Times, The Wall Street Journal,* and Cleveland's *The Plain Dealer.* She and her book, *Retire Smart, Retire Happy,* were the focus of a 90-minute PBS special, "Retire Smart, Retire Happy." Her new book, *Revitalizing Retirement* develops the importance of paying attention to one's psychological portfolio. Her second edition of *Overwhelmed: Coping with Life's Ups and Downs* has been translated in Japanese and is used widely in training. Her textbook, *Counseling Adults in Transition: Linking Schlossberg's Theory With Practice in a Diverse World,* with Mary Anderson and Jane Goodman, is now in its fourth edition. She currently is an invited blogger for *Psychology Today.*

Stephanie A. Shields

Stephanie A. Shields, Ph.D., a Professor of Psychology and Women's Studies at The Pennsylvania State University (University Park). I coordinate the dual-title Ph.D. in Women's Studies and Psychology. I served as Director of Women's Studies at Penn State and previously the University of California, Davis, where I also was founding director of the Consortium for Research on Women and Gender.

My research is at the intersection of the psychology of emotion, the psychology of gender, and feminist psychology. I focus mainly on the micropolitics of emotion, the use of one's own or others' emotions to assert or challenge status and power. I have also developed an experiential teaching exercise (aka, board game) for faculty and administrators that demonstrates the nature and cumulative effects of apparently minor biases in the academic workplace (http://wages.la.psu.edu/).

I am determined to be more organized about this last phase of my career than I have been up to now. Besides a long list of writing projects, I plan to continue my obsession with Argentine tango, learn how to draw, find a way to become involved in community activism around biodiversity, and, at long last, master conversational Spanish.

Rachel Josefowitz Siegel

Rachel Josefowitz Siegel. Born in Germany in 1924 of Lithuanian Jewish parents. I grew up in Switzerland and came to the U.S. with my family in 1939. I graduated from Simmons College in 1944, married Benjamin M. Siegel, raised two sons and a daughter, and became a homemaker, faculty wife, and community volunteer.

In 1973 I earned my MSW at age 49. I opened a private practice after 3 years at the local Mental Health Clinic, and became a
Feminist Therapist. I have been active on the steering committees
of FTI and the Jewish Caucus at AWP. I also presented at international conferences of the National Women's Studies Association.
My primary professional interests have been in the areas of Jewish
women, old and aging women, and cultural diversity. I retired
gradually, phasing out around age 76. Now widowed and retired,
I continue to write. In 2007 I moved to Kendal, a local retirement
community.

My professional papers have been deposited with the
Schlesinger Library at Radcliffe. In 2005 I was honored nation-
ally with the Doris Howard Lifetime Achievement Award of
the Association for Women in Psychology, and locally with the
Laura Holmberg Award, presented by the Women's Fund of the
Community Foundation of Tompkins County.

Bonnie Ruth Strickland

Bonnie Ruth Strickland, Ph.D., was born in 1936 and educated
in the public schools of Alabama. She received her Bachelor of
Science degree from Alabama College in 1958, her Master's
degree (1960) and Ph.D. in Clinical Psychology from The Ohio
State University in 1962. A Diplomat in Clinical Psychology, she
has been on the faculties of Emory University and the University of
Massachusetts as administrator, clinician, consultant, researcher,
and teacher. She retired in 2002.

A recipient of numerous awards and honors, Dr. Strickland
has published more than a hundred scientific and scholarly works,

including two Citation Classics in psychology. She has served as President of the American Psychological Association (APA) and held major offices within APA as well as numerous other organizations.

At a personal and political level, Dr. Strickland has been involved in the major social actions of her time from the civil rights movement of the 1960s through the gay rights movement of today. Her commitment to social justice is long standing and she has been a staunch advocate for minority concerns.

Lillie Weiss

Lillie Weiss is a psychologist in Scottsdale, Arizona and the author of seven books, including *Dream Analysis in Psychotherapy*, *Women's Conflicts about Eating and Sexuality* and *Therapist's Guide to Self-Care*. She received her Ph.D. in clinical psychology from the State University of New York at Buffalo in 1968. After working at several inpatient and outpatient settings in Buffalo and Jerusalem, she moved to Phoenix in 1970 where she held two half-time positions, one at Maricopa County Medical Center and the other at Arizona State University where she was in charge of a long-term research project in assessing and teaching therapeutic skills to graduate students. Throughout her career, she has simultaneously held clinical and academic positions, combining direct services with teaching, training, research and writing. She maintained her university affiliation after she went to work at Good Samaritan Medical Center in 1974 and after going into private practice in 1984, continuing to teach and supervise, collaborating on many projects, developing psycho educational intervention programs and at times serving as director of the ASU Psychology Clinic. She closed down her practice in 2006. She received the Distinguished Contribution to the Practice of Psychology Award from the Arizona Psychological Association in 2009.

Diane J. Willis

Diane J. Willis, Ph.D., a member of the Kiowa Tribe, is Professor Emeritus, Department of Pediatrics, University of Oklahoma Health Sciences Center in Oklahoma City. She served as Director of Psychological Services and Training at the U of O's Child Study Center for 23 years. A founding editor of the *Journal of Pediatric Psychology* and past editor of the *Journal of Clinical Child Psychology*, she has co-edited four books and published 68 articles/ chapters. She has received numerous awards throughout her career, and is a member of Divisions 12, 18, 29, 35, 37, 42, 45, 53, and 54 of the American Psychological Association. Dr. Willis has devoted her career to the education and training of psychologists and the development of new service models for meeting the mental health needs of culturally diverse and difficult-to-serve populations.

Judith Worell

Judith Worell, Professor Emerita, University of Kentucky, Lexington. A native New Yorker, I grew up in Greenwich Village where residents typically led unconventional lifestyles and favored social/ political activism. After graduating with honors in Psychology from Queens College, I earned my Ph.D. in Clinical Psychology from Ohio State University. Working with many now-famous professors, I was well-grounded in Social Learning

Theory, with a deep respect for the place of research in clinical practice. My first husband was also a clinical research psychologist. He taught at four different colleges and universities that did not welcome women in academia. Thus, I found alternative employment as a family therapist, a researcher in a psychiatric hospital, a part-time instructor in undergraduate programs, a researcher with a 7-year NIMH grant on interpersonal conflict, and finally was hired fulltime at the University of Kentucky. This was not in psychology, since their nepotism rule precluded spouses teaching in the same department. I found a niche in the Department of Educational and Counseling Psychology, where I attained Full Professor, then Director of Clinical Training and finally Department Chair. I have been retired for the past 9 years, but remain busy with writing and organizational activities.

Considering my experiences of academic exclusion, it was no accident that I became active in women's concerns, and found a comfortable and challenging home in feminist psychology.

CPSIA information can be obtained at www.ICGtesting.com
Printed in the USA
LVOW071453310712

292376LV00012B/25/P